How to Do *Everything* with

Illustrator® CS

D1318567

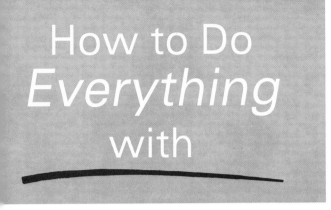

How to Do *Everything* with

Illustrator® CS

David Karlins

McGraw-Hill/Osborne

New York   Chicago   San Francisco   Lisbon
London   Madrid   Mexico City   Milan   New Delhi
San Juan   Seoul   Singapore   Sydney   Toronto

The McGraw·Hill Companies

McGraw-Hill/Osborne
2100 Powell Street, 10th Floor
Emeryville, California 94608
U.S.A.

To arrange bulk purchase discounts for sales promotions, premiums, or fund-raisers, please contact **McGraw-Hill**/Osborne at the above address. For information on translations or book distributors outside the U.S.A., please see the International Contact Information page immediately following the index of this book.

How to Do Everything with Illustrator® CS

1234567890 DOC DOC 019876543

ISBN 0-07-223092-4

Publisher	Brandon A. Nordin
Vice President &	
Associate Publisher	Scott Rogers
Executive Editor	Jane Brownlow
Acquisitions Editor	Katie Conley
Project Editor	Patty Mon
Technical Editor	Carrie Gatlin
Copy Editor	Kathy Krause
Proofreader	Pam Vevea
Indexer	Karin Arrigoni
Composition	Lucie Ericksen, Elizabeth Jang
Illustrators	Kathleen Fay Edwards, Melinda Moore Lytle, Lyssa Wald
Series Design	Lucie Ericksen
Cover Series Design	Dodie Shoemaker
Cover Illustration	Bruce K. Hopkins

This book was composed with Corel VENTURA™ Publisher.

Dedication

Dedicated to every illustrator
who needs to enhance his or her skills to get a job!

About the Author

David Karlins teaches graphic and interactive design at the University of California Extension and in San Francisco State University's Multimedia Studies Program. He is a graphic and web consultant and designer and the author of a dozen books on graphic and web design, including *Build Your Own Web Site* (McGraw-Hill/Osborne, 2003) and *Adobe Illustrator 10 Virtual Classroom* (McGraw-Hill/Osborne, 2001). Contact David through his web site, www.davidkarlins.com.

About the Illustrator

Bruce K. Hopkins is the lead illustrator for this book. He has been a freelance illustrator for 20 years, the last 12 of which he has also worked as a fine artist. Bruce has produced artwork for a variety of illustration projects, including educational toys, novelty prints for apparel, catalogs and packaging, digital illustration for technical manuals, patent drawings, and a teaching book for children. For the last two years he has been focusing much of his energy on creating fine art and promoting himself as a fine artist. His fine art works include an ongoing botanical series painted in gouache, a series of more than 200 geometric digital giclee prints called the "Space" series, an ongoing collection of nude figure studies on paper, and, most recently, a series of local landscapes. Contact Bruce through his web site at www.bkhopkins.com or via e-mail at bruhopk@aol.com.

Contents at a Glance

Contents

Acknowledgments

Creating this book presented a unique and special mission. We set out to create a book that both clearly and completely explained "how to do everything" in Illustrator *and* used artwork that provided real-world examples and creative inspiration.

A unique and special group of people helped me meet that challenge. In creating the basic content of this book, I drew heavily on my experiences teaching Illustrator and on the questions, discoveries, complaints, and inspiration provided by my students. I've also drawn from my professional design interactions with clients, and the book includes insights from those experiences as well.

To solve the challenge of providing creative, useful, and aesthetic illustrations throughout the book, I turned to three sources. First and foremost, I drew on the amazing portfolio of Bruce K. Hopkins. Bruce has literally done it all in the realm of Illustrator artwork, ranging from fine art to technical illustrations. Being able to access, dissect, rearrange, and just plain mess with Bruce's amazing inventory of projects was a huge element of making this book the combination of technique and aesthetics that we were aiming to produce.

I also drew on projects created by students in my online Illustrator course in San Francisco State University's Multimedia Studies Program. Those students generously shared the results of hours of their hard work and creativity.

And I had the audacity to ask the most successful graphic designers in the business to let me share and deconstruct some of their best projects for the "Behind the Scenes" gallery at the end of this book.

Finally, this book required exponentially more blood, sweat, and tears (of joy—of course!) from the editors, artists, and production folks at McGraw-Hill/Osborne. My appreciation to all of them!

Introduction

A Unique Approach to Learning Illustrator

This book provides a clear, concise, and coherent introduction to Adobe Illustrator CS. Illustrator has an overwhelming set of tools, features, and effects. Some of these features are relatively esoteric, and part of my job as author of this book was to identify the Illustrator features you *really need* as an aspiring graphic designer or digital artist.

To do that, I've emphasized and gone into detail about how to use the Pen tool, how to create and manage illustrations, and how to prepare your illustrations for various forms of output. This knowledge is the key to understanding Illustrator (and other vector art programs), and you'll use it nearly every time you use the program, regardless of your level of experience.

Illustrator's vector-based logic can be disorienting. I've been teaching and writing about vector-based graphic tools since before you were born. OK, maybe not—but for 16 years. In that time, I've learned (through trial and error) how to demystify Illustrator and make the learning process both effective and fun.

How Is this Book Organized?

There are two possible approaches to using this book. You can go through it cover to cover. Or you can use it as a reference to look up features you need. The book will work either way. If you're new to Illustrator, I'd strongly suggest setting aside some quality time and working through the book from beginning to end. It will be helpful to at least familiarize yourself with the exploration of the Illustrator interface in Chapter 1 before either proceeding from beginning to end or jumping around in the book.

As you read and refer to this book, take time to check out the artwork used to illustrate the feature you're exploring. Since many of the projects used as models in the book are plundered from the archives of Bruce K. Hopkins, you'll get a chance both to see a feature demonstrated and to see how that feature is used in the real world trenches of professional design and illustration.

At any point in the process (including right now), feel free to jump to the back of the book and check out the "Behind the Scenes: A Gallery with Techniques from the Pros" section. There you'll find a representative selection of accessible projects (a poster, a map, a CD cover, a business card, and more) created for the "real world." Turn to this section for inspiration, to see the techniques you're mastering applied to completed projects, or just to browse some very cool projects. The artwork in the "Behind the Scenes" section is deconstructed so you can see how professional artists and designers created it.

Illustrator is used widely in both Macintosh and PC environments. We've done everything we could to make this book "bilingual" for Mac and PC users. Where keystroke or menu commands are different for different operating systems, you'll find it easy to identify the instructions for your operating system and environment. Where there are different keystrokes for Mac and Windows (PC), I'll put the Windows keystrokes in parentheses. For instance, where the instructions say to hold down the OPTION (ALT) key, Mac users will hold down the OPTION key and PC users will hold down the ALT key. If a menu option works one way in OSX, and differently for Windows and OS9 users (we tried to make this book as backward-compatible as possible), then the instructions will be spelled out explicitly. For instance, if I want you to access the Preferences dialog box, I'll tell you to choose Edit | Preferences in OS9 or Windows, or Illustrator | Preferences in OSX. And we've kept the screen shots as closely cropped as possible so you won't be distracted by operating system elements foreign to your own work environment. Finally, I've compiled separate lists of the most useful Illustrator keyboard shortcuts for Mac and PC and included this list inside the back cover of the book.

Who Is this Book Written For?

This book is written for the beginning or intermediate user of Illustrator who is interested in learning to use Illustrator for professional or personal projects. Because Illustrator's vector logic is so different from the underlying structure of programs such as Photoshop, even folks who have used Illustrator find it somewhat intimidating.

If you're brand new to Illustrator, you'll find that this book is just what you need. If you've been using Illustrator for years but remain confused by some of the features or wonder if you're doing things the most efficient and effective way, you'll find this book highly valuable, too.

Part I

Prepare Your Illustrator Project

Chapter 1

Introducing Illustrator CS and Its Interface

How to...

- Understand Illustrator's role in the world of digital illustration
- Get your hands around vectors
- Identify elements of a vector
- Fit Illustrator into the world of digital graphics
- Publish Illustrator artwork
- Navigate Illustrator's palettes
- Manage Illustrator's tools
- Find new features in Illustrator CS

Understand Illustrator's Role in the World of Digital Graphics

Adobe Illustrator is an almost supernatural program for generating print and digital artwork. Illustrator's drawing tools provide micro-control over drawings. Its gigantic set of graphical effects, combined with its almost limitless control over sizing, scaling, perspective, and fills, allows Illustrator to give expression to any artistic inspiration. There's no other design software that provides such powerful control over lines and curves, fills, and color effects.

Illustrator's unique set of graphical tools are based on *vectors*—mathematically based curves. Vectors give Illustrator its muscle, versatility, and subtlety, but many artists find vectors unintuitive and even frustrating.

No fear. This book will demystify and break down the art of vector art. Step by step you'll learn to orchestrate curves and fills to generate unique artwork.

Get Your Hands Around Illustrator's Curves

Adobe Illustrator is often compared and contrasted to its graphical sibling, Adobe Photoshop. Photoshop allows artists to create or edit illustrations by defining and editing individual pixels. A *pixel* (from *picture element*) is the tiny dot that is the smallest element of a graphical object. A file that records the location, color, and quality of a bunch of pixels is called a *bitmap* or *raster file*, and images generated using pixel editing software are called *bitmap* or *raster images*.

FIGURE 1-1 Zoomed in, the hand is revealed to be composed of identically sized square pixels with a different color assigned to each pixel.

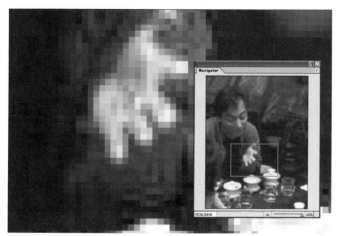

Barbara Mercer

Vector-based graphics are quite different. Adobe Illustrator is the most widely used vector art program, but others include Macromedia Freehand and CorelDRAW. Macromedia Flash is also based on vector graphics. Other graphical software options, such as Macromedia Fireworks, are hybrid programs that combine both vector and pixel editing tools.

Figure 1-1 shows a bitmap image in Adobe Photoshop. When you examine it in detail, you can see that the illustration is composed of thousands of pixels—each one individually colored and defined.

By contrast, vector art is defined by line segments that are controlled by anchor points. The enlarged section of the illustration in Figure 1-2 shows that the birds in the drawing are defined not by individual pixels but by many curved lines.

FIGURE 1-2 Each bird, and each element in each bird, is defined by a set of curves.

Bruce K. Hopkins

To break this down a bit, vector *magnitude* incorporates elements such as length, outline color, outline thickness, and fills. Vector *direction* means that the lines go from point A to point B, although not necessarily in a straight line.

Vector art is scalable. The files you create in Illustrator can be printed on a postage stamp, a business card, a full-sized poster, or a billboard over Sunset Strip without losing quality or even increasing in file size! For example, the Illustrator file in Figure 1-3 was used to create both a postcard and full-sized framed posters for exhibit in galleries.

FIGURE 1-3 Illustrator artwork is scalable—with no loss in resolution, and no increase in file size.

Understand Paths, Anchor Points, and Fills

Each version of Adobe Illustrator has piled on new tools, effects, and techniques for manipulating curves and fills. Illustrator's tool kit can be pretty overwhelming to new users, part-time users, and even long-time graphic design professionals who are upgrading.

The key thing to keep in mind is that all the tools in Illustrator essentially manipulate paths, anchor points, and fills. *Paths* are lines, which can be straight or curved. *Closed paths* are objects such as circles or stars, in which the start and end of the path are the same point. *Open path* objects do not have the same start and end points. Figure 1-4 shows both an open and a closed path.

Anchor points are the start and end points in a path (line), as well as other points along the path that control the direction and curvature of that path. The paths in Figure 1-4 each have three anchor points.

"SPACE" — a series of digital prints by Bruce K. Hopkins

Bruce K. Hopkins

To get a bit Zen about the whole process of working in Illustrator…you will go down many paths as you create artwork. But at the heart of every object in Illustrator, you'll find anchors and paths.

Paths can have fills, or not. Much of this book will be devoted to exploring various fill options, and how to apply them. But if you keep in mind that all Illustrator objects essentially boil down to paths and fills, the complex set of features will at least make sense.

FIGURE 1-4 On the top is an open path, and on the bottom is a closed path. Each path has three anchor points.

Use Illustrator with Other Programs

Many complex illustrations mix both bitmap and vector art. Illustrator can incorporate bitmaps into illustrations, and provides some rudimentary editing features for bitmaps. But in general, you (or a collaborator) will create bitmaps in a program such as Adobe Photoshop and bring them into Illustrator in a basically finished state.

Artwork produced in Illustrator is ultimately destined for either a digital display device (such as a monitor or digital projection screen) or some form of hardcopy (such as a poster, framed art, or a picture in a book, magazine, or brochure). Sometimes entire projects are created and printed directly from Illustrator, but most Illustrator artwork ends up in another software program. Artwork destined for the Web will likely be managed through programs such as Macromedia Dreamweaver, Microsoft FrontPage, or Adobe's own GoLive web design software. Illustrations destined for print will likely be integrated into a publication using desktop publishing programs.

Illustrator drawings can be easily integrated into desktop publishing programs such as Adobe PageMaker, Adobe InDesign, and QuarkXPress. These programs, and others, support Illustrator's native AI file format, and even more programs support Illustrator's EPS file format that preserves the features of your illustration for export.

Caution *Presenting Illustrator artwork on the Web is a bit of a challenge because native mainstream browser support for images is limited to bitmap file formats such as JPEG and GIF. Additional formats require plug-ins. However, Illustrator provides extremely powerful and easy-to-use export-to-web tools that make it easy to convert your Illustrator vectors to web-compatible bitmaps.*

Get Around in Illustrator

Just as the concept of vector art takes some getting used to, the Illustrator interface can be rather intimidating to the uninitiated. If you are coming to Illustrator from Photoshop, you'll find familiar faces in the Toolbox and floating palettes. Whether you're new to the Photoshop/Illustrator interface, or just need to acclimate to Illustrator's set of features, it's worth taking some time to walk through the Illustrator interface.

Illustrator features are found both in the menu structure and in floating sets of tools called *palettes*. In many cases, the features found on the menus and on palettes overlap—you can access a feature from either a menu or a palette.

One way to display a palette is by selecting it from the Window menu. As you select a palette, it appears on your screen. The Toolbox is a special palette in that it provides handy access to dozens of most-used features for creating, selecting, editing, and colorizing objects.

 In the course of this book, you will explore menu options and palettes as you learn new image editing techniques. But you'll find that process more friendly if you put some work into experimenting with the environment first.

Open a File

The process of setting up the Illustrator environment for a new file is somewhat complex. That's because Illustrator needs to know (if possible) what kind of file you are creating—a web graphic, printed artwork, and so on. And Illustrator needs to know how you'll be managing color in your document. Since this process involves making a number of informed decisions even before you start work, Chapter 2 in this book is devoted to showing you how to prepare to create an Illustrator file.

On the other hand, opening an existing Illustrator file is easy. Just choose File | Open, and navigate to the folder and file you wish to work with. With your file open, you can use the horizontal and vertical scrollbars to navigate around your image. (Sorry, Adobe steadfastly refuses to provide support for mice with scrollbar wheels.) If you are new to Illustrator, you might want to open one of the sample art files available from the File | New From Template menu option. With a file open, you can more easily familiarize yourself with Illustrator's navigation features and tools.

You can change the magnification of an illustration by using the Zoom drop-down menu on the left side of the status bar at the bottom of the Illustrator window. To see your entire artwork, choose Fit On Screen, as shown in Figure 1-5.

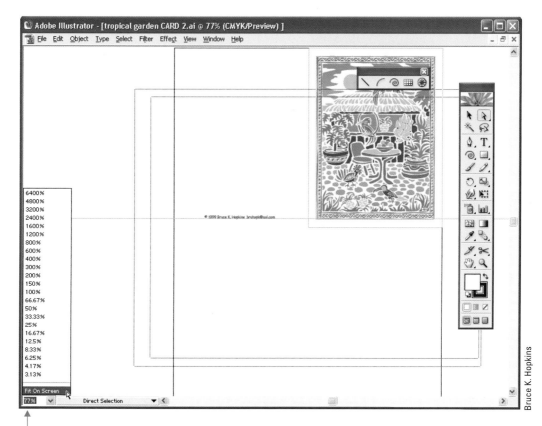

Zoom display

FIGURE 1-5 Displaying an entire document in the Illustrator window

Use the Window Menu to Organize Views

The Window menu allows you to view more than one file at a time. If you have several open windows, you can display more than one document at a time by choosing Window | Tile or Window | Cascade.

One useful technique is to open a document in two different windows. You can do this for an open document by choosing Window | New Window. You can then view different parts of your artwork at different sizes, as shown in Figure 1-6.

Because Illustrator files can be large, and because Illustrator's constant generation of curves draws a lot of your computer processor's resources, you will often want to avoid having two Illustrator files open at the same time.

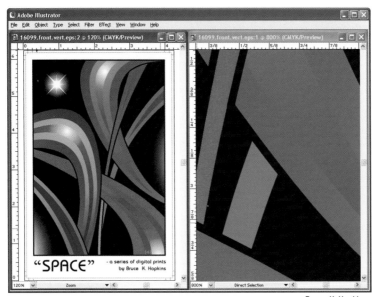

FIGURE 1-6 Zooming in and zooming out—viewing the same illustration in two windows

Work with Palettes

You can display (or close) a palette by selecting (or deselecting) that palette from the Window menu. Figure 1-7 shows the Window menu, with the Tools palette selected.

Most palettes (with the exception of the Toolbox) have pop-up menus, accessed by clicking the right-pointing triangle in the top-right corner of the palette. You'll want to familiarize yourself with palettes if you're not already at home with Adobe's palette system. Try selecting any palette from the Window menu, and then deselecting it.

FIGURE 1-7 The Window menu displays or hides the Toolbox and Illustrator's palettes.

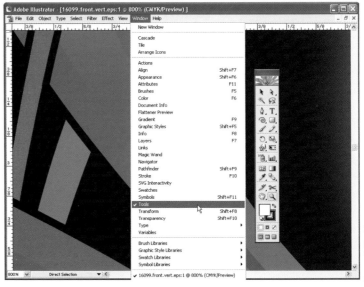

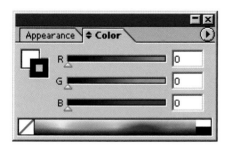

With a palette displayed, experiment with the palette properties. Some palettes are docked with other palettes. These display as tabs at the top of the palette and can be dragged away from their docking mates, as shown in Figure 1-8.

You can close a palette either by deselecting it in the Window menu or by clicking on the palette's close box.

Use Illustrator's Toolbox

Much of the power of Illustrator is stored in the tools in the Toolbox. In addition, the color and screen buttons at the bottom of the Toolbox let you quickly assign (or remove) colors from objects and easily toggle between different views of your workspace.

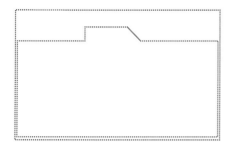

FIGURE 1-8 Separating docked palettes

Unfortunately, the majority of the Illustrator tools are initially hidden. You see them only when you click on a tool pop-out (indicated by a small triangle in the lower-right corner of the tool icon).

All this can be a bit overpowering until you learn your way around the Toolbox. You will eventually get comfortable finding needed tools, but I wanted to provide a clear, easy map to the Toolbox right away and explain very briefly what each tool does. That way you'll be able to find your way around, and in the process, you'll get a quick introduction to much of what Illustrator can do.

Most of the tools in the Illustrator Toolbox are actually just front icons for *sets* of tools. These sets of tools are sometimes called *tearoffs* because they can be "torn off" the Toolbar, revealing the hidden set of tools under the main display tool.

If you click and hold down your mouse button on a tearoff tool, the entire set of underlying tools is revealed, as shown in Figure 1-9.

Any tool in the Toolbox with a tiny triangle in the lower-right corner of the tool icon is covering up a tearoff tool set. To tear off a set of tools from the main Toolbox, first reveal the tearoff, and then click the Tearoff icon, as shown in Figure 1-10.

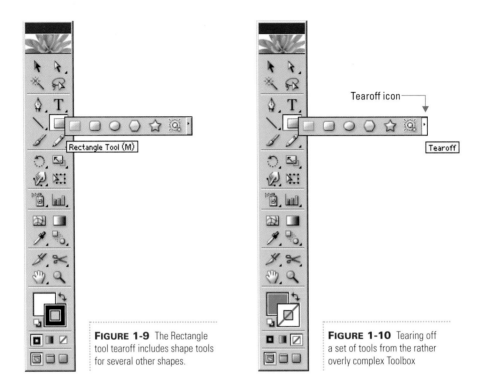

FIGURE 1-9 The Rectangle tool tearoff includes shape tools for several other shapes.

FIGURE 1-10 Tearing off a set of tools from the rather overly complex Toolbox

Identify Tools in Illustrator

You can identify a tool by hovering over it. Illustrator will display a tooltip, and a shortcut key if one exists for that tool.

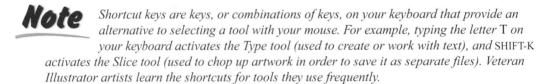 *Shortcut keys are keys, or combinations of keys, on your keyboard that provide an alternative to selecting a tool with your mouse. For example, typing the letter* T *on your keyboard activates the Type tool (used to create or work with text), and* SHIFT-K *activates the Slice tool (used to chop up artwork in order to save it as separate files). Veteran Illustrator artists learn the shortcuts for tools they use frequently.*

The following sections in this chapter will identify each tool in each tearoff of the Toolbox. You will return to many of these in other chapters in this book, but you can use the following sections for easy reference to find tools.

Find Illustrator's Default Displayed Tools

By default—until you start choosing other tools—a set of tools is visible in the Toolbox. Those tools are identified in Figure 1-11.

FIGURE 1-11 The default tools displayed in Illustrator's Toolbox

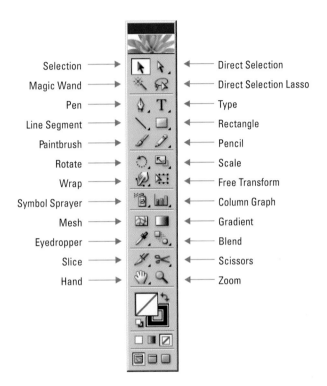

Selection → ← Direct Selection
Magic Wand → ← Direct Selection Lasso
Pen → ← Type
Line Segment → ← Rectangle
Paintbrush → ← Pencil
Rotate → ← Scale
Wrap → ← Free Transform
Symbol Sprayer → ← Column Graph
Mesh → ← Gradient
Eyedropper → ← Blend
Slice → ← Scissors
Hand → ← Zoom

Explore the Tearoffs

Most of the tools in the Toolbox will be explored in depth in different chapters of this book. But here you'll get a quick introduction to all of them.

Some tools in the Toolbox are not part of tearoff sets. The Selection tool is used to select objects for editing. The Magic Wand tool selects objects with similar attributes—color, stroke weight, and so on. The intuitively named Paintbrush tool draws freehand lines that look like brush strokes. The Mesh tool is used for complex gradient fills and reshaping objects. The Lasso tool is used to select irregularly shaped areas of your illustration.

The Free Transform tool allows easy resizing and reshaping of objects. The Gradient tool defines gradient fills. And the Zoom tool allows you to zoom in and out. Figure 1-12 shows an illustration with a gradient fill being edited with the Free Transform tool. The Zoom tool was used to draw a marquee (border) around the area that is displayed.

FIGURE 1-12 Sizing the gradient that will be the background for a CD sticker using the Free Transform tool

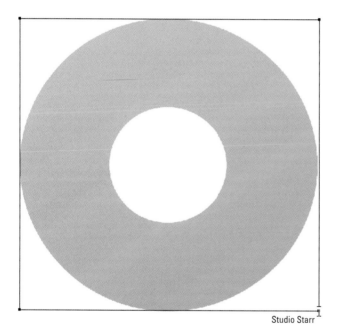

Studio Starr

While a few of the most commonly used tools are not associated with tearoffs, most tools are part of tearoff sets. You'll get introduced to each of these sets of tools in this section of the chapter, and you'll get a quick preview of how some of the most frequently used tools are used in illustrations.

The bottom section of the Toolbox, which displays icons for other useful techniques, will be discussed in the next section, "Identify Tools for Fills and Views."

Peruse the Pen Tools

The Pen tools are the essence of Illustrator. They are used to draw and edit curves. The Pen (P) tool is used to generate curved and straight lines. The Add Anchor Point (+) and Delete Anchor Point (−) tools allow you to add new anchor points or delete existing anchor points from a curve. The Convert Anchor Point (SHIFT-C) tool changes sharp angles to curves, and vice versa, and allows you to tweak the exact character of a curve.

Figure 1-13 shows the Pen tool tearoff, along with a drawing created mainly by drawing curves with the Pen tool.

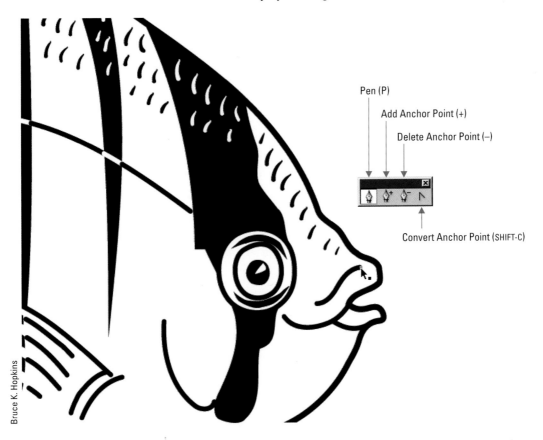

Pen (P)

Add Anchor Point (+)

Delete Anchor Point (−)

Convert Anchor Point (SHIFT-C)

Bruce K. Hopkins

FIGURE 1-13 Touching up a Pen tool curve

Look at the Line Segment Tools

Some of the uses for the Line Segment tools are pretty obvious. The Line Segment (\) tool draws straight lines; the Arc tool draws arcs. The Spiral tool draws spirals, and the Rectangular

Grid and Polar Grid tools quickly generate grids. Each of these tools and its use is illustrated in Figure 1-14.

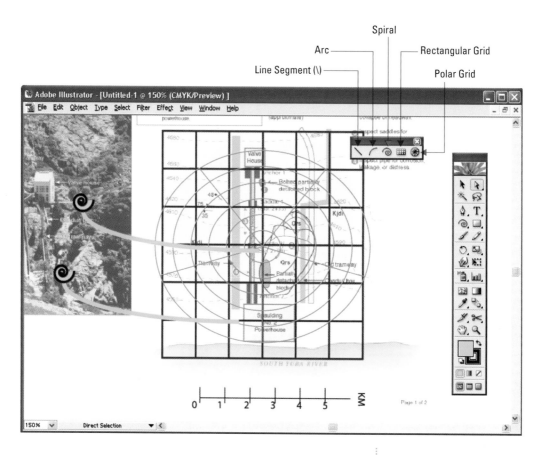

FIGURE 1-14 Line segments, arcs, spirals and grids

Reveal the Rotate Tools

Rotate tools are used to rotate selected objects clockwise or counterclockwise and to create mirror images of selected objects. The Rotate (R) and Reflect (O) tools are displayed in Figure 1-15.

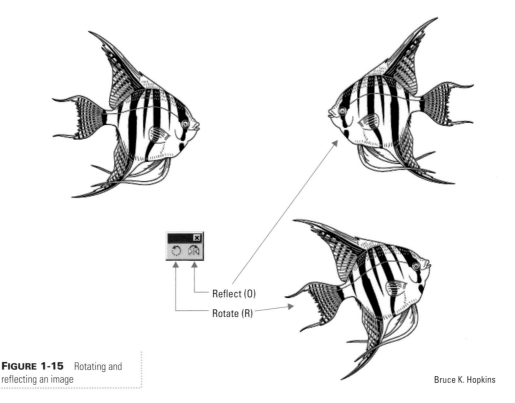

Reflect (O)
Rotate (R)

FIGURE 1-15   Rotating and reflecting an image

Bruce K. Hopkins

View the Warp Tools

The Warp (SHIFT-R), Twirl, Pucker, Bloat, Scallop, Crystallize, and Wrinkle tools are referred to as the *liquify* tools because they can apply interesting sets of distortion to objects. These tools are illustrated in Figure 1-16.

 *Some of Illustrator's tools, such as the liquify set, have pretty unpredictable results. You'll simply use experimentation and trial-and-error to discover effects you want to preserve.*

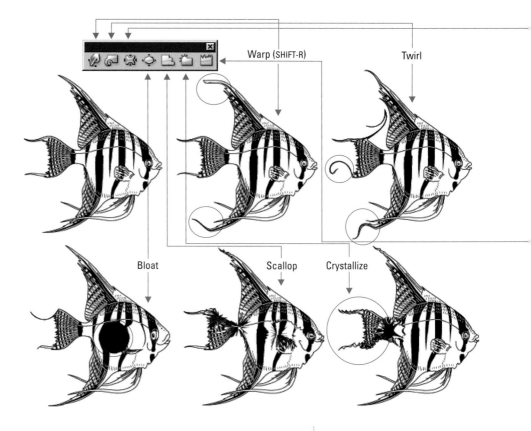

Warp (SHIFT-R)   Twirl

Bloat   Scallop   Crystallize

FIGURE 1-16   Changing an image's appearance using the liquify tools

Survey the Symbol Sprayer Tools

The symbol feature is a sophisticated technique for creating many *instances* of a single object. You'll be introduced to this technique in Chapter 21.

The Symbol Sprayer (SHIFT-S) paints selected symbols on the screen as if you are using a paintbrush. The Symbol Shifter, Symbol Scruncher, Symbol Sizer, Symbol Spinner, Symbol Stainer, Symbol Screener, and Symbol Styler tools are used to modify the appearance of symbols in your document.

The Symbol tools are illustrated in Figure 1-17.

Eye the Eyedropper Tools

The Eyedropper (I) and Paint Bucket (K) tools are used to grab colors. The Eyedropper tool is used to grab colors from objects on the screen, while the Paint Bucket tool assigns your defined fill color (shown in the Fill palette at the bottom of the Toolbox) to selected objects. (The Fill palette will be discussed in the next section, "Identify Tools for Fills and Views.")

When you select the Measure tool, you can click and drag to reveal the distance and direction of any dimension in your document, as shown in Figure 1-18.

See the Slice Tools

Slicing tools are used to break illustrations into more than one savable section. This is especially helpful in preparing large illustrations for the Web. You'll investigate slicing in Chapter 23.

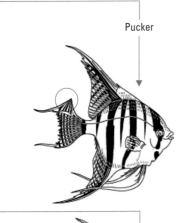

Pucker

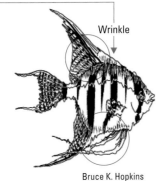

Wrinkle

Bruce K. Hopkins

Slice (SHIFT–K)   Slice Selection

Symbol Sizer
Symbol Scruncher
Symbol Shifter
Symbol Sprayer
(SHIFT-S)

Symbol Spinner
Symbol Stainer
Symbol Screener
Symbol Styler

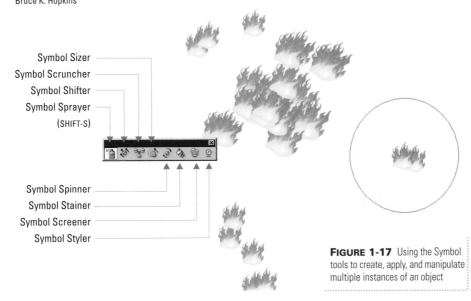

FIGURE 1-17 Using the Symbol tools to create, apply, and manipulate multiple instances of an object

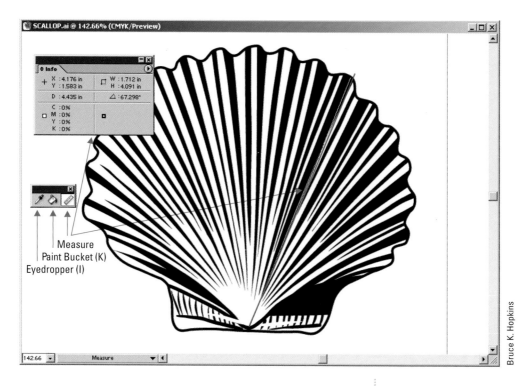

FIGURE 1-18 Measuring angle and distance within the shell

Handle the Hand Tools

The Hand (H) tool functions as a grabber hand and allows you to drag your document around in your monitor window. The Page tool can be used to redefine page size for printing.

Hand (H)   Page

Detect the Direct Selection Tools

The Direct Selection (A) tool is used to select a specific anchor point or line segment within an illustration. The Group Selection tool selects grouped objects within a larger object.

Direct Selection (A)   Group Selection

Tour the Type Tools

In the course of this book, you'll explore Illustrator's ability to create, edit, and shape type in detail. Along with the Type (T) tool—used to type and edit text—the Type tool tearoff reveals the Area Type, Path Type, Vertical Type, Vertical Area Type, and Vertical Path Type tools.

Type tools can be used to flow text around an object, or to fill an object, as shown in Figure 1-19.

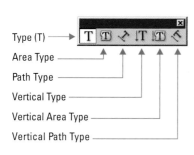

Type (T) →

Area Type

Path Type

Vertical Type

Vertical Area Type

Vertical Path Type

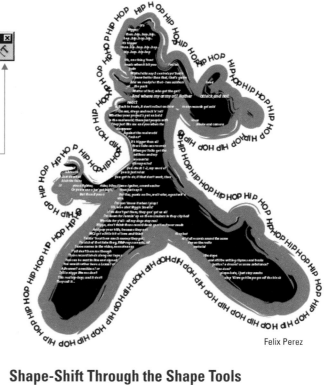

Felix Perez

FIGURE 1-19 The Path Type tool flows text around the drawing, and the Area Type tool is used to fill the figure with lyrics.

Shape-Shift Through the Shape Tools

The Rectangle (M), Rounded Rectangle, Ellipse (L), Polygon, and Star tools create shapes familiar to everyone who's ever created an illustration. These tools create objects that lay the basis for a wide variety of drawings, even very complex ones.

The Flare tool is somewhat out of place in the shapes family. It creates an outer-space-type effect. All these shape tools are found on the Rectangle tool tearoff, as shown in Figure 1-20.

Scale the Scale Tools

The Scale (S), Shear, and Reshape tools allow you to resize and reshape objects. The Scale tool opens a dialog box with properties that control exactly how much to enlarge or shrink a selected object. The Shear tool is used to skew shapes—for instance, to turn a rectangle into a parallelogram. You click

Rectangle (M)   Rounded Rectangle   Ellipse (L)   Polygon   Star   Flare

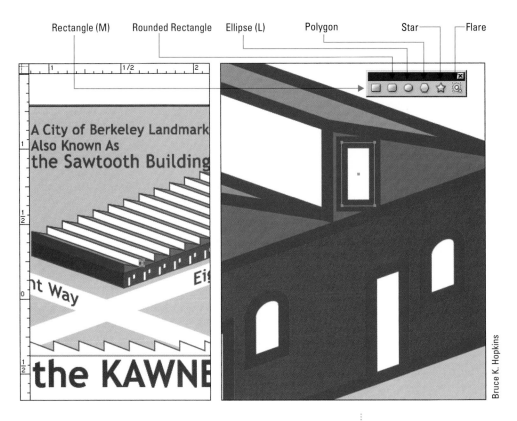

Bruce K. Hopkins

FIGURE 1-20 Basic shapes, such as the rectangle and circle, form the basis of many elements of professional graphic design projects.

and drag with the Reshape tool to interactively reshape objects. Figure 1-21 shows an illustration being resized with the Scale tool.

Pass Through the Pencil Tools

Expert Illustrator designers use the Pen tool to draw with because of the intricate control that tool provides over curve segments. The Pencil (N), Smooth, and Erase tools are Illustrator's concessions to users who are new to vector drawing, or who just never make the adjustment to the Pen tool's challenging but powerful features.

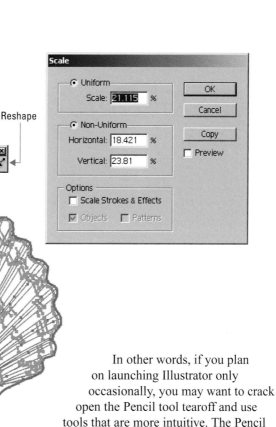

Bruce K. Hopkins

FIGURE 1-21 Resizing an illustration using the Scale tool dialog box

In other words, if you plan on launching Illustrator only occasionally, you may want to crack open the Pencil tool tearoff and use tools that are more intuitive. The Pencil tool works the way a real pencil does—you draw with your mouse or on your drawing tablet to create lines and curves in the Illustrator document. The Smooth tool smoothes out awkward or jaggy lines, while the Erase tool works like a pencil eraser. Figure 1-22 shows the Pencil tool in action.

Chart the Graph Tools

Illustrator's graphing tools are an interesting combination of not very powerful and confusing. Serious graphing is done with dedicated graphing programs, or even the graphing tools found in spreadsheet programs such as Excel. The good side of graphing in Illustrator is that you can touch up your graph with Illustrator's powerful array of editing features.

Those who must whip up a quick graph in Illustrator select the Column Graph (J), Stacked Column Graph, Bar Graph, Stacked Bar Graph, Line Graph, Area Graph, Scatter Graph, Pie Graph, or Radar Graph tool from the Graph tearoff and draw a marquee that indicates the size of the graph. A data grid appears after you draw the graph area. Enter values to graph in the rows and columns as shown in Figure 1-23.

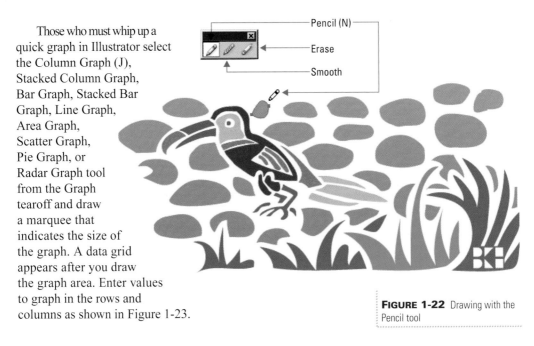

FIGURE 1-22 Drawing with the Pencil tool

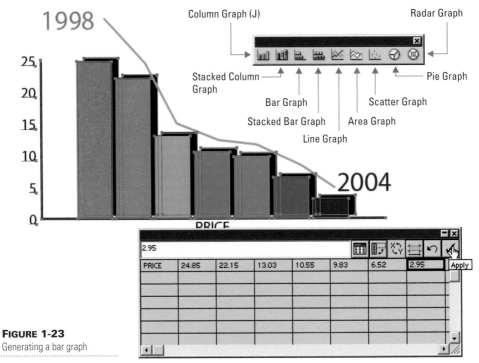

FIGURE 1-23
Generating a bar graph

After you enter graph values in the grid, you click the
Apply check icon (as shown in Figure 1-23) to add or update
the graph data.

Buzz Past the Blend Tools

The Blend (W) and Auto Trace tools share the Blend tool tearoff,
and both are essential in creating artwork in Illustrator. Blends
generate images that transition between two objects. They are
used to create many objects at once, or to generate transitions
so smooth that they look like gradients.

Each update of Illustrator improves the Auto Trace tool's
ability to convert scanned or imported bitmap images into vectors.
Both the Blend and Auto Trace tools will be invoked throughout
this book. Figure 1-24 shows an illustration with both a step
blend and a smooth blend.

FIGURE 1-24 The fence, the
steps, and the Slinkys are step
blends. The path and the doorway
were generated with smooth blends.

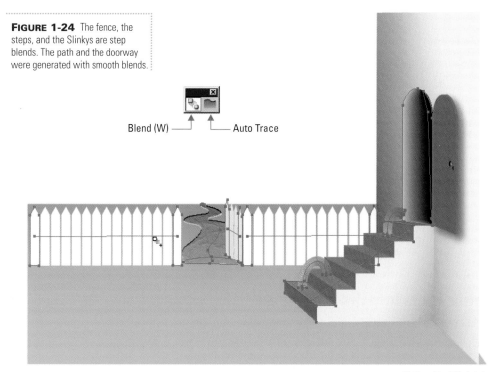

Blend (W) ——⌐ ⌐—— Auto Trace

Nathan Alan Whelchel

Knife Through the Scissors Tools

As is the case with many tools in Illustrator, the Scissors (C) and Knife tools are alternatives to other options. These tools are used for cutting sections of illustrations. Most designers use cropping instead of these tools, but they are handy for occasional trimming of shapes, objects, or paths. Figure 1-25 illustrates both the Knife and Scissors tools.

FIGURE 1-25 The Scissors tool breaks up paths, the Knife tool cuts through objects.

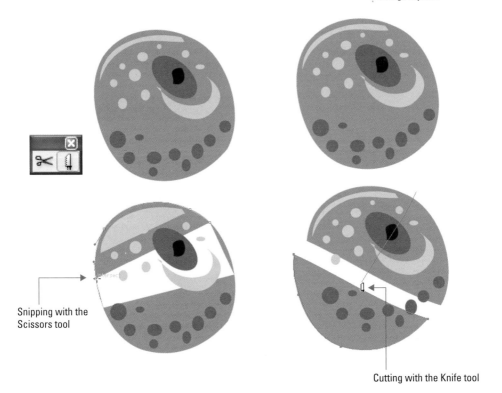

Snipping with the Scissors tool

Cutting with the Knife tool

Identify Tools for Fills and Views

Now that you've been quickly introduced to Illustrator's vast tool set, it's time to investigate the final elements of the Toolbox. Underneath the default tool set in the Toolbox you'll find icons that provide quick access to stroke and fill color and display.

The Fill (X) icon displays the currently selected fill color that will be applied to newly created objects. The Stroke (X) icon displays the currently selected color that will be assigned to the outline of a new object. They both have the same keyboard shortcut (X) because that key toggles between the Fill and Stroke icons. The smaller Swap Fill and Stroke (SHIFT-X) icon reverses the fill and stroke of a selected object. The Default Fill and Stroke icon (D) assigns a black stroke and white fill to an object.

The Color (<) button activates Illustrator's Color palette and allows you to choose a new color for Fill or Stroke (depending on whether the Fill or Stroke icon is active when the Color button is clicked).

The Gradient (>) swatch assigns gradient fills—fills that merge two or more colors from one point in an object to another, and the None (/) icon assigns no color to either Fill or Stroke.

The bottom row of the Toolbox defines view. The Standard Screen mode displays Illustrator in a window within your operating system. The Full Screen with Menu Bar option displays only Illustrator, along with a menu bar. The Full Screen Mode button is used to preview your illustration without any interface display (except for the Toolbox and open palettes).

Tip   *The screen options all have the same shortcut key (F) because it toggles between the three viewing modes.*

FIGURE 1-26 The bottom tools in the toolbox control stroke and fill color along with viewing modes

These tools at the bottom of the Toolbox are displayed in Figure 1-26.

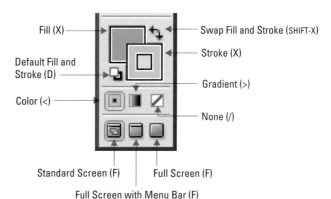

As you work on an illustration, you can move the Toolbox out of the way by clicking and dragging the blue bar at the top of the Toolbox.

Use New Features in Illustrator CS

Illustrator CS refines a program that has been used by graphic art professionals for years. It's more stable, manages memory better in OSX and Windows XP, and includes a few new features.

One of the most dramatic additions to Illustrator is the inclusion of 3-D effects similar to, but very much scaled down from, those that came with Adobe's semi-abandoned Dimensions 3-D imaging program. You'll experiment with these 3-D tools in Chapter 14.

The other area of dramatic improvement is in text formatting and control. Illustrator CS introduces much smoother and more helpful tools for paragraph formatting, flowing text between blocks, and better dictionary and search and replace tools. Find and Replace features are beefed up and allow searches for special characters (such as paragraph or line breaks). You'll explore these improved text features in Part III of this book.

Note *Because type and font management is so improved in Illustrator CS, when you open a file created in an older version of Illustrator, you'll be prompted to convert that "Legacy" (Adobe's term for older versions of Illustrator) type to type that utilizes the new features of Illustrator CS.*

Illustrator CS has added much more powerful support for extended Open Type character sets. Open type makes it possible to include hundreds of characters in a single font set, and Illustrator's new type features make Open type characters easy to use.

Other updates include Illustrator's ability to save to new graphic formats (JPEG 2000) and to export more accurately to Adobe's InDesign desktop publishing program. Illustrator CS artwork even meshes better with Microsoft Office programs than artwork created in version 10 does.

While Illustrator CS fine tunes and improves on versions 9 and 10, readers using those versions will have little trouble using this book as a guide. You'll simply note a missing feature here and there. If you find you need that feature, upgrade. If not, use this book with your old version of Illustrator.

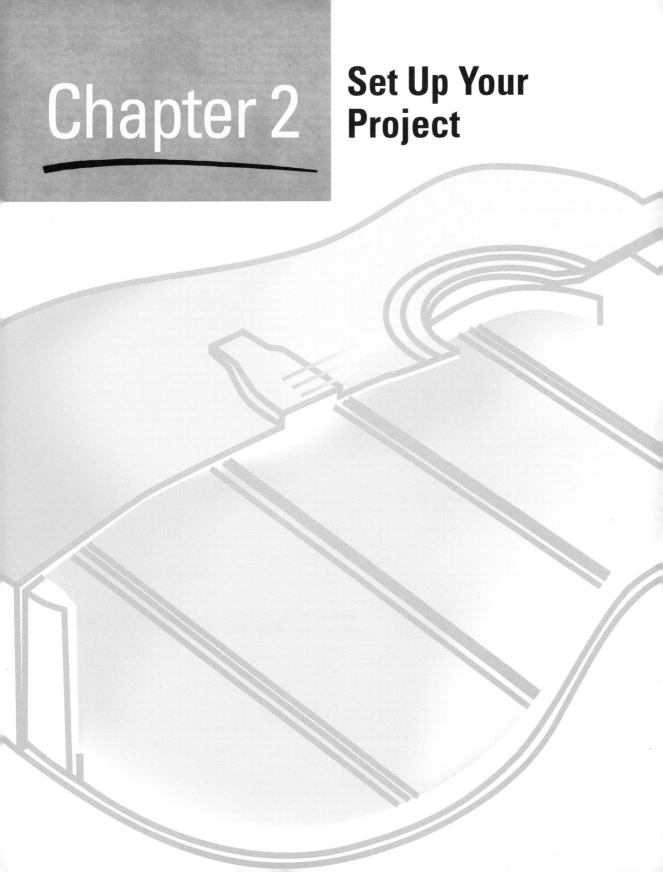

Chapter 2

Set Up Your Project

How to...

- Set up a new document
- Define color options
- Set preferences
- Define page size
- Define custom page sizes
- Navigate your page

Illustrator CS is highly adaptable. You can design a postage stamp, a billboard, a web graphic, or artwork for a Flash animation in the same document window. But you'll want to define a different working environment for each type of project.

Most veteran Illustrator artists will advise you to work backwards when you set up your document window. You can save time and energy if your page size, color settings, units of measurement, and so on match the project you are working on. That said, Illustrator is forgiving and flexible enough to allow you to rather easily change your mind and resize and reformat your illustration.

That means that you should do your best to define your document settings before you begin work. But feel free to crack this book open to this chapter at *any point* in the design process to alter your document settings.

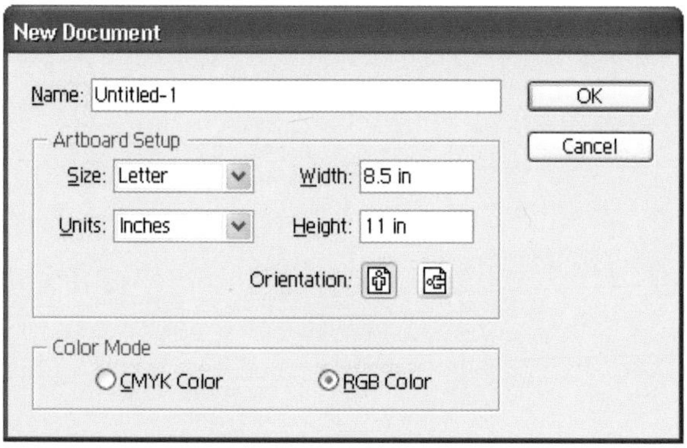

FIGURE 2-1 Creating a new document

Set Up a New Document

To create a new document, choose File | New, or press COMMAND-N (CTRL-N). The New Document dialog box opens, allowing you to define the size and color system for your illustration. The New Document dialog box reflects the settings you last used to define your document, so yours might well look different than the one in Figure 2-1.

If you are starting Illustrator for the first time, you might see the "Welcome to Adobe Illustrator CS" splash screen. Unchecking the "Show this dialog at startup" check box will make this superfluous interface go away the next time you launch Illustrator.

If you wish, you can simply accept the existing settings in the New Document dialog box. In that case, you can change document settings later by choosing File | Document Setup. But in general, you'll want to define document settings in advance that correspond to the type and size of artwork you are creating.

The New Document dialog box presents you with three decisions: you need to assign a filename to your illustration, you need to set up your illustration's workspace (called the *artboard*), and you need to decide which set of colors to use in your illustration.

Assigning a name in the New Document dialog box does not save your file. But when you choose File | Save from the Illustrator menu, the document name you assign will be the default filename. The size of the artboard and the color palette you select should reflect how you plan to produce your illustration.

Scratch area   Artboard

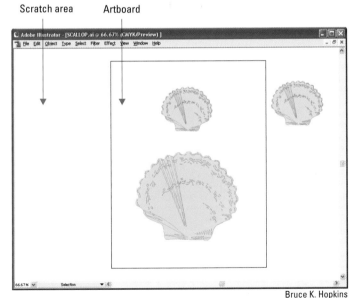

Bruce K. Hopkins

FIGURE 2-2 Only objects on the artboard print.

Set Up the Artboard

You should define an artboard size that corresponds to the size of your final output and a color palette that will be the same as the one used when your illustration is produced.

The artboard defines the size of the area of the workspace that will be produced when you print your illustration. Figure 2-2 shows the artboard, along with the scratch area outside the artboard.

The imageable area is the part of your illustration that will be printed, but all objects in the workspace are saved with your file.

The artboard is also important when you are preparing illustrations for the Web. You can size the artboard to 800×600 pixels, or other dimensions typical of the size of web browsers.

To define the size of the artboard, follow these steps:

1. In the Artboard Setup area of the New Document dialog box, select a unit of measurement for your artboard from the Units drop-down list. Typically you will chose pixels for images headed for the Web and inches, picas, points, millimeters, or centimeters for illustrations destined for printed output.

2. Use the Size drop-down list to choose from one of the preset output sizes, or choose Custom from the Size drop-down list and use the Width and Height boxes in the dialog box to define a size not listed.

3. Use the Orientation buttons to toggle between portrait and landscape orientation for your artboard. The "sideways" icon (which looks like a horizontal piece of paper) represents landscape orientation.

 *Don't click OK just yet! You still need to define a color mode for your document.*

Define Color Options

The New Document dialog box offers two options for defining colors: Cyan-Magenta-Yellow-Black (CMYK) or Red-Green-Blue (RGB).

You will explore the use of color in artwork in many chapters of this book, and you'll look at defining print color modes in detail in Chapter 22 and web color in detail in Chapter 23. But for now, a quick introduction to the two basic coloring methods will be enough to get you started on your illustration.

RGB is a method of defining colors displayed on monitors. As you might guess, these colors are generated by combining various levels of the colors red, green, and blue. Figure 2-3 shows a graphic intended for the Web using the RGB color scheme. Note that the Color palette displays colors defined as combinations of red, green, and blue.

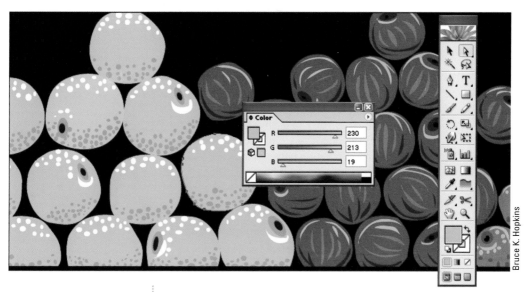

Bruce K. Hopkins

FIGURE 2-3 Using the RGB Color palette to select a color

In the CMYK color scheme, cyan is a shade of green, magenta is a bluish purple, yellow is of course yellow, and black is represented with a K so as not to be confused with blue. These colors are applied in layers during four-color printing to produce a wide array of colors. Figure 2-4 shows an illustration using CMYK.

FIGURE 2-4 Defining colors using CMYK mode—the selected color is pure cyan

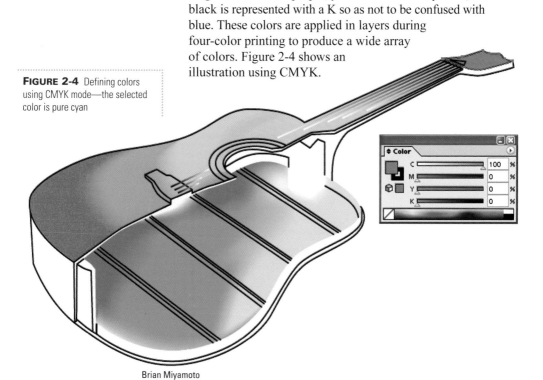

Brian Miyamoto

There are many variations on these options. For example, a set of 216 RGB colors is supported by all (or mostly all) operating systems. These colors are commonly known as browser-safe RGB colors.

If you change your mind about document settings, you can change them by choosing File | Document Setup to open the Document Setup dialog box. Here you can change the size of your artboard. Or choose File | Document Color Mode to open a pop-out menu that allows you to toggle between the CMYK (printed color) or RGB (web or monitor output color) modes.

In short, you will generally want to choose CMYK for printed output and RGB for monitor or web output.

Once you have selected a document name, artboard setup, and color mode, you can click OK to close the New Document dialog box and open your new file.

Customize Preferences

With eight sets of customizable preferences, Adobe almost lets you design your own custom version of Illustrator. I won't detail every customizable option here. In many cases, I'll note preference options throughout the book where they are relevant to the feature being explored. But you will want to be aware of some preferences as you start out in Illustrator. To access the whole set of preferences, choose Edit | Preferences in Mac OS9 and Windows or Illustrator | Preferences in Mac OSX and choose from one of the sets of definable options.

Once you open the Preferences dialog box, a drop-down menu at the top of the dialog box allows you to switch between any of the sets of preferences. The following sections summarize the customizing features available in each set of preferences.

Set General Preferences

The general set of preferences is a real mixed bag of features hardly anyone uses, but some features are important to know about.

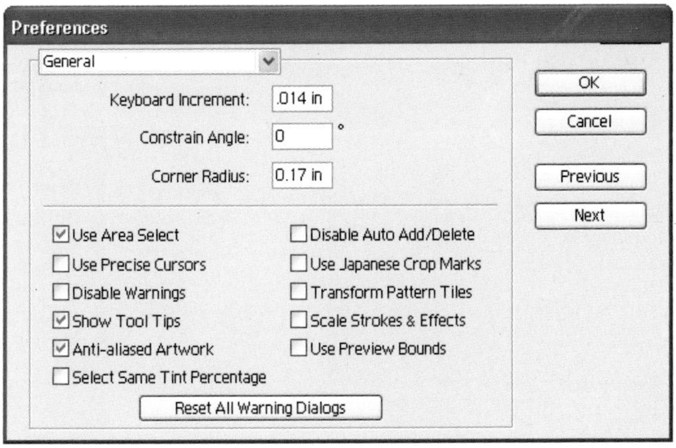

FIGURE 2-5 Defining general preferences

One of the more useful options, the Keyboard Increment setting defines how far a selected object moves when you press the up, down, right, or left arrow key on your keyboard.

The Corner Radius box defines how round the corners generated by the Rounded Rectangle shape tool will be. Higher values create more rounded rectangles.

You'll probably want to leave the rest of the general settings at their default state, as shown in Figure 2-5, unless you recognize one you know you want to change.

Set Default Type & Auto Tracing Preferences

The Type Options area of this dialog box defines how type is altered when you use special keyboard shortcuts for type formatting features such as type size and leading (space between lines), tracking (space between characters), and baseline shift (the distance by which superscript characters are raised and subscript characters are lowered). These features are used by type specialists. The keyboard settings can be defined by choosing Edit | Keyboard Shortcuts.

Auto tracing preferences define how the Auto Trace tool works when it converts imported bitmaps to vectors. Auto trace tolerance values can range from 0 to 10. This setting determines how carefully the Auto Trace tool adheres to the shape of the object being traced. Lower values trace more accurately, while higher values smooth out irregularities in the outline of the traced bitmap.

The auto trace gap setting defines how large a gap between lines to ignore when a bitmap image is traced when converted to a

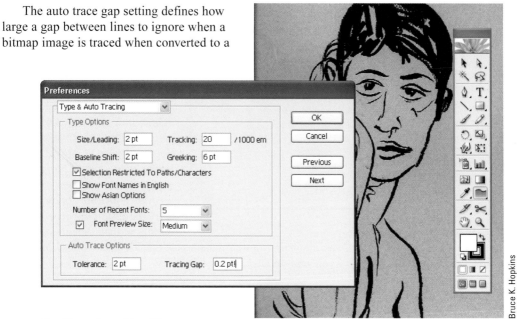

vector. Smaller values allow Illustrator to connect lines that come close to connecting in the original traced bitmap. The range for gap settings is from 0 to 2, as shown in Figure 2-6.

FIGURE 2-6 A low auto tracing gap setting will produce more accurate conversion from bitmap to vectors.

Define Units & Display Performance

The units preferences define units of measurement for objects in Illustrator. You can define three separate units of measurement:

- General defines the unit of measurement used to size objects, determine your page size, and so on.

- Stroke sets a unit of measurement for stroke (outline) thickness.

- Type defines a unit of measurement for text size (usually points for printing projects, and occasionally pixels for text destined for the Web).

Figure 2-7 shows typical settings for printed copy. Printed output often uses points, inches, or centimeters as units of measurement.

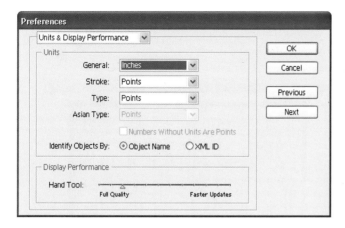

FIGURE 2-7 Setting units of measurement for a typical print output project

The display performance settings regulate how your graphical memory manages movement around your image with the Hand tool. Dragging the slider toward the Full Quality (left) side of the scale maintains a more accurate image as you scroll with the Hand tool, while dragging the slider towards the Faster Updates (right) edge of the scale allows the image to re-resolve more quickly as you scroll with the Hand tool.

Previous to Illustrator CS, older versions of Illustrator allowed you to define how much memory to set aside for undo operations (Edit | Undo) in the Preferences dialog box. Illustrator CS automatically allows as many undos as your system's memory will support.

 The Object Name and XML ID option boxes are used for the very complex and rather esoteric programming of objects in Illustrator and are beyond the scope of this book.

Set Guides & Grid Preferences

Grids are sets of regularly spaced horizontal and vertical lines that don't print but are used to make it easier to locate objects. *Guides* are custom-defined horizontal or vertical lines that are used the same way.

The preferences for grids and guides define how customized these elements appear on your page. You'll learn to define and view grids and guides in the "Turn on Grids and Snap Options" section coming a bit later in this chapter.

Define Smart Guides & Slices Preferences

Smart Guides are different than the just-mentioned *guides*. They're not lines on your page, but instead they display helpful information about objects that you point to or select. This info is especially useful when you are getting acquainted with Illustrator.

If you're using Smart Guides to help you get familiar with how Illustrator works, you'll probably want to leave the default settings in this dialog box alone so that you get the most possible help when you point to an object. In Figure 2-8, the Smart Guides are identifying an anchor point. You turn Smart Guides on (or off) by choosing View | Smart Guides from the menu.

Slicing cuts an image into separate regions that can be saved separately. The Slice options make it easier to keep track of slices. Slices are explained in Chapter 23 as part of discussing how to prepare illustrations for the Web.

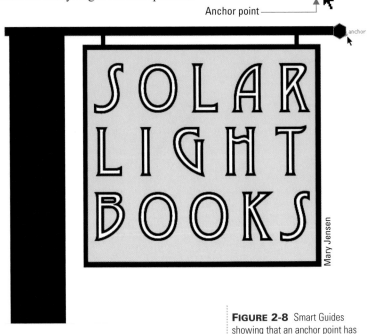

Mary Jensen

FIGURE 2-8 Smart Guides showing that an anchor point has been selected

Control Hyphenation Preferences

The hyphenation preferences allow you to choose a language dictionary from which to apply hyphenation to text. Choose a language from the Default Language drop-down list.

The Hyphenation dialog box also allows you to create a list of words that you don't want Illustrator to hyphenate. Or, if you want to add a word with preferred hyphenation, you can enter a word with a hyphen where you want hyphenation to occur. (For instance, type **non-fiction** to ensure that "nonfiction" is always hyphenated between the *n* and the *f*.)

Define Up Plug-Ins & Scratch Disks Preferences

The plug-in preferences allow you to define a folder with any plug-in programs you might have that are compatible with

Illustrator. The Scratch Disks preference dialog box has two drop-down menus, Primary and Secondary, which define where Illustrator will store temporary files while the program is running.

Pick fixed disks (not R/W CD, Zip, or floppy disks) because you are defining where files essential to the operation of Dreamweaver will be temporarily stored, and if you assign these files to a zip drive, R/W CD or other removable medium, Dreamweaver won't work properly when those disks are removed from your computer.

Set Default File & Clipboard Settings

The file and clipboard settings preferences define how files are saved and how objects are saved through the clipboard. Leave the clipboard setting at AICB because it supports more features than PDF. The best files setting to use will differ depending on your operating system. Mac users can append extensions (such as AI) to files, which make them more accessible to PC users.

The Update Links drop-down menu defines how linked images within a file are updated. You'll explore how linked images work in the next chapter in this book, when you learn to import bitmaps (and other files) into Illustrator documents.

Set Up Workgroup Preferences

The workgroup preferences are used with files that are shared over a server. They're used when several designers are working with the same set of files. These preferences allow you to have Illustrator prompt for approval when a file is checked out from the server or updated to the server.

Control the Status Bar Display

The status bar at the bottom of the Illustrator window has a Zoom menu and also displays a variety of information about your project or your selected tool.

On the far left of the status bar, the Zoom percentage pop-up menu allows you to define zoom levels. To the right of the Zoom menu is a customizable display.

By default, the status bar displays your selected tool. This can be changed to display date and time, free memory, the remaining number of undos and redos available, or the document color profile. You change the information displayed in the status bar by clicking on the existing information, which opens a pop-up menu with other display options.

Turn on Grids and Snap Options

Very often, designers want to be able to easily and quickly constrain objects to set sizes. Illustrator offers a variety of features for setting up your workspace with rulers, grids, and guides. You can elect to snap to rulers, grids, or even other objects.

View Grids

Grids make it easy to locate or size objects as you create them. To view grid lines, select View | Show Grid from the menu. Figure 2-9 shows grids being used to help draw an illustration.

    To make your grid lines sticky—so that objects drawn *near* the grid jump to the grid—select View | Snap to Grid.

    To control the spacing between grid lines, the display color, or the subdivisions within (between) grid lines, choose Illustrator (Edit) | Preferences | Guides & Grid and change the settings.

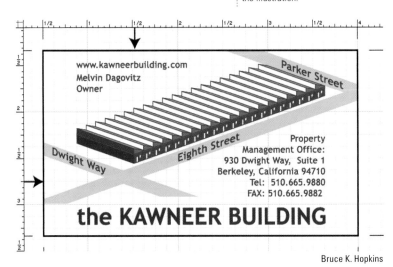

FIGURE 2-9 Grid lines help constrain the size of objects in the illustration.

www.kawneerbuilding.com
Melvin Dagovitz
Owner

Parker Street

Dwight Way

Eighth Street

Property
Management Office:
930 Dwight Way, Suite 1
Berkeley, California 94710
Tel: 510.665.9880
FAX: 510.665.9882

the KAWNEER BUILDING

Bruce K. Hopkins

Show Rulers and Create Guides

Rulers display on the horizontal and vertical borders of the Illustrator window. Choosing View | Show Rulers displays rulers, and View | Hide Rulers removes them. The unit of measurement will be determined by the settings in the Units & Display Performance dialog box discussed earlier in this chapter.

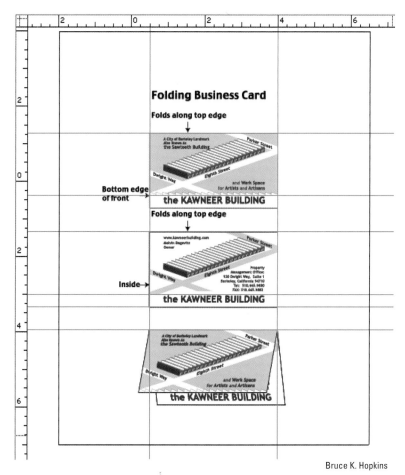

Folding Business Card

Folds along top edge

Bottom edge
of front

the KAWNEER BUILDING

Folds along top edge

Inside→

the KAWNEER BUILDING

the KAWNEER BUILDING

Bruce K. Hopkins

FIGURE 2-10 Custom guides (in red) help size a folding business card.

You can create guides—custom-defined horizontal or vertical alignment rules—by dragging a horizontal or vertical ruler onto your page. Custom guides can define your page size or other parameters useful in a drawing, as shown in Figure 2-10.

By default, guides are locked. If you want to move them, first choose View | Guides and deselect Lock Guides. Then you can select guides with the Select tool and drag them to new locations. Or you can select a guide and delete it by pressing the DELETE key.

 Remember, guides are visible *but they* do not print. *To see your document without guides, choose View | Guides | Hide Guides.*

Navigate Your Page

Once you open or create a document, you'll find that Illustrator has a number of features that help you navigate. It might seem that navigation wouldn't be an issue with small projects, such as business cards or postcards. But because you might well want to magnify your document hundreds of times, even a postage stamp can be difficult to find your way around in.

You can zoom in and out of a document using the Zoom pop-up menu on the left side of the Illustrator window status bar. A quick, easy way to view your entire illustration is to choose Fit On Screen from this menu.

 The Zoom pop-up menu is visible only when you have your document window maximized within Illustrator.

The Navigator palette is a great aid in navigating around a large document. Display this palette by choosing Window | Navigator. The Navigator palette has its own Zoom slider that allows you to control magnification. Once you set magnification with the Zoom slider, you can use your cursor as a grabber hand within the Navigator palette to define which section of the illustration shows up in the main document window, as shown in Figure 2-11.

FIGURE 2-11 Defining a zoom area in the Navigator palette

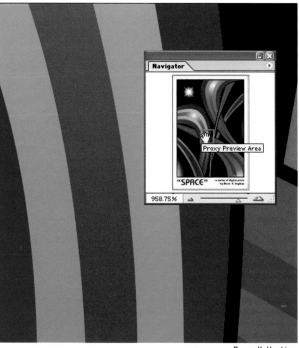

Bruce K. Hopkins

Proper Setup Saves Time

Experienced pros spend serious time defining default settings for a project. The right sized artboard, the right color model, the right units of measurement, are all essential to create projects in Illustrator.

For instance, for printed projects, you'll likely want to define page size (and rulers) in inches, but stroke thickness (for image border, for example), in points. For web projects, you'll want to define your "page" size in pixels—and use a size appropriate for the kinds of web graphics you'll be designing.

That said, you'll always end up adjusting your default settings as you work on a project. The nice thing about Illustrator is that you can change things like units of measurement or page size at any time, and your document is automatically associated with the new parameters you define.

Chapter 3

Import Artwork

How to...

- Choose between importing and linking embedded artwork
- Use embedded bitmaps
- Use linked bitmaps
- Place artwork in your document
- Trace imported bitmaps
- Use an imported bitmap as a non-printing tracing layer
- Organize bitmaps with the Links palette
- Manage linked bitmaps
- Set a default editor for linked objects
- Replace a linked image

Illustrator files often include objects from other sources. If you simply want to combine objects from more than one Illustrator file, you can copy and paste them between documents. But if you want to include artwork from Photoshop, PowerPoint, a scanned photo, or other artwork with another file format, you'll use Illustrator's Place features to insert that artwork.

Placed artwork can be from another vector graphics program (such as Freehand or CorelDRAW), or it can be a bitmap image. Imported pixel-based files present some special challenges because they come from the world of bitmaps and aren't easily edited with Illustrator's vector art tools. This chapter will explain how to effectively combine artwork from other sources—especially bitmaps—with an Illustrator project.

Chapter 19 will take a quick look at Illustrator's limited bitmap editing tools. For most bitmap editing, the folks at Adobe would prefer that you turn to Illustrator's cousin, Photoshop.

FIGURE 3-1 Using a scanned bitmap (gray and black) as a model for drawing (in color)

Bruce K. Hopkins

Imported bitmap

Drawing on top of bitmap

FIGURE 3-2 The onion is an imported Photoshop (PSD) file, and the text was created in Illustrator.

Bruce K. Hopkins

Import Art

Imported artwork can be either vector objects or bitmaps. There are no special requirements for importing vector objects. Once they are copied and pasted, or imported, into an Illustrator document, they behave just like other Illustrator vectors. Imported bitmaps are often managed differently. Let's look at three scenarios for importing bitmap art.

Scenario #1   You want to use a charcoal or pen drawing as a non-printing layer in your illustrations, and trace over it using Illustrator tools. Then you'll be able to use Illustrator's full set of tools and effects on the artwork. Figure 3-1 shows a drawing being used as a tracing layer for Illustrator's drawing tools.

Scenario #2   You want to import a sketch, but *leave it alone* as a bitmap, and simply include it as part of your illustrations (mixing bitmap and vector art in the same Illustrator file). Figure 3-2 shows an illustration that includes both an imported bitmap and vector art.

Scenario #3   You want to import a bitmap image (such as a scanned drawing) and use Illustrator's tracing tools to convert that bitmap object into a vector object.

You'll explore all three scenarios in this chapter.

Choose Between Importing and Linking

Before you bring files into Illustrator, you need to decide whether to embed them or link them. *Embedded* images are saved in your Illustrator file as part of your illustration. *Linked* files remain independent files.

Illustrator text

Imported bitmap

You have the option of linking or embedding imported artwork regardless of whether that artwork is bitmap art, another Illustrator file, or a file from another vector art program. However, there is usually not much reason to choose the link option for imported vector art, because there isn't the same need to preserve the ability to edit that art in another program.

Use Embedded Images

Embedding images is simpler and more reliable than linking them. Embedding is safer because you don't have to worry about sending a bunch of linked images along with your Illustrator file to a client, or about whether you've broken links to images by changing your file folder structure in the process of transferring Illustrator files.

By not selecting the Link check box when you place an image in Illustrator, you embed the file. Images you copy and paste into Illustrator will be embedded, not linked.

You can convert linked objects to embedded images by selecting a linked file, either on the artboard or in the Links palette, and then choosing Embed Image from the Links palette menu.

Use Linked Images

Linked images are saved as separate files and must be transferred *along with* your Illustrator file. For example, if you use several linked images, and you save your Illustrator file to a zip drive, you must save the linked bitmaps to the *same folder* on the zip drive (or CD/R or whatever media you use).

The advantage of maintaining images as linked files is that you can more easily *substitute different* linked images. For instance, if a technical drawing includes a photo of a product that is frequently updated (while the drawing is not), you might choose to link the photo so that another file with the same name can easily be used in place of the original.

 *When you transfer an Illustrator file to a client, you should almost always embed images. Don't count on your client (or your printer) to accurately keep your Illustrator file and your associated image files together.*

FIGURE 3-3 Importing a
Photoshop file as a linked image

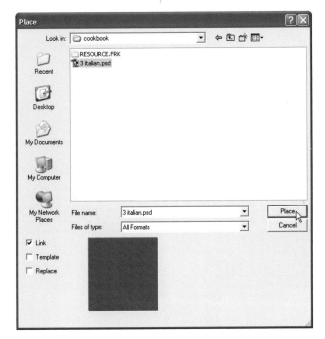

Place Artwork in Your Document

Once you've decided whether you will be embedding or linking files, you can place artwork in an open Illustrator file by choosing File | Place. The Place dialog box opens. Navigate to the folder that contains your linked file.

When you select a new object for embedding or linking, the Link and Template check boxes become active in the Place dialog box, as shown in Figure 3-3. If you want to import your image as a linked file, select the Link check box.

A placed bitmap will look like any other vector object on your artboard. You can move it and apply many effects and filters.

The Template check box in the Place dialog box will import your image as a non-printing, non-editable template layer. This feature is discussed later in this chapter in the "Use an Imported Bitmap as a Non-printing Tracing Layer" section.

Trace Imported Bitmaps

One option for working with imported bitmaps is to use Illustrator's Auto Trace tool to automatically generate vector lines and fills from the artwork. This works for simple drawings that can be traced easily. Or you can use the Auto Trace tool to start converting a bitmap to a vector object and finish up the job using Illustrator's drawing tools.

There are two adjustable properties for the Auto Trace tool. Oddly enough, they're not found in an Auto Trace dialog box or anything associated with the tool itself. Instead, you must select Illustrator (Edit) | Preferences | Type & Auto Tracing from the main Illustrator menu to open the Type & Auto Tracing section of the Preferences dialog box. Here you can define tolerance and gap settings.

Tracing tolerance can be defined on a scale of 1–10, and tracing gap can be set anywhere from 0 to 2 pixels. A setting of 0 tolerance allows you to select very specific sections of an imported bitmap to convert to vectors, while a setting of 10 unleashes Illustrator to convert bigger chunks of the bitmap to vectors each time. A gap setting of 0 will stop conversion to vectors whenever there is a break in a line, while a setting of 2 will allow the generation of a continuous curve whenever a break of 2 points or smaller is encountered.

 The bottom line is that you'll end up experimenting with both tolerance and gap settings when you convert a bitmap using the Auto Trace tool.

Figure 3-4 shows a drawing scanned with both high and low gap settings. The low setting is on the left, and the high setting is on the right.

Low gap setting

Untraced original

High gap setting

Bruce K. Hopkins

FIGURE 3-4 The Auto Trace tool converts larger sections of the bitmap to a single path when a high gap setting is used.

Use an Imported Bitmap as a Non-printing Tracing Layer

Imported bitmaps are often used as tracing layers. Sometimes this is done to simply duplicate an image with an accuracy and detail not available with the Auto Trace tool. Other times the

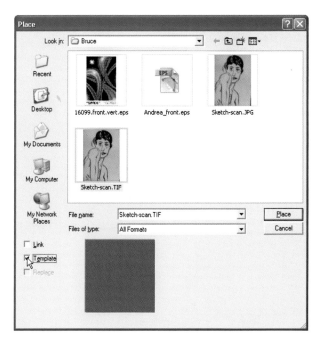

underlying tracing layer is used as a basis for artwork that is not intended to exactly follow the original scanned or imported image.

To import artwork as a non-printing tracing layer, choose File | Place. Navigate to and select the file you are importing, but don't click Place in the dialog box just yet. First, select the Template checkbox, as shown in Figure 3-5. Then click Place.

You'll find that you can't move, edit, or delete your imported artwork. But you can draw on top of it. When you print, the placed template art will not be visible.

FIGURE 3-5 Using a bitmap as a non-printing template

Note *You can convert a template layer into a printing layer. This is covered in Chapter 20, which explores layers in detail.*

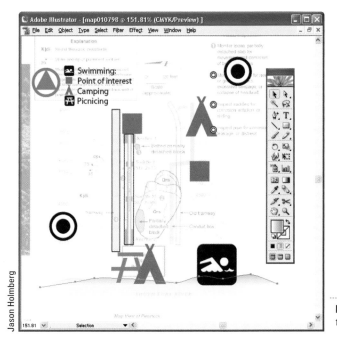

Jason Holmberg

FIGURE 3-6 Drawing over a template

Figure 3-6 shows a tracing layer being used as a basis to create a new sketch in Illustrator.

Organize Bitmaps with the Links Palette

When you open an Illustrator file that includes linked bitmaps (or other linked files), the linked files will automatically be opened in the document. The Links palette helps you view, find, and manage all the embedded and linked images in your open document. To view the Links palette, choose Window | Links. All linked and embedded bitmaps will display in the Links palette, as shown in Figure 3-7.

 Oddly enough, the so-called "Links" palette is actually used to manage both linked and embedded images.

To sort the display of linked and embedded images by name, choose Sort by Name from the Links palette menu. You can also use the Links palette menu to sort by file type or status (linked or embedded). The same menu also allows you to show all images (choose All from the menu) or just embedded images (choose Embedded from the menu). To change the size at which linked and embedded images are displayed on the palette, choose Palette Options from the Links palette menu and select from the thumbnail size options.

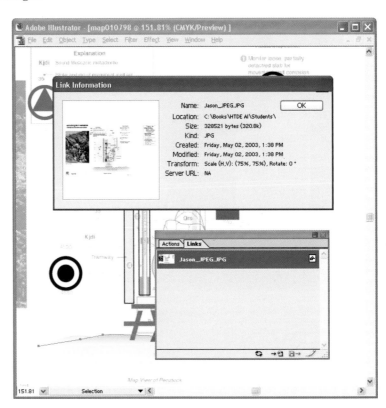

FIGURE 3-7 The Links palette shows a list of placed files. Double-clicking on a link opens

Manage Linked Files

In the course of this book, you'll learn to apply many effects and filters to artwork that will distort, contort, recolor, and reshape objects. When you place a file as a linked object, you can assign all the effects and filters you wish in Illustrator.

Those effects stay with the imported file, even if the picture is edited in its original application. Let's say, for example, that you've imported a photo from Photoshop, and you have applied several effects in Illustrator. Then let's say that you later edit the photo back in Photoshop. When you update the link in Illustrator, the effects you applied will still be associated with the photo, but any changes made to the photo in Photoshop will also be applied to the photo in Illustrator.

To define how you want this updating to work, choose Illustrator (Edit) | Preferences | Files & Clipboard. The Preferences dialog box offers three Update Links options, as shown in Figure 3-8.

FIGURE 3-8
Defining link update options

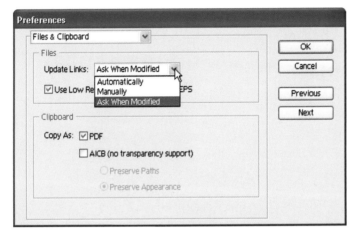

If you choose the Automatically option, Illustrator will modify the linked image whenever you change the file in another program. The Ask When Modified option prompts you to accept or reject changes. The Manually option requires you to click an object in the Links palette and choose Update Link from the Links palette menu before a newer version of your image will be substituted.

You're better off choosing the Ask When Modified option. You'll have a chance to reject changes if you want to.

Set a Default Editor for Linked Objects

You can conveniently edit a linked image in your system's default bitmap editor by choosing Edit Original from the Links palette menu. After you edit a linked image in your bitmap program, exit the program, and you'll be prompted to apply the changes to the version of the linked image in Illustrator.

How does Illustrator know what bitmap editor to launch when you edit a linked file? This is defined in your operating system, not in Illustrator. In Windows, choose Start | Settings | Control Panel, and double-click on Folder Options. In the Folder Options dialog box, choose the File Types tab. Select a file format (such as TIFF or JPEG) and use the Change button to define a new application to associate with that file format.

In OSX, select a file, then choose the Get Info command. On the Info palette, under the Open with menu, select the

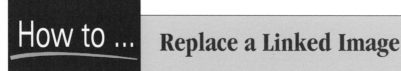

Replace a Linked Image

You can not only edit a linked image in your bitmap editor and have it change in Illustrator, but you can also replace a linked image with a different linked image and still retain all the effects you applied in Illustrator.

Try the following steps to see how you can replace a linked image in Illustrator without losing your changes:

1. Choose File | Place and place a picture in an Illustrator file. Be sure to select the Link check box in the Place dialog box as you import the image.

2. Move the image.

3. View the Links palette (Window | Links), and select the image to be replaced in the Links palette.

4. Choose Replace from the Links palette menu. The Place dialog box opens.

5. Navigate to the bitmap image file you wish to substitute for the selected image, and click on the Place button in the Place dialog box.

The new image will replace the old one, in the same location.

 After you place the image, all the effects and other editing you applied to the original image are applied to the new bitmap.

appropriate application. Then click Change all to make that application the default for this file type.

Fix Missing Links

If you try to open an Illustrator file in which a linked image has been deleted or moved, you will be prompted with a dialog box asking if you want to replace the file for that image with another one.

If you have moved the image file or have another file you want to use, click Yes. The Replace dialog box will open. It's just like the Place dialog box; you can use it to navigate to and select a new image (or find a moved image). When you select a replacement image, click the Replace button in the Replace dialog box to substitute the new (or moved) file.

Part II

Draw Objects

Chapter 4

Draw with the Pencil and Brush Tools

How to…

- Get a handle on paths and anchors
- Draw with the Pencil tool
- Use the Erase tool to edit drawings
- Draw nice, smooth curves
- Draw strokes with brushes
- Define brush stroke attributes
- Define stroke thickness
- Set stroke and fill colors
- Copy stroke and fill colors from one object to another

FIGURE 4-1 A complex drawing based on Pencil-drawn objects

In Illustrator, you create and edit drawings by defining anchor points and the paths between them. Before you start drawing lines and curves, you'll find it helpful to have an introduction to the basic way paths and anchors work.

Understand Paths and Anchors

In this chapter, you'll learn to use the Pencil, Line Segment, Arc, Spiral, Rectangular Grid, and Polar Grid tools to generate a variety of paths and anchors. Figure 4-1 shows an illustration that depends on the Pencil tool.

An *anchor* (or *anchor point*) is the end of a line segment, and it controls the curve and finish location of that line segment. The line that connects the start and end of a group of anchors is often called a *path*. OK, enough theory for now, time to start drawing!

Draw with the Pencil Tool

The Pencil tool has a split personality. If you start from that understanding, then you won't get as disoriented when odd things happen when you use this tool.

The Pencil tool can be used as a quick-and-dirty way to draw lines. It's also a way to *redraw* existing lines to smooth out edges or tweak an illustration.

As a drawing tool, the Pencil tool has its limitations. Even experienced Illustrator artists, who use drawing tablets to facilitate more accurate drawing, usually start from a sketch created with an old-fashioned pencil, piece of charcoal, or paintbrush. When you want to create a complex illustration, you'll often want to create artwork on paper first, and scan your artwork into Illustrator. But the Pencil tool provides a flexible way to either draw with your mouse or drawing tablet or trace a scanned image.

The Pencil tool also has its limitations as a redraw tool. Artists who become comfortable with using the shape, line, and arc tools and the Pen tool generally stay away from the Pencil tool since it duplicates the features of those tools, but not as well. That said, many designers who are new to Illustrator find the Pencil tool more intuitive than its big brother, the Pen tool. You'll use the line and arc tools later in this chapter and the Pen tool in Chapter 6.

FIGURE 4-2 Stroke is set to red, and fill is set to None

Set Stroke and Fill Color

Before you start drawing with any tool, you'll want to set a stroke and a fill color. To define a visible stroke color, click on the Stroke icon at the bottom of the Toolbox, and then choose a color in the Color palette that appears.

You can choose a fill color by clicking on the Fill icon in the Toolbox and then clicking on a color in the Color palette. Figure 4-2 shows a red stroke color and no fill color being assigned.

Bruce K. Hopkins

To assign no *fill to your drawings, click the Fill icon in the Toolbox and then click the None button below the Fill/Stroke icons in the Toolbox. It might be helpful to avoid color fill as you experiment with drawing tools.*

Define Pencil Tool Preferences

Before you start sketching away with the Pencil tool, double-click the tool to open the Pencil Tool Preferences dialog box. Use the Fidelity slider to define how many anchor points to generate as you draw. The fidelity value tells the program how faithful it should be (in pixels) to the user's actual mouse movements.

A low fidelity value, for example, tells Illustrator to stay very close to your mouse (or drawing tablet) movements. Low fidelity values create more angular curves. A high fidelity value allows Illustrator more freedom to stray from the path you draw to create a smoother curve. A low value generates more anchor points, while a high fidelity value creates a smoother line. Figure 4-3 shows fidelity and smoothness settings in the Pencil tool dialog box.

Figure 4-4 shows the same drawing, done twice. The drawing on the left was done with a low fidelity value, while the smoother drawing on the right was done with a high fidelity value.

FIGURE 4-3 The low fidelity value and high smoothness settings mean that the Pencil tool will draw smooth curves that do not adhere closely to the path you draw with your mouse or drawing tablet.

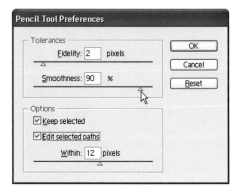

Smoother lines produced by higher fidelity values

FIGURE 4-4 The drawing on the left, produced with a low fidelity value, is more jagged than the one on the right, produced with a higher value.

The Smoothness slider in the Pencil dialog box works in a similar fashion: a high setting evens out your drawing.

If the Keep Selected check box is checked, after you draw a curve with the Pencil tool the anchor points will all be selected. This feature is useful if you expect to edit your anchor points after you draw with the Pencil tool. Selecting the Edit Selected Paths check box enables the Pencil tool to function like an editing tool, changing the size and direction of selected paths.

Caution *The Edit Selected Paths check box option can be a little disorienting because it's sometimes hard to tell whether your Pencil tool is in a state where it will add to a drawing or edit it. Higher settings on the Edit Selected Paths slider make the Pencil tool less sensitive to nearby curves. If you find that you're often trying to draw new paths but the Pencil tool keeps editing nearby paths, increase the value of the slider. If you find that it's just too confusing to have one tool do two different things, you can turn off the editing feature of the Pencil tool by deselecting the Edit Selected Paths check box.*

Draw with the Pencil Tool

Draw with the Pencil tool as if you were holding a pencil. Hold down your mouse button or use your drawing tablet tool and, with the Pencil tool selected, simply start drawing, as shown in Figure 4-5.

FIGURE 4-5 Drawing with the Pencil tool

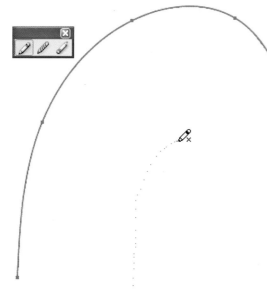

If you enabled the Keep Selected check box in the Pencil Tool Preferences dialog box, the object that you draw will automatically be selected as if you had clicked on it with the Selection or Direct Selection tool. This makes it easier to *edit* the drawing by redrawing the generated path.

As you draw with the Pencil tool, Illustrator generates paths. You can ask Illustrator to smooth those curves out (to varying degrees) as you draw. Or you can use a special tool on the Pencil tear-off, the Smooth tool, to soften your curves after you draw with the Pencil tool.

However you generate paths with the Pencil tool, if you examine them you'll see they are made up of anchor points and line segments. Try it. Select a curve you've drawn with the Pencil tool, and take a close look at the anchor points you generated. You'll want to be aware of these anchor points as you begin to edit your line.

Edit Drawings with the Pencil Tool

All three of the tools in the Pencil tool tearoff can be used to edit curves. You can use the Pencil tool itself to not only draw curves but to modify existing curves. The Smooth tool irons out zigs and zags, making your curves flow more smoothly. And the Erase tool works like a pencil eraser to eliminate part of a curve.

To use the Pencil tool to edit a curve, first select that path (line) with a selection tool. Select the Pencil tool again, and then click and drag on a curve to change that curve, as shown in Figure 4-6.

Smooth a Line

The Smooth Tool Preferences dialog box works much like the Pencil Tool Preferences dialog box does. You open it by double-clicking the Smooth tool.

Fidelity as applied to the Smooth tool defines how closely Illustrator adheres to the smoothing line you draw over an existing curve. Higher fidelity values remove more anchor points as you "sweep" over a curve. A fidelity value that is too high removes all nuance and detail from the drawing. A high smoothness setting smoothes out more rough edges in your drawing.

To use the Smooth tool, first double-click the Smooth tool and define the degree of fidelity and smoothing you want to use, and click OK. Then use the Selection (or Direct Selection

FIGURE 4-6 Redrawing a selected line segment using the Pencil tool

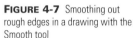

or Lasso) tool to select the curve to be smoothed. Finally, click and drag with the Smooth tool along the path you want to apply smoothing to, as shown in Figure 4-7.

Erase a Line

The Erase tool deletes selected sections of a path. There are no preference settings for the Erase tool; it simply does its thing and deletes anchor points and the line segments between them. The

FIGURE 4-7 Smoothing out rough edges in a drawing with the Smooth tool

concept to keep in mind is that you are deleting *anchor points,* not bunches of pixels (as you would with an eraser tool in a program such as Photoshop).

 In addition to deleting points, you can use the Erase tool to remove sections of a path between two points. Illustrator then adds new end points to the new path segments.

To erase a section of a drawing, follow these steps:

1. Select an object using the Selection tool or Lasso tool.

2. With the object selected, click the Erase tool (in the Pencil tool pop-out).

3. Click and drag with the Erase tool along the outline of the selected object to erase a section of the path, as shown in Figure 4-8.

 To make a line less smooth, you can choose Effect | Distort And Transform, and then experiment with using the Roughen, Twist, or Zig Zag effects to add wrinkles and twists.

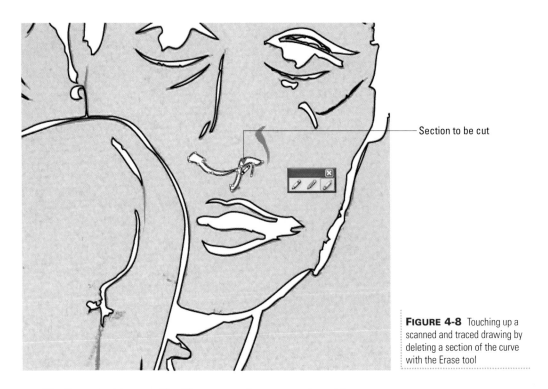

Section to be cut

FIGURE 4-8 Touching up a scanned and traced drawing by deleting a section of the curve with the Erase tool

The Erase tool is versatile. You can use it on any path and in any place within a line. If you want to make a clean cut in a line, click and drag across the line (as if cutting with a knife).

 *If you just point and click on a path with the Erase tool, you'll delete the entire line segment. If you need help zeroing in on anchor points with the Erase tool, you can convert the display from the Erase icon to cross hairs by pressing* CAPS LOCK *on your Mac or PC keyboard. This approach sometimes makes it easier to identify exactly where you are erasing.*

Edit Anchor Points with the Direct Selection Tool

You can edit objects by selecting and moving anchor points with the Direct Selection tool. If the anchor selected with the Direct Selection tool is associated with a curved line, that *smooth anchor* will have control handles that allow you to manipulate the curve of the line.

Editing smooth anchors can be quite complex. In later chapters of this book, you'll be introduced to various ways of tweaking anchor points. But the short story is that by clicking and dragging anchor points, you can change the angle of the curve, and by lengthening or shortening the handle, you can alter the size of the curve.

As mentioned earlier, clicking on the Direct Selection tool on a path between smooth anchor points, *handles* appear connected to each anchor. Clicking and dragging on these handles changes the angle of the curve, as shown in Figure 4-9.

FIGURE 4-9 Dragging on an anchor point with the Direct Selection tool to alter a path

Draw Straight Lines and Curves

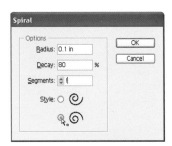

Illustrator's Line Segment tool pop-out provides a set of tools for drawing lines, arcs, spirals, rectangular grids, and polar grids.

Each of the tools in the Line Segment tool pop-out can be used two ways: you can interactively click and drag to create an object; or you can select the tool, click once on the artboard, and then define the parameters of the object in a dialog box such as the one shown in Figure 4-10 (for spirals).

The Arc, Rectangular Grid, and Polar Grid tools include four clickable corner buttons in the upper-left corners of their dialog boxes. You use these clickable corners to determine where you want to start your object. You can define the insertion to start the drawing at the top left, top right, bottom left, or bottom right of the object you generate.

Draw Straight Line Segments

To draw a line, select the Line Segment tool, then click and drag. Hold down SHIFT as you draw to constrain your line to 45-degree angles. If you hold down OPTION (ALT) as you click and drag, you will draw your line symmetrically, around a central radius. You can combine these features—holding down SHIFT-ALT as you draw—to create lines that expand from a center point and are at increments of 45 degrees.

FIGURE 4-10 Generating a spiral from the Spiral dialog box

 If you're looking for tools to draw rectangles, ovals, stars, and polygons, you'll find those features discussed in Chapter 5.

Draw Arcs, Spirals, Rectangular Grids, and Polar Grids

You can draw a symmetrical arc, spiral, rectangular grid, or polar grid by simply selecting any of these tools and clicking and dragging. Most folks find that it's easier to draw an arc interactively on the artboard than it is to generate one from a dialog box. Just click and drag to approximate the length, direction, and curvature of your arc. When you release the mouse button, your arc is complete.

You can rotate, resize, or reshape a curve using the Free Transform tool.

You can help yourself draw symmetrical curves by holding down SHIFT to constrain arcs to increments of 45 degrees, or holding down OPTION (ALT) to draw an arc starting from a center point.

Since spirals, rectangular grids, and polar grids can be rather complex sets of paths, it's often easier to use the click-and-define technique for generating these shapes. First select a tool, and then click on the artboard. An associated dialog box appears, allowing you to define the exact configuration of the resulting object.

The Spiral tool options allow you to define the radius (distance from the center to the edge), the decay (degree of spiraling), and the number of segments. A decay angle of anything less than 50 produces something more like a curve than a spiral. A decay angle close to 100 percent creates a very tight spiral.

The number of segments defines how many times the spiral winds around, with each wind containing four segments. As you increase the segment number, it creates more winds in the center of the spiral. A small number of segments creates a choppy-looking curve, while a large number creates a smoother curve.

The highest possible setting for a decay value is 150 percent.

Rectangular grids are defined by their size, the number of horizontal dividers, and the number of vertical dividers. The Polar Grid dialog box defines the number of concentric dividers (rings) and radial dividers (pie slices). The Rectangular Grid and Polar Grid definition dialog boxes both have Skew sliders. These sliders warp your grid to make it asymmetrical—with dividers grouped more closely on the left or right, outside or inside, or top or bottom of an object, as shown in Figure 4-11.

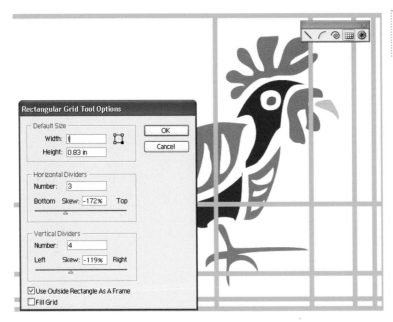

Draw with Paintbrushes

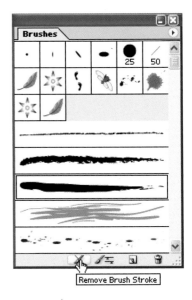

The Paintbrush tool draws using a defined shape as the brush. Simply select the Paintbrush tool and draw as you would with the Pencil tool to create a curve. The default (plain) setting creates flowing, ribbon-like curves.

You can also use the Paintbrush tool to "paint" curved lines using all kinds of symbols and images. You can choose from a wide variety of brush types that come with Illustrator, or you can even create your own brush shapes.

 Chapter 18 explains how to define custom brushes.

Change Brush Stroke Symbols

To choose from Illustrator's gallery of available brushes, choose Window | Brushes (or press F5 on your Mac or PC keyboard) to display the Brushes palette. The Brushes palette is shown in Figure 4-12.

Scroll down the Brushes palette and click a symbol you wish to use as a brush shape. With a brush selected from the palette, you can use the Paintbrush tool to paint curves using the selected symbol.

FIGURE 4-12 Viewing the Brushes palette

4

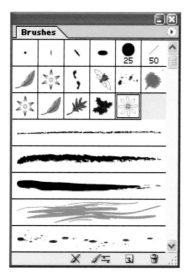

FIGURE 4-13 Adding a floral brush to the Brushes palette

To turn off a brush stroke (so that it won't be used when you use other drawing tools), click the Remove Brush Stroke button at the bottom of the Brushes palette (as shown in Figure 4-12). Each time you select the Paintbrush tool in the Toolbox, you'll turn the selected brush stroke back on, and it will apply to any drawing tool.

Use Additional Brush Strokes

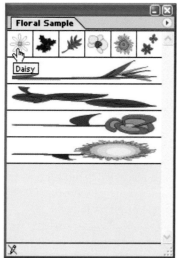

You can add brushes to the Brushes palette by choosing Window | Brush Libraries and choosing from one of the available sets of brushes. A new palette with brush symbols appears.

Clicking a symbol in the new Brush Library palette adds a symbol to your working Brushes palette, as shown in Figure 4-13.

Once you add brush symbols to your regular Brush palette, you can use them like any other brush shape. Figure 4-14 shows a drawing using a brush loaded with a fill from the Brushes palette.

Define Strokes and Fills

The most basic way to assign a stroke (outline) or fill color to an object is to select the object, click the Fill or Stroke icon at the bottom of the Toolbox, and then click a color in the Color palette.

There are many other options for assigning colors to strokes or fills. And there are other stroke and fill attributes that you can define. In this section, you'll learn to define thickness and different styles (such as dashes) for strokes.

FIGURE 4-14 A leaf brush was used for this drawing.

You can also pick up a color from anywhere on your screen and apply it to selected objects using the Eyedropper tool. You'll explore that technique in this section as well.

Define Stroke Attributes

You define stroke thickness and style by using the Stroke palette. You can also use the Stroke palette to define how lines end and how they join (connect) with each other. Choose Window | Stroke (or press F10) to view the Stroke palette.

To define the weight (thickness) of a selected line, choose a dimension from the Weight drop-down list, as shown in Figure 4-15.

The units of measurement in the list are defined in the Preferences dialog box. (Choose Illustrator (Edit) | Preferences | Units & Display Performance, and select a unit of measurement from the Stroke drop-down list in the Preferences dialog box.)

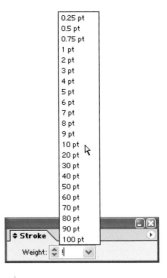

FIGURE 4-15 Setting stroke at 10 points

Define Caps and Joins

A Line segment can end at its anchor point (butt style), be rounded (round style), or project past the anchor point (projecting). Line segment options for a selected line segment are visible if you choose Show Options from the Stroke palette menu.

Choose a line cap style for a selected line segment by clicking one of the three cap buttons. All three cap styles are shown in Figure 4-16.

The three join buttons (miter, round, and bevel) control how corner line segments connect. Rounded joins create curved corners, and beveled joins create cut-off corners instead of sharp corners. You can limit mitered joins by choosing a value in the Miter Limit spin box. A high enough value will prevent beveling.

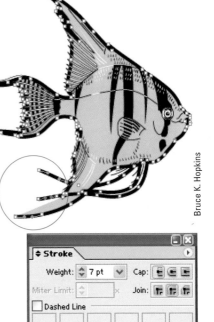

Bruce K. Hopkins

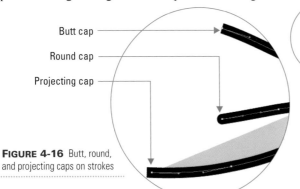

Butt cap

Round cap

Projecting cap

FIGURE 4-16 Butt, round, and projecting caps on strokes

You can assign dashed lines to selected line segments by clicking the Dashed Line check box. If you want to define custom dashed lines, you can use the gap area(s) to define spacing between dashes. The Dash boxes allow you to define a dash of a set length (like "12 pt" for a 12 point dash). The Gap areas can be defined in length as well.

Assign Stroke or Fill Colors with the Eyedropper or Paint Bucket Tool

You can "steal" colors from other strokes or fills by using the Eyedropper tool. Or you can easily apply the currently selected color for a fill or stroke using the Paint Bucket tool. Follow these steps to select a color using the Paint Bucket tool:

1. Using a selection tool (such as the Selection tool), select the object from which you want to copy stroke and fill settings.

2. Click the Paint Bucket tool in the Toolbox.

Tip   *The Paint Bucket tool is on the Eyedropper tool tearoff.*

3. Use the mouse to move the Paint Bucket tool cursor over a section of the illustration to which you want to assign the fill and stroke colors, and click. The color you point to will be assigned the fill of the selected object, as shown in Figure 4-17.

The Eyedropper tool can grab stroke and fill colors from any object. First, select the object *to which* you want to apply a fill and stroke color. Then select the Eyedropper

Paint Bucket

FIGURE 4-17 The stroke and fill colors of the object clicked on with the Paint Bucket will be assigned from the selected circle in the upper left corner.

tool, and point and click on an object *from which* you will copy stroke and fill colors. In Figure 4-18, the stroke and fill of the ball are being used as a source for the sky color.

Nathan Alan Whelchel

Eyedropper

FIGURE 4-18 The sky was selected, then the Eyedropper was used to "borrow" the fill from the ball.

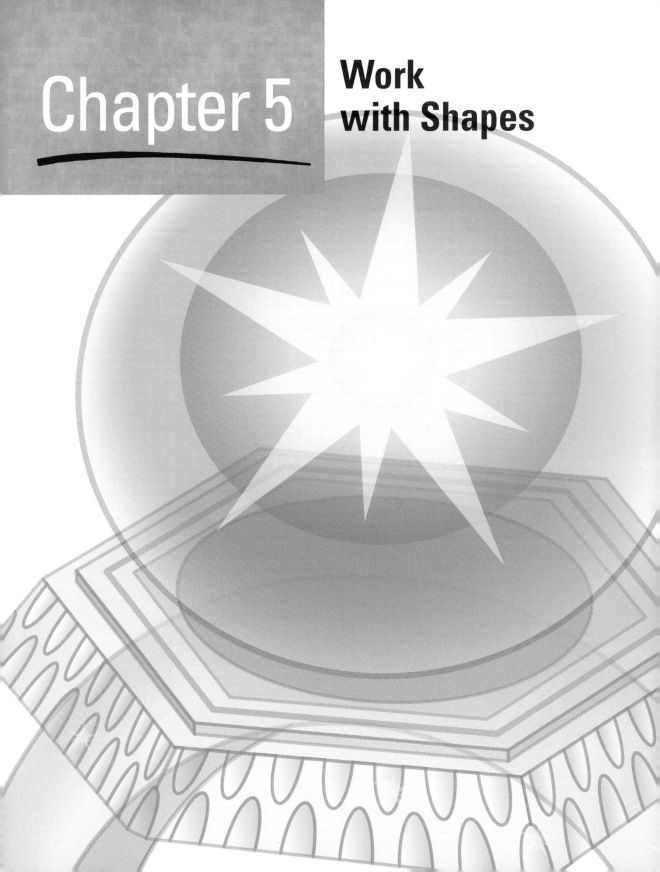

Chapter 5

Work with Shapes

How to...

- Draw rectangles
- Size a rectangle precisely
- Draw a rounded rectangle
- Draw ellipses and circles
- Draw polygons and stars
- Generate effects with the Flare tool
- Combine objects with the Pathfinder tools

Many complex illustrations start out with, and are built on, basic shapes. Experienced Illustrator artists stretch, fill, and add effects to simple shapes such as ovals, rectangles, and stars to create projects. This chapter will show you how to create and combine shapes.

In this chapter, you'll also explore Illustrator's powerful set of *Pathfinder tools*. These tools allow you to create any possible interaction between overlapping shapes. You'll see how you can combine, split apart, merge, or break up shapes using these tools.

How useful are the modest shape tools? The illustration in Figure 5-1 is 95 percent shapes, altered in some cases with rotating tools (covered in Chapter 7), and tweaked with just a bit of gradient fill (covered in Chapter 17).

Bruce K. Hopkins

FIGURE 5-1 Look closely—the bulk of this illustration is composed of stars and other shapes.

Draw Rectangles

The Rectangle, Rounded Rectangle, Ellipse, Polygon, and Star tools are found on the Rectangle tool tearoff. Joining them, but out of place on this tearoff, is the Flare tool. The easiest way to use these tools is to simply click and drag. Alternatively, you can generate shapes from a dialog box that opens when you click any of the shape tools and then click on the artboard.

 The odd-duck Flare tool works differently. You double-click on the Flare tool to open the dialog box. Alternatively, you can select the tool and then click and drag or click on the artboard and then click again in the document window to generate a flare.

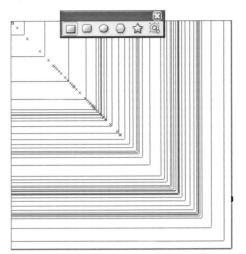

To draw a rectangle, select the Rectangle tool and then click and drag anywhere on the artboard. If you hold down SHIFT as you click and drag, you constrain the rectangle to a square. If you hold down OPTION (ALT) as you click and drag, the location from which you start to click and drag becomes the center point for the rectangle instead of a corner of the rectangle. Holding down SHIFT *plus* OPTION (ALT) as you draw creates a square with the initial point being the center of the square.

Holding down the tilde key (~) as you draw a rectangle generates multiple rectangles, as shown in Figure 5-2.

FIGURE 5-2 Drawing a square and generating many squares using SHIFT and the tilde key

Size a Rectangle Precisely

The other way to define a rectangle is to select the Rectangle tool and click anywhere on the artboard without clicking and dragging. The point where you click becomes the upper-left corner of the rectangle. The Rectangle dialog box appears, as shown in Figure 5-3.

This technique of defining a shape size in a dialog box can be applied to all shapes (except, of course, the otherworldly Flare tool).

FIGURE 5-3 Defining a rectangle by entering width and height values

Draw a Rounded Rectangle

To draw a rounded rectangle, select the Rounded Rectangle tool from the Rectangle tool tearoff. As with the regular Rectangle tool, you can either click and drag to interactively define the rounded rectangle, or you can click once on the artboard to define the rounded rectangle in a dialog box.

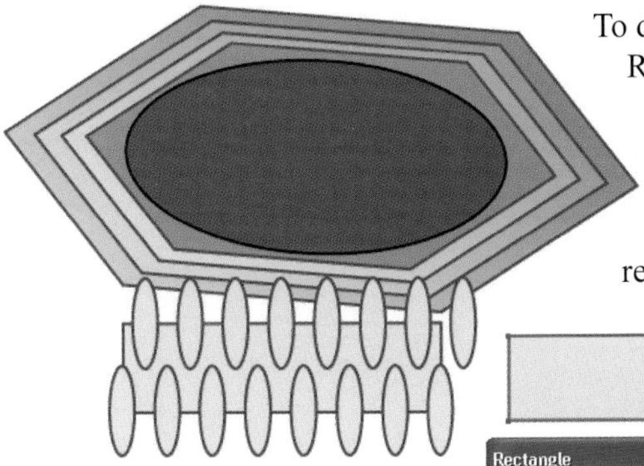

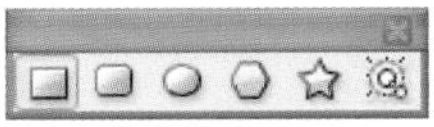

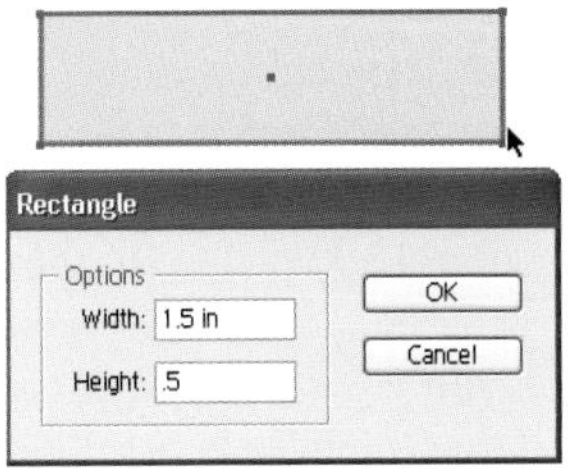

The Rounded Rectangle dialog box differs from the regular Rectangle dialog box only in that you can also define the size of the corner radius. The size of the radius determines how much rounding to apply: larger values increase the rounding. Once you define a radius, it applies to each rounded rectangle you draw.

If you want to change the units that appear in the shape dialog boxes, select Illustrator (Edit) | Preferences | Units & Display Performance. In the Preferences dialog box, change the selected unit of measurement in the General drop-down list to pixels, points, inches, or one of the other measurement options.

Draw Ellipses and Circles

To draw an ellipse (oval), select the Ellipse tool and then click and drag anywhere on the artboard. If you hold down SHIFT as you click and drag, you constrain the ellipse to a perfect circle. If you hold down OPTION (ALT) as you click and drag, you define the circle from a center point.

As with other shapes, you can hold down the tilde key as you click and drag to generate multiple ellipses as you draw.

The other way to define an ellipse is to select the Ellipse tool and click anywhere on the artboard without clicking and dragging. The Ellipse dialog box appears, and you can enter an exact width and height.

Draw Polygons and Stars

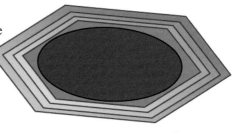

The Polygon and Star tools work like the other shape tools: you can interactively draw on the artboard, or you can click and define the polygon or star in a dialog box. Because polygons and stars can have anywhere from 3 to 1000 points or sides, you'll probably want to define the number of points and sides in a dialog box before you start drawing.

To define sides or points for a polygon or star, select the tool and click on the artboard. Use the dialog box to define the number of sides or points you want, and then click OK. If necessary, delete the just-created star or polygon by pressing DELETE or BACKSPACE. Then draw on the artboard. The stars or polygons will have the number of points or sides you just assigned in the dialog box.

When you draw a star or polygon, you can *rotate* the shape as you draw. First, draw the shape itself, at the size you want it to appear. Then, *without releasing your mouse button,* you can move your mouse clockwise or counterclockwise to tilt the shape, as shown in Figure 5-4.

Holding down the SHIFT key as you draw a star or polygon locks the alignment of the shape so that the base is parallel with the edge of the artboard. With the SHIFT key down, you cannot rotate stars or polygons as you draw.

FIGURE 5-4 Rotating a polygon as you draw

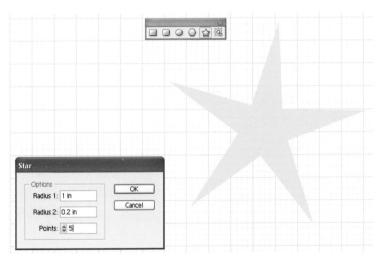

Normally, one dimension of a star is the outer dimension, defining the points of the star, and the second dimension is the inner radius, defining the inside circumference of the internal star points. By adjusting the ratio between Radius 1 (the first dimension of the star) and Radius 2 (the second dimension of the star), you can

FIGURE 5-5   The Radius 2 value for this sharply pointed star is much smaller than the Radius 1 value.

control the type of star you draw. To create a very pointed star, such as the one in Figure 5-5, use a Radius 2 value that is much smaller than the Radius 1 value. The star in the figure has a Radius 2 value that is 1/5 the value of the Radius 1 value.

Tip   *Alternatively, you could transpose the values in the above example—if the second dimension of the star is five times the first dimension, you'll get a star with the same degree of pointiness. To generate a shape instead of a star, set both dimensions to the same value. For instance, a "4-point" star with both dimensions set at equal values will produce an octagon (an eight-sided shape).*

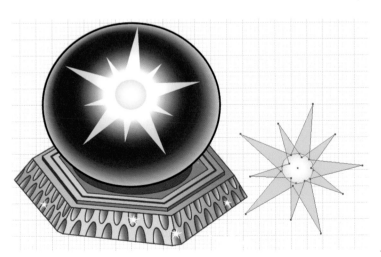

Another useful technique is to create stars that look like they're twinkling by placing a smaller star on top of a larger one. In Figure 5-6, two stars are combined to put a shine on the top of the ring jewel.

FIGURE 5-6   The glittering star is created by placing a smaller star (rotated) on top of a larger star. A similar technique was used to provide gleam in the jewel setting. Other ring elements were created with polygons and ellipses.

Space Out with the Flare Tool

The Flare tool might as well be from outer space—both because it doesn't really fit with the other tools on the Rectangle tearoff, and because it generates effects that can be used in science-fiction-style illustrations.

To draw a flare, start by selecting the Flare tool and then clicking and dragging to create the first part of the flared object. During this *first* click and drag, you'll define the radius of the flare. To complete the flare object, click a second time on the artboard to create the second part of the flare, as shown in Figure 5-7.

Alternatively, you can click once and use the Flare Tool Options dialog box to define the details of your flared object.

FIGURE 5-7 Adding flare to space

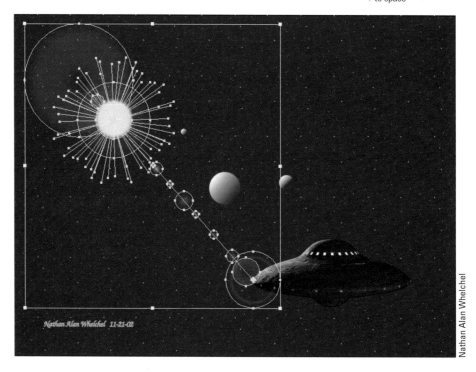

Nathan Alan Whelchel

Combine Objects with the Pathfinder Tools

The ten tools in the Pathfinder palette basically allow you to combine and divide two or more intersecting paths. These tools provide a quick way to apply some complex anchor point and path changes that would be tedious if you did them with tools such as the Pen tool or the Direct Selection tool.

When the tools in the Pathfinder palette combine two objects, the object on the bottom usually assumes the fill and stroke attributes of the object on top. So before you apply a Pathfinder effect, select Object | Arrange, and move objects in front of or behind other objects to define how fill and stroke attributes will be handled.

Note *There are a couple of Pathfinder tools that are exceptions to this rule: the use of these tools will cause the* top *shape to assume the properties of the* bottom *shape instead. Those odd tools are the Subtract From Shape Area and the Crop tools.*

You'll explore how to move objects in front of or behind each other in detail in Chapter 11, but here it will be helpful to have a quick preview of how to do that. To move an object in front of other objects, select the object and choose Object | Arrange from the menu. You'll have the option of moving a selected object in front of or behind other objects, or all the way to the front or all the way to the back of other objects on the artboard. Figure 5-8 shows an example of a typical Pathfinder technique. One ellipse has been placed on top of another oval. The Trim tool on the Pathfinder palette will use the top ellipse to "trim away" a section of the bottom ellipse. This new shape will then help create the perspective at the base of the ring.

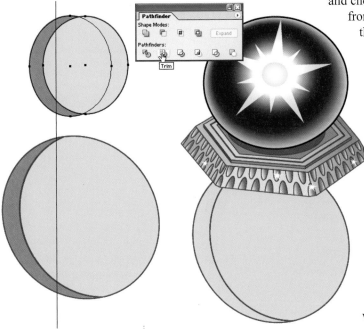

FIGURE 5-8 Using one shape to trim another with the Pathfinder palette

Caution *Pathfinder tools work with vector objects, including gradient fills. However, they don't work with bitmaps.*

Identify the Pathfinder Tools

To access the tools in the Pathfinder palette, choose Window |
Pathfinder. Figure 5-9 identifies each of the tools and shows
how they work.

Change Pathfinder Options

To access the Pathfinder palette
options, open the Pathfinder palette
menu and choose Pathfinder Options.

The Pathfinder Options dialog
box appears, as shown in Figure 5-10.
The options define how intersecting
objects will be combined. The
Precision value determines how
accurately intersecting objects will
be combined or divided. The default
setting works fine.

The Remove Redundant Points
and the Divide and Outline Will
Remove Unpainted Artwork check
boxes are useful. Each of them
removes elements of a combined (or
divided) object that aren't functional,
simplifying the resulting paths.

It's a good idea to activate the
Remove Redundant Points and Divide
and Outline Will Remove Unpainted
Artwork options. Usually you'll want to
invoke these helpful features to clean up
the result of your crop, trim, and so on.

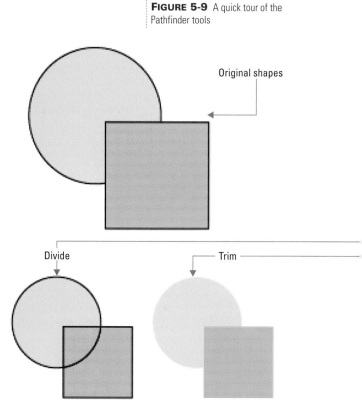

FIGURE 5-9 A quick tour of the
Pathfinder tools

*Caution* *Pathfinder palette options are retained during your Illustrator session, even if you
close the palette and re-open it. However, if you quit the application and restart,
the options are reset to the default values.*

Use Shape Modes

The Pathfinder tools are divided into two rows:
the Shape Modes and the Pathfinders. The
Shape Mode tools generate *new* shapes from
intersecting shapes.

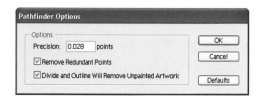

FIGURE 5-10 Choosing
Pathfinder options

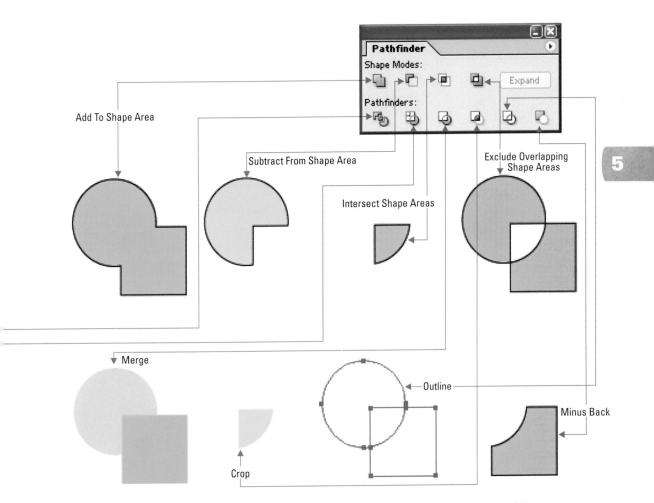

The Add To Shape Area tool combines selected objects into a single shape. The Subtract From Shape Area tool deletes the top shape from the bottom shape. The Intersect Shape Areas tool removes everything but overlapping areas of selected shapes. The Exclude Overlapping Shape Areas deletes shared areas of two overlapping selected objects.

 The Add To Shape Area Pathfinder tool was called the Unite button in Illustrator 9 and earlier versions.

After you apply a Shape Modes tool, the resulting path is a compound shape. Compound shapes are kind of like grouped shapes (explored in detail in Chapter 11), but Shape Mode tools more thoroughly combine the selected objects.

To break a compound shape back up into its components, choose Release Compound Shape from the Pathfinder palette menu.

Expand Compound Shapes

To convert a compound shape created with a Shape Modes tool into a completely editable, single object, click the Expand button in the Pathfinder palette. Expanding a compound shape completely removes all remnants of the original shapes and results in a single, new shape.

Figure 5-11 shows the differences in paths once generated shapes have been expanded. Note the missing anchors and paths in the expanded objects.

FIGURE 5-11 Generated vs. expanded shapes—note the missing and changed anchors in the expanded versions.

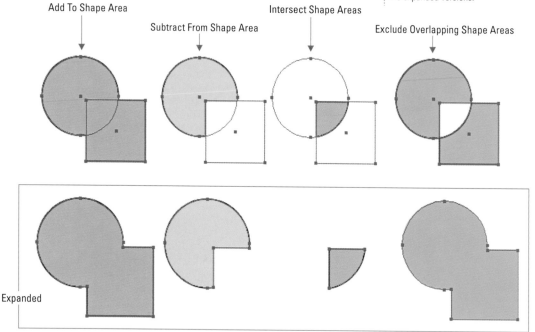

Add To Shape Area

Subtract From Shape Area

Intersect Shape Areas

Exclude Overlapping Shape Areas

Expanded

Clip, Crop, and Split with the Pathfinder Tools

The Pathfinders—the second row of tools in the Pathfinder palette—perform more complex transformations to overlapping objects than the Shape Modes tools do.

 In early versions of Illustrator, these Pathfinders were referred to as divide tools, which give a little hint as to what they are used for.

One basic function of Pathfinders is to combine overlapping objects and then break them into a variety of new objects that can be ungrouped and moved, deleted, or edited individually.

The Divide tool splits selected objects into individual shapes created by intersecting paths. The Trim tool deletes the covered portion of the bottom shape. The Merge tool is similar to the Trim tool, but it merges contiguous shapes if both have the same color fill.

The Crop tool uses the top object like a cookie cutter to cut away parts of the bottom object that do not fit within it. The Outline tool converts fills to outlines; the color of the fill becomes the color of the outline stroke.

The Minus Back Pathfinder tool uses the bottom object as a cookie cutter to strip away intersecting areas from the front object.

After you apply one of the Pathfinders, the result is a grouped object. You can split that group and edit the newly generated shapes by choosing the group and selecting Object | Ungroup from the menu.

Sometimes the results of the Merge and Trim Pathfinder tools are the same. The only time the results are different is if there is a contiguous, divided area with the same color fill.

How to ...   Examine Hard and Soft Mixes

Hard and Soft mix options are one way, but not the best way, to combine colors in overlapping shapes. Nowadays, Illustrator users take advantage of transparency to mix the colors of overlapping objects. You'll get your hands around transparency features in Chapter 17.

You can access these effects, and the rest of the Pathfinder tools, from the menu by choosing Effect | Pathfinder and then selecting a Pathfinder effect.

Note *Older versions of Illustrator (version 9 and older) displayed Hard and Soft mix options in the Pathfinder palette. In Illustrator CS, Hard and Soft mixes live on the Pathfinder menu.*

Since the arrival of transparency back in Illustrator 9, you now have a more reliable way to combine colors in overlapping objects. Transparency produces color mixes that stand up better when sent to hardcopy or web output. Hard and Soft mixes remain on the Effect | Pathfinder menu, but they are no longer an important part of the Illustrator arsenal. That said, if you want to try them, group objects before applying a Hard or Soft mix. Hard mixes add the values of overlapping colors—as if you were overprinting hardcopy colors. Soft mixes are similar to transparency.

Cut with Knife and Scissors

The choice of tools for chopping up objects in Illustrator seems to be endless. The Pathfinder tools you just explored earlier in this chapter are some of the more powerful and useful. In Chapter 6, when you explore the Pen tool, you'll learn to select and edit individual anchors. That method provides very fine control over reshaping objects, but it is also the most tedious way to alter a shape.

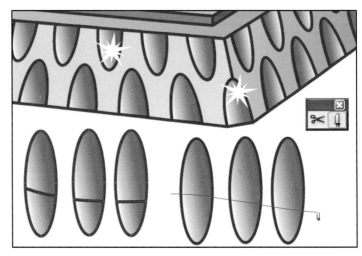

FIGURE 5-12 Cutting shapes with the Knife tool

Somewhere in between these techniques lie the Scissors and Knife tools. Because these tools are more tedious than the Pathfinders, and less powerful than the Pen tools, experienced designers don't use them much. But they're worth a quick look.

Drag the knife tool across any object or objects to cut them into separate sections, as shown in Figure 5-12.

 *Objects have to be selected before you can slide through them with the Knife tool.*

The Scissors tool is similar to the Knife tool in that it can dissect objects. However, with the Scissors tool, you click on a path to instantly sever that path. You can click at two points on a path to break an object into two parts. Or just click once—converting a *closed* object (one with identical starting and ending points) into an *open* object (one with different starting and ending points).

Chapter 6

Draw with the Pen Tool

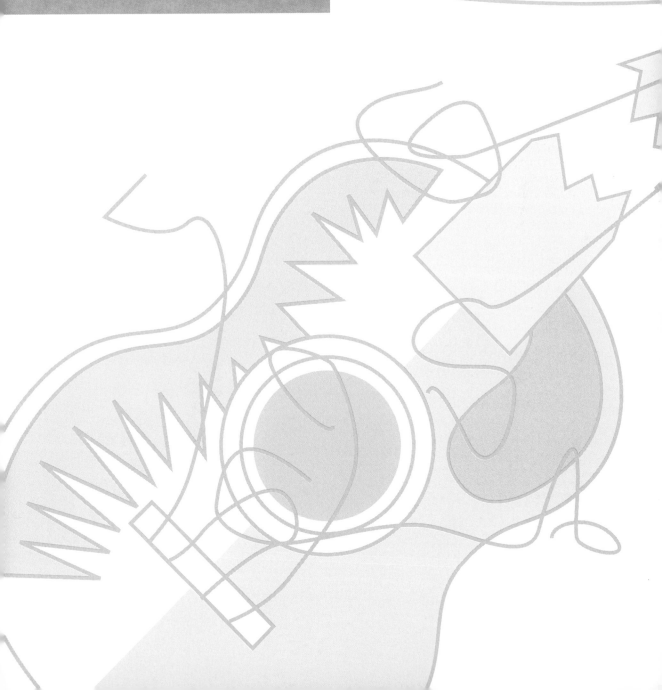

How to...

- Understand pens and paths
- Use vectors to help you draw
- Draw lines with the Pen tool
- Define anchor point angles
- Draw and manipulate curved paths
- Draw waves
- Modify curved paths with Control Points
- Add and delete anchor points
- Edit drawings with the Pen tool
- Clean up stray anchor points

The unique power of vector drawing programs such as Illustrator lies in their ability to generate perfect curves. It's amazing how much freedom you have to create illustrations by combining straight lines and curves. And the ultimate curve tool in Illustrator's arsenal is the Pen tool.

The Pen tool isn't easy to master, and it isn't intuitive. When you draw in "real life," you don't consciously think of generating paths controlled by anchor points that define the curvature of a path. But that's how the Pen tool works. You don't "click and drag" with the Pen tool as you do with the Pencil tool (or a real pencil). Instead, you click to define the location of anchor points, and then manipulate control points associated with those anchors to define the curvature of your path. All this takes much practice.

Few digital artists sit down and "free-flow" design with the Pen tool. Instead, it's more often used to trace scanned artwork or generate exact curves based on a template or model. That said, the Pen tool is the single most effective, fine-tuned, and essential resource in Illustrator.

Pens and Paths

Other tools, such as the Pencil or the shape tools, are sufficient for creating already defined shapes or imprecise drawings. But to really unleash Illustrator's ability to generate and control curves, you'll need to pick up the mighty Pen tool. The Pen tool provides unlimited control over the curvature of line segments and how they connect with each other.

In this chapter, you'll learn techniques that will demystify the process of generating curves with the Pen. And you'll learn tricks for creating smooth, precise illustrations with this most powerful of Illustrator tools.

The Math of Paths

Without the math underlying Illustrator, you'd be without the freedom to create beautiful, accurately defined curved paths.

An Illustrator vector object is a combination of anchor points and the line segments in between those anchor points (along with a defined fill). Illustrator saves programming code (called PostScript, a page-description language) that defines the nature of each path. This vector-based method of saving graphic files is rooted in the mathematical formulas for defining curves pioneered by a French engineer named Pierre Bézier.

Bézier's curves revolutionized the way graphic files were saved. Vector images are often smaller in file size and, as explained briefly in Chapter 1, they are always more easily resizable than bitmap images. Vector graphics are, indeed, an efficient way to save illustrations. But they are also a dynamic and unique way to create drawings.

Did you know?

Vectors Help You Draw

In the movie *Zoolander*, Ben Stiller's character was determined to found an institution for kids who "can't write good." Illustrator's vector drawing tools aren't exactly the remedy for folks who "can't draw good," but they can be a big help. Illustrator compensates for our humanly imperfect drawing skills. And, while we marvel at the drawings of M.C. Escher, even the most accomplished artist can't duplicate the precision and control that Illustrator provides over curves.

Tip   *If you're unfamiliar with the groundbreaking work of M.C. Escher, you can visit http://www.worldofescher.com/gallery/ to be introduced to some of his work. Preceding the era of digital art, he nevertheless incorporated new discoveries in math and philosophy in his amazing drawings.*

If you don't count yourself among the drawing elite, you can still create perfect curves. The most powerful and versatile tool for generating and altering curves is the Pen tool. The Pen tool creates anchor points and the line segments between them.

The nature of a segment (curved or straight) is defined by the anchor points at either end of the segment. Anchor points that connect (or end) straight lines are referred to as *corner anchor points* (or *corner anchors* or *corner points* for short). Anchor points that connect (or end) curved lines are referred to as *smooth anchor points* (or *smooth anchors* or *smooth points* for short). Anchor points that connect a curved path segment with a straight path segment are called *combination anchor points*.

Smooth anchor points are manipulated by moving the anchor control points associated with the anchor points. The direction lines that connect control points to their associated anchor point make it easier to get a feel for how moving a control point affects the curve associated with a smooth anchor point. The following illustration shows a drawing that is composed of a combination of smooth, corner, and combination anchor points.

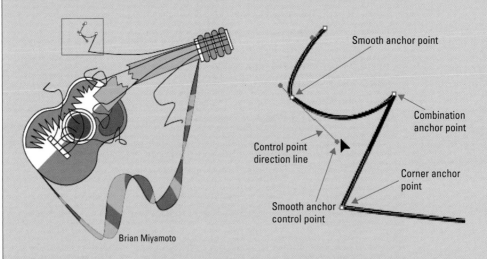

As you explore and experiment with the Pen tool, you'll gain a wizard-like ability to draw with it. And with some practice, it will become an extension of not just your hand but your imagination.

Draw Line Segments with the Pen Tool

The easiest and most basic type of line segment you can create with the Pen tool is a straight segment: a line segment with two corner points. To draw a straight line with the Pen tool, click once and then click again at another location on the artboard.

Complete the straight corner point by clicking a third time anywhere on the artboard, as shown in Figure 6-1. Finish the path segments by clicking on another tool (like the Selection tool), or holding down the COMMAND (CTRL) key and clicking with the Pen tool.

As with all of Illustrator's drawing tools, the Pen tool cursor can be displayed as cross hairs for more accuracy. To display the Pen tool cursor as cross hairs, press CAPS LOCK on your keyboard. Pressing CAPS LOCK again reverts to the normal cursor display.

FIGURE 6-1 Three clicks and you're on—drawing a corner with the Pen tool

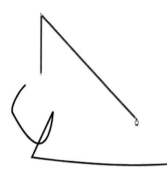

End a Pen Segment

The Pen tool stays active and continues to add on to your path until you indicate that you're done. When you have completed the set of line segments, hold down COMMAND (CTRL) and click to deselect the Pen tool.

Another way to deselect the Pen tool is to simply select another tool. A quick, easy way to do this is to use a keystroke shortcut (such as the letter V, which selects the Selection tool) to quickly deselect the Pen tool. You can press P or select the Pen tool from the Toolbox to begin a new set of line segments.

Alternatively, you can end a series of straight line segments by closing the path. Just move the Pen cursor over the original anchor point and click. As you move the cursor over the starting anchor point, the Pen tool cursor displays with a circle next to it, as shown in Figure 6-2.

FIGURE 6-2 Closing a path with the Pen tool

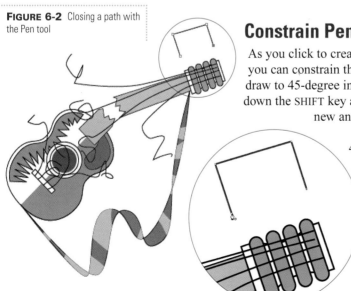

Constrain Pen Angles

As you click to create straight corner points, you can constrain the line segments you draw to 45-degree increments by holding down the SHIFT key as you click to create new anchor points.

If you turn on Smart Guides, 45- and 90-degree angle points are illustrated. (Choose the View menu and make sure Smart Guides is selected.) You can add more angles or edit the default settings for Smart Guide angle constraints by choosing Illustrator (Edit) | Preferences | Smart Guides & Slices. You can choose angle options from the Angles drop-down menu or type in exact angles in the boxes in the Angles area. So, for instance, if your illustrations require many 30-degree angles, you can program the Smart Guides to help you draw that angle.

Create and Edit Smooth Anchor Points

Curved line segments are defined by the length and location of their associated control points. Direction lines that connect control points to smooth anchors make it a bit more intuitive to manage curves by manipulating control points. As you get more comfortable with the Pen tool, you cannot only use it to generate anchor points, but you can also, simultaneously, manipulate anchor control points as you draw.

To create and fine-tune a smooth anchor point as you draw with the Pen tool, follow these steps:

1. Select the Pen tool and click on the artboard to create the first anchor point.

2. Move your cursor (without clicking and dragging) to the location of a second anchor point, and click. Don't release the mouse button.

3. With your mouse button still down, drag from the new anchor point to create a control point (indicated by the resulting direction line) and generate a smooth anchor.

4. Click on a third point on the artboard.

5. Press COMMAND (CTRL) and click to finish the path, as shown in Figure 6-3.

FIGURE 6-3 Generating a smooth anchor as you draw with the Pen tool

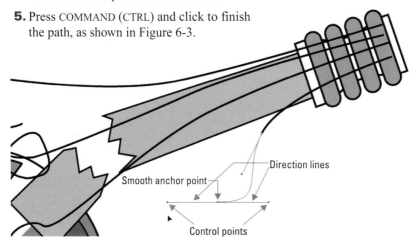

Draw Wave Forms

FIGURE 6-4 Generating a wavelike curve with the Pen tool

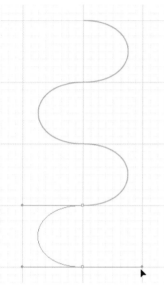

Waves are a widespread phenomenon in nature, and therefore in art as well. One of my favorite uses of the Pen tool is to generate smooth, flowing, and easily altered waves. The exercise of drawing a wave is also a good way to get a feel for how curves are defined by manipulating control points and their associated direction lines.

Follow these steps to draw a set of waves with the Pen tool:

1. To get help drawing evenly spaced waves, select View | Show Grid and then select View | Snap To Grid.

2. Select the Pen tool, and click and drag horizontally to create a horizontal direction line.

3. Draw a second horizontal direction line lower on the page. Remember, you're not drawing a line now, you're manipulating a control point to define a smooth anchor point. You'll create the actual line when you define the next anchor point.

4. Press COMMAND (CTRL) and click to end the path, as shown in Figure 6-4. To create a set of wave-form paths, duplicate the generated path.

Note *After you draw a wave, you can use all the transformation tools (discussed in Chapter 7) to resize, rotate, and otherwise distort your waves for effect.*

Manipulate Control Points

FIGURE 6-5 Shortening a direction line to make a curve shallower

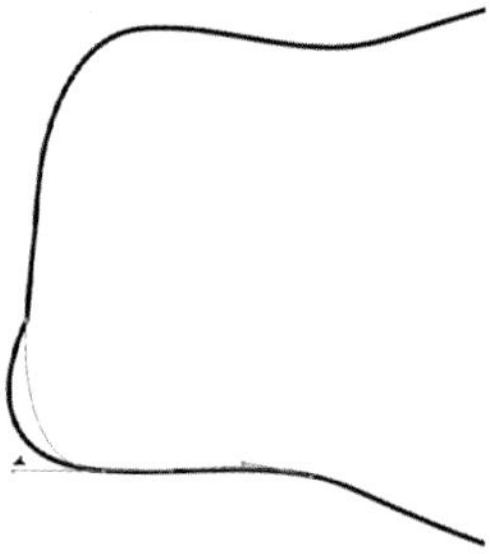

When you generate a smooth anchor point, you can manipulate the curve of the attached line segment(s) by moving the control points. You can make a curve steeper by extending the control points away from the anchor point (lengthening the Direction lines). Make a curve more shallow by shortening the direction lines, as shown in Figure 6-5.

Nathan Alan Whelchel

Select an anchor point and activate the control points by clicking on the anchor point with the Direct Selection tool. Locating an anchor point with the Direct Selection tool can be tricky, however. As you hover over an anchor point, the Direct Selection tool cursor turns into a tiny open square. It's easier to identify anchor points if you turn on Smart Guides (choose View | Smart Guides from the menu).

In addition, you can alter the angle of the intersection of curved line segments by rotating the direction line by dragging on a control point. To change the direction or length of a direction line, use the Direct Selection tool to select the anchor point. As you do, the direction line(s) become visible. Click and drag on the control point at the end of a direction line to lengthen or rotate the direction line, as shown in Figure 6-6.

Combine Straight and Curved Segments

Complex drawings mix and match both straight corner and curved corner anchor points. To create a complex path of both curved and straight segments, use the Pen tool to generate your curve by clicking to create anchor points.

For those anchor points you want to act as smooth anchors, click and drag to generate a pair of control points for the anchor. For straight corner points, simply click. Try clicking and dragging with the Pen tool to generate one smooth anchor point. Remember, you can always change the height and direction of a curved segment by later manipulating the direction lines. The basic technique is this: first rough out your path, and then fine-tune the curve by clicking and dragging on control points to manipulate the direction handles. This method provides a very high degree of control over the curvature of paths.

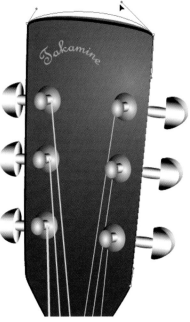

FIGURE 6-6 Changing the radius of a curve by rotating a direction line

 You can move an anchor point by selecting the anchor with the Direct Selection tool and then clicking and dragging that point to a new location.

Add or Delete Anchor Points

After you generate a path with the Pen tool, you can easily add or remove anchor points with the Add Anchor Point or Delete Anchor Point tool—both found on the Pen tool tearoff.

With the Add Anchor Point tool selected, click anywhere on a path to create a new anchor. The new anchor point is created with the attributes (curved or straight) of the existing segment. So, for instance, if you click a straight line segment with the Add Anchor Point tool, you'll create a new straight corner point. Similarly, you can use the Delete Anchor Point tool to remove unwanted anchor points. Select the tool and point and click an existing anchor point, and it's gone.

FIGURE 6-7 Reducing the number of anchors with the Simplify dialog box. The original set of anchors is illustrated in red, the resulting set in blue.

Automatically Create or Delete Anchors

You can also add anchor points automatically between every pair of anchor points in a selected path. Perform this task by first selecting the path and then choosing Object | Path | Add Anchor Points. You'll instantly double the number of anchor points, providing more flexibility in manipulating the path.

To automatically reduce the number of anchor points (and thus smooth out a curve), select Object | Path | Simplify. The Simplify dialog box appears. The Simplify dialog box has Curve Precision and Anchor Threshold sliders, as well as check boxes for Straight Lines, Show Original, and Preview. Higher Curve Precision values increase the number of anchors that will be left after simplifying. The Angle Threshold slider can be used to prevent some angle anchors from being smoothed into curves. The Straight Lines check box changes curved paths to straight lines.

The great thing about the Simplify dialog box is that you don't need to really grasp these settings to manage the process. If you click both the Show Original and the Preview check boxes, your original anchors will display in red, while the anchors that result from simplifying display in blue. Tweak the angle threshold and curve precision settings to experiment, observing the changes in your drawing as well as the net reduction in anchors that will result from your settings, as shown in Figure 6-7.

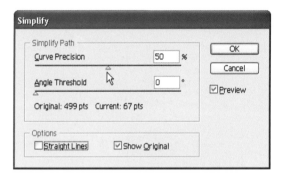

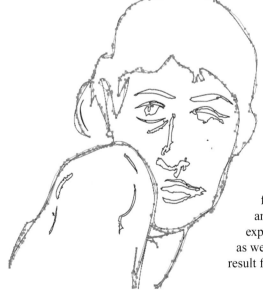

The Simplify feature is effective in many important ways. It can be used to clean up extraneous anchors in scanned and traced objects. It can clean up unnecessary Pen-generated anchors. And simpler curves mean smaller file sizes, so when you can remove anchors without distorting your illustration, it's a good idea to do so.

FIGURE 6-8 Converting a smooth anchor point to a corner anchor point

Change Anchor Types

You can transform anchor points from corner to smooth, or vice versa. The easiest way to perform this task is to use the Convert Anchor Point tool (in the Pen tool tearoff).

When you point and click on an anchor point with the Convert Anchor Point tool, curved points are instantly converted to straight corner points. In Figure 6-8, the curved anchor point is about to be converted to a corner point.

If you convert a straight point to a curved point, you can immediately click and drag to define and manipulate control points to edit the line segments that connect to that point. In Figure 6-9, a straight corner anchor has been converted to a smooth anchor with the Convert Anchor Point tool, and the control points are being maneuvered to define the curve.

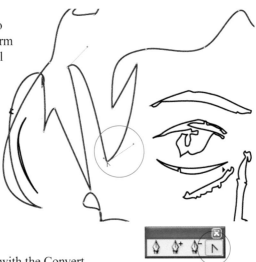

Edit with the Pen Tool

You'll almost always want to modify curves that you create with the Pen tool. Often you'll want to quickly switch back and forth between touching up your curves and creating new ones. Illustrator provides many tricks for doing this. Depending on when and how you use it and which keyboard keys you hold down, the Pen tool converts to several related tools.

In addition, Illustrator provides features for automatically smoothing or touching up your Pen-drawn curves,

FIGURE 6-9 Adjusting the control points on a converted anchor

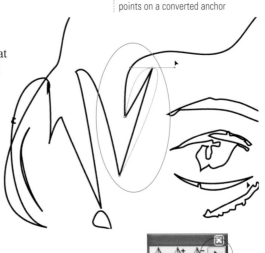

including the ability to line up anchor points, delete stray anchor points, and simplify a curve.

Because the Pen tool is the most powerful and useful tool in Illustrator, you'll have it selected most of the time as you create a drawing. By moving the cursor to different parts of a path, or by pressing COMMAND (CTRL) or OPTION (ALT), you can temporarily change the functioning of the tool.

You can use the Pen tool to add segments to an existing path and to add or delete anchor points to a path. The Pen tool can even be converted so that it temporarily functions like the Convert Anchor Point tool.

Add Segments to a Path

To add segments to an existing path, move the Pen tool over an endpoint in the path. As you do, the cursor displays as a slash (/).

With the Pen tool cursor displaying with a slash, click the current endpoint in the path. Then click again to define a contiguous segment, as shown in Figure 6-10.

FIGURE 6-10 Extending a line with the Pen tool

Tip *If you click and drag instead of just clicking, you'll define a new curved anchor point.*

Add, Delete, and Adjust Anchor Points with the Pen Tool

When you point to an anchor point, the cursor displays with a minus (–) sign, and the Pen tool takes on the persona of the Delete Anchor Point tool. Move the Pen tool over an existing anchor point, look for the minus sign cursor, and click. The selected anchor point disappears.

When you point to a path (but not an anchor point on the path), the Pen tool temporarily assumes the identity of the Add Anchor Point tool. Click to create new anchor points. The new anchor point assumes the characteristics of the line segment to which it is added. So a new anchor point on a curved line segment will be a curved anchor point.

Control Pen Tool Mode

When you hold down COMMAND (CTRL), the Pen tool changes to the most recently chosen selection tool. After you've jumped to the Direct Selection tool once, for example, the next time you need to toggle from the Pen tool to the Direct Selection tool, just press COMMAND (CTRL) to convert the Pen tool on the fly to the Direct Selection tool.

One frequent scenario that uses this technique is when you have added an anchor point by pointing and clicking on a path. You can then press COMMAND (CTRL) to convert the Pen tool to the Direct Selection tool. Now you're ready to adjust the control points on the new curved anchor point.

Manage Paths

You can use menu options to close a path and to "average" a path to align points. These options help create symmetrical, clean drawings.

You can also use menu options to find and clean up those stray anchor points that are created when you click with the Pen tool but don't generate a path. Somehow, those darn things always seem to litter a complex illustration.

Align Points by Averaging Paths

Illustrator allows you to align specific anchor points within a path. This trick can be handy when you need to create symmetrical or aligned objects. Generally, when you average paths, you'll want to apply the averaging only to selected points. Otherwise averaging tends to mush your path into an unrecognizable mess.

 If you are trying to look up how to align objects (not anchor points), jump ahead to Chapter 11.

To average points in a path, follow these steps:

1. Use the Direct Selection tool to select two (or more) anchor points in a path.

2. With two or more points selected, choose Object | Path | Average. The Average dialog box appears.

3. Select Horizontal to align the selected points on a horizontal plane; select Vertical to line the points up vertically. If you select both, the selected points will move to the same location (and merge into one point).

4. Click OK to apply the changes to the path, as shown in Figure 6-11.

FIGURE 6-11 Horizontal averaging on two points in a path

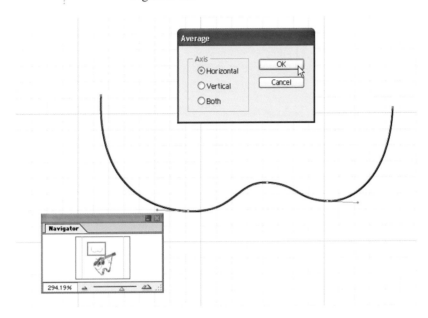

To close an unclosed path, select all the line segments and choose Object | Path | Join. A line segment is generated between the first and last anchor point in the path. If you select two anchor points that are already in the exact same place and choose Object | Path | Join, you convert them into a single anchor point. If one of the anchor points is a smooth anchor and the other is a corner point, you can use the Join dialog box to choose whether to convert the newly merged point to a smooth or corner point.

The easiest way to select just two anchor points is to select one and then hold down SHIFT *and select a second point.*

Because anchor points are tiny, it's sometimes hard to tell if they are selected. Selected anchor points display as filled squares instead of hollow squares, and they are easier to identify in

Outline view. To view your illustration in outline view, choose View | Outline. You can revert to Preview view by choosing View | Preview.

Clean Up Stray Anchor Points

A click here, a click there, and suddenly your artboard is littered with a bunch of invisible (unless selected) anchor points. Although they don't print, they mess up your project by adding space and size to exported files. And they cause confusion by appearing when you select objects and find you've also grabbed a few stray anchor points. You can see stray anchor points in Outline view, and you can delete them manually.

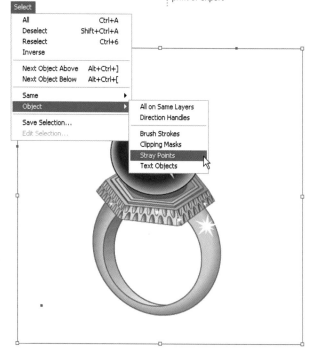

FIGURE 6-12 Cleaning up stray anchor points prepares the file for print or export

Thankfully, Illustrator also allows you to identify and delete these stray anchor points automatically. Just choose Select | Object | Stray Points and press DELETE to clean them up. Figure 6-12 shows stray anchors selected all around the illustration—ready for deletion.

Another way to clean up stray points is to select Object | Path | Clean Up. This strategy opens the Clean Up dialog box, with check boxes that allow you to get rid of stray points, unpainted objects, and/or empty text paths.

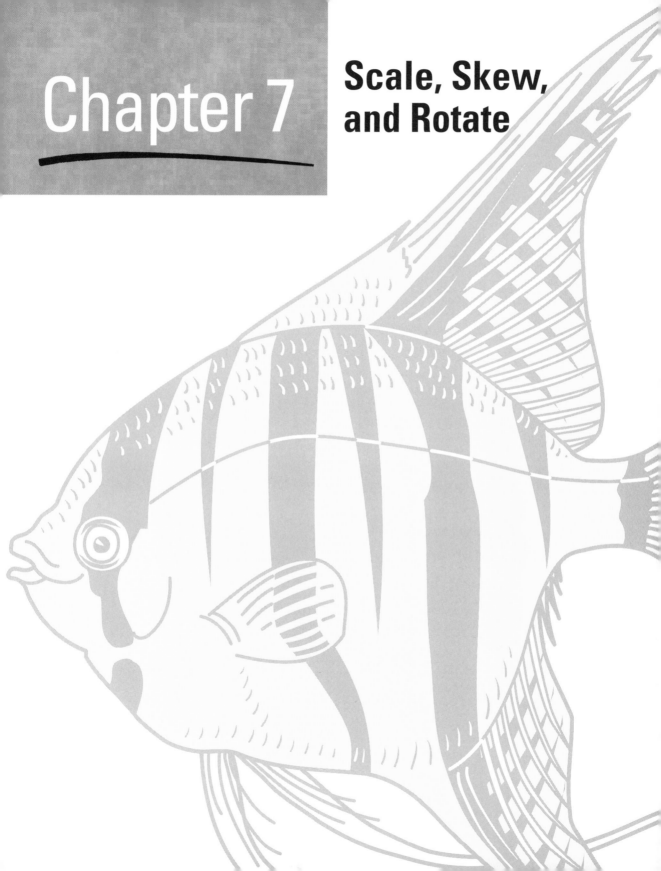

Chapter 7

Scale, Skew, and Rotate

How to...

- Group objects
- Select objects within a group
- Resize and reshape with a bounding box
- Resize and reshape with the Free Transform tool
- Resize precisely with the Scale Tool
- Rotate objects precisely

Much of the power of Illustrator is expressed in the ability to stretch, shrink, skew, and rotate objects *without losing any image quality.* Since Illustrator is such a powerful tool for distorting objects, there are many tool options for resizing and reshaping. Just as people living in snowbound areas of the planet have developed a vocabulary to cover every shade of white, Illustrator offers multiple options for sizing, reshaping, rotating, and flipping objects or groups of objects.

You can transform a simple drawing in an infinite number of ways by using Illustrator's escalating set of transforming tools. You can apply these tools to single objects, sets of selected objects, or grouped objects.

Get Ready to Size, Scale, and Rotate

You can elect to display bounding boxes on your artboard, which provide convenient anchor points around selected objects for sizing, mirroring, or rotation. For basic resizing or rotating, the Free Transform tool usually does the trick. For more precise sizing or rotation, the Scale and Rotate tools allow you to assign exact size changes and rotation angles. Further, they allow you to select anchor points that stay in one place as you interactively resize or rotate an object.

The more esoteric Reflect, Shear, and Reshape tools provide more options for distorting selected objects. In this chapter, you'll examine and learn to use each of these resizing and reshaping tools.

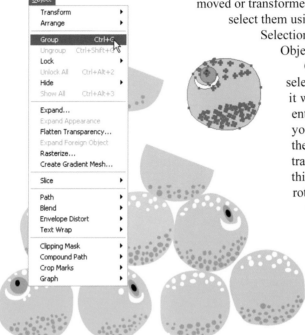

FIGURE 7-1 Grouping selected objects

Group Objects First

Before you begin to modify objects, it will be helpful to understand how objects can be grouped together and then moved or transformed together. To group objects, first select them using a selection tool (such as the Selection tool or the Lasso tool). Then choose Object | Group, as shown in Figure 7-1. Once objects are grouped, you can select the entire group by clicking within it with the Selection tool. With the entire set of grouped objects selected, you apply fill or stroke changes to the entire group. In a similar way, the transforming tools covered in the rest of this chapter (such as those that resize or rotate an object) generally apply to the whole selected group of objects.

Select Within a Group

If you want to change just one object within a group, you can ungroup the objects and then select an individual object within the group. That can get tedious, however, especially if you're frequently switching back and forth between changes to a bunch of grouped objects and changes to a single object (or a few objects) within the group.

The solution to this problem is to use the Group Selection tool found in the Direct Selection tool tearoff. The Group Selection tool allows you to select any object(s) within a group. So, for example, if you wanted to change the fill color of just the spots on a lemon, you could use the Group Selection tool, hold down SHIFT, and click on the spots, as shown in Figure 7-2. Holding down the SHIFT key allows you to use the tool to select several objects.

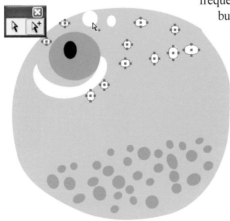

FIGURE 7-2 Selecting within a group with the Group Selection tool

To more or less permanently ungroup a set of objects, select the group and choose Object | Ungroup (or use the shortcut keys COMMAND-SHIFT-G [CTRL-SHIFT-G]). Groups can themselves be grouped again.

 The keyboard shortcut for grouping is COMMAND-G (CTRL-G).

 If you're going to get into multiple levels of grouping, you'll probably be better served by organizing collections of objects into more powerful layers. You will learn to do that in Chapter 20.

An alternative way to select several objects is to hold down SHIFT while clicking with the Selection tool. Be aware that each level of grouping has to be ungrouped in turn. So if you've grouped a group within a group, you'll have to choose Object | Ungroup more than once to ungroup all the objects.

Change Objects with a Bounding Box

A bounding box is an imaginary, non-printing border around an object or group of objects. It facilitates some basic transformations, including resizing, reshaping, mirroring (flipping), and rotating objects. Illustrator's object editing tools provide detailed control over any kind of tweaking you wish to apply to an object or group of objects.

You'll explore each of those powerful tools shortly, but first here's the quick-and-dirty way to change an object. When you just want to quickly and (relatively) crudely resize, rotate, or flip an object or quickly experiment with all these changes to an object, the simplest way to do so is to use a bounding box.

View a Bounding Box

To view a bounding box around a selected object, choose View | Show Bounding Box (if this is not already selected). When you do, a bounding box with four small, square side anchor points and four corner anchor points appears, as shown in Figure 7-3.

Bounding box

FIGURE 7-3 The bounding box enables quick-and-dirty resizing and rotating.

Most editing is the same, whether or not a bounding box is displayed. For example, you move an object or group with the bounding box displayed by clicking on a path or fill within the bounding box and click and drag to a new location on the artboard.

Tip   *Holding down* ALT *as you click and drag makes a copy of the object(s) at a new location.*

FIGURE 7-4 The height-to-width ratio is maintained as the squirrel is resized with a bounding box.

Resize and Reshape with a Bounding Box

To resize an object, click and drag on a side or corner anchor point while holding down SHIFT. Holding down SHIFT maintains the height-to-width (aspect) ratio of your object(s) as you resize. Figure 7-4 shows a group being resized using a bounding box with the SHIFT key.

The bounding box around this set of grouped objects provides easy access to basic transformation actions. If you want to resize without maintaining the height-to-width ratio of your object(s), click and drag a side anchor point to change height or width, or a corner anchor point to resize both height and width independently of each other. With this technique, you can make an object or group wider, narrower, shorter, or taller.

Rotate and Flip with a Bounding Box

Displaying a bounding box around selected objects also makes it easy to rotate or mirror (flip) these objects. To rotate a selection, choose the Selection tool, and move your cursor near a corner or side anchor point. As you do, a rotation cursor appears, as shown in Figure 7-5. Click and drag with the rotation cursor to rotate the selected object(s) around the center point of the selection.

You can also use a bounding box to mirror (flip) an object horizontally or vertically. The routine for mirroring an object is similar to the one for resizing, except that you drag an anchor point across the box, and post the opposite edge of the bounding box, creating a mirrored version of the object.

FIGURE 7-5 Using the rotation cursor with a bounding box

If you hold down the OPTION (ALT) key as you mirror an object with the bounding box, the object mirrors using the center of the selected object as an axis. If you hold down the SHIFT key as you mirror, the object retains its height-to-width ratio but also flips horizontally and vertically, as shown in Figure 7-6.

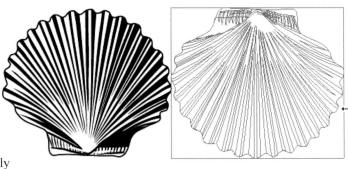

FIGURE 7-6 Quick mirroring with the bounding box

  If you want to rotate your object around an axis other than the center point, jump ahead to the "Rotate Objects Precisely" section.

Resize and Reshape with the Free Transform Tool

Enabling a bounding box around selected objects has its merits: it makes rotation, sizing, and mirroring easy to accomplish. The downside is that you have to put up with a bounding box popping up on your screen whenever you select an object or group of objects.

If the bounding box is getting in your way, choose View | Hide Bounding Box (or COMMAND-SHIFT-B [CTRL-SHIFT-B]) to make it disappear.

The Free Transform tool applies a functioning bounding box to selected objects. Use it to rotate, resize, or mirror a selected object. When you select a different tool, the bounding box created by the Free Transform tool disappears.

If you are an artist or designer who is new to Illustrator, or if you don't need precision sizing and rotating, you will find the Free Transform tool useful. It's versatile, intuitive, and easy to use. You can quickly resize a selected object using the Free Transform tool by clicking and dragging on a side or corner anchor point. Hold down SHIFT as you drag to maintain the height-to-width ratio as you resize the object.

To rotate a selected object with the Free Transform tool, hover over a corner or side anchor point and click and drag to rotate clockwise or counterclockwise. You can easily mirror (flip) a selected object using the Free Transform tool by clicking and dragging on a side anchor point. To mirror the object horizontally, drag a right or left side anchor point over and past the other side anchor point. To mirror vertically, click on the top anchor point and drag past the bottom anchor point.

As mentioned, using the Free Transform tool is very similar to displaying a bounding box—it's really a matter of your preference as to whether you want and need the bounding box displayed all the time.

For more precise control over sizing and rotating, you'll want to use the Scale and Rotate tools. These tools allow you to enter sizes or rotation angles digitally, and to rotate an object around any of the anchor points—not just the middle of the object.

Resize Precisely with the Scale Tool

The Scale tool has a couple of advantages over sizing freehand with a bounding box or the Free Transform tool. The Scale tool allows you to resize to an exact percentage—so, for instance, you can resize an object to 50 percent to make it exactly half size. And you can use the Scale tool to resize an object from a defined point, as opposed to just scaling from a selected anchor point with the Free Transform tool.

Using the Scale tool interactively is a bit like driving on an icy road—controlling the process is a bit scary until you get comfortable with the tool.

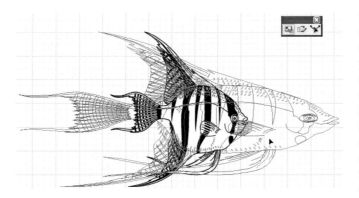

FIGURE 7-7 Using the SHIFT key with the Scale tool to change only width while maintaining the original height

When you resize using the Scale tool, you simply click and drag on a selected object to change the size. If you hold down the SHIFT key and click and drag out at about a 45-degree angle from a corner handle, you can maintain the height-to-width ratio of the original drawing. If you hold down the SHIFT key and drag up or down, you will change only the height *or* the width, as shown in Figure 7-7.

By default, when you resize a selected object with the Scale tool, the center of the object is used as the point from which the object is enlarged or compressed. You can change that point by clicking within a selected object with the Scale tool. Then, when you resize the object, the newly selected point is the pivot and hub from which the object is resized, as shown in Figure 7-8.

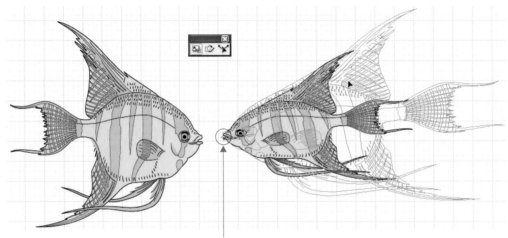

Fixed point

The Scale dialog box resizes digitally—no clicking and dragging required. It also allows you to control whether to rescale an object's stroke (outline) proportionally as you rescale the object. To resize using the Scale dialog box, follow these steps:

1. Select any object(s).

2. With the object(s) selected, double-click the Scale tool. The Scale dialog box appears.

3. Use the Scale box in the Uniform section to enter a percentage if you want to resize the object while maintaining the same height-to-width ratio.

4. Use the Horizontal and Vertical boxes in the Non-Uniform section of the dialog box to enter different percentages if you want to resize the height and width independently.

5. Click the Preview check box to see the object interactively resize on the artboard as you enter values in the sizing boxes.

6. Click the Scale Strokes & Effects check box if you want to proportionally resize strokes and effects.

7. Click the Objects check box to resize objects. You'll almost always want to select this option; otherwise, the object itself won't resize.

For the very rare occasions when you want to resize the pattern fill in an object but not the object itself, deselect the Objects check box. You'll explore pattern fills in Chapter 18.

FIGURE 7-9 The rescaled fish with unchanged stroke now has proportionally thicker lines.

8. Click the Patterns check box to proportionally resize patterns within a shape.

9. When your object is correctly resized, click OK (or press ENTER).

Figure 7-9 shows an object rescaled with and without rescaling the associated stroke.

Original

Rescaled with stroke unchanged

Rescaled with stroke rescaled

Rotate Objects Precisely

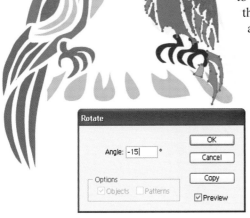

The Rotate tool rotates objects with the same kind of precision and control that the Scale tool uses. As with the Scale tool, you can use an associated dialog box to define rotation to a precise angle. And, as with the Scale tool, the Rotate tool can be used to define a rotation point that acts as a fulcrum as you interactively rotate an object.

To rotate a selected object (or set of objects) precisely with the Rotate dialog box, double-click the Rotate tool. The Rotate dialog box appears, as shown in Figure 7-10.

FIGURE 7-10 Defining rotation for a selected object—-the negative value in the Angle box indicates that the bird is being rotated counterclockwise

The value you enter in the Angle box of the dialog box defines the degree of rotation. The Copy button creates a second, rotated version of your selected object while leaving the original unchanged. The Preview check box allows you to view changes on the artboard as you make them in the dialog box, before your press ENTER or click OK. The Objects and Patterns check boxes allow you to elect to rotate objects and/or their fill patterns independently.

The Rotate tool also allows you to rotate around a selected anchor point in a selected object. To rotate an object around a selected anchor point, follow these steps:

Rotation anchor point

1. Select the object (or objects).

2. Click the Rotate tool.

3. Click an anchor point on the selected object to establish the rotation point.

4. Click and drag a different anchor point to rotate the object around the selected point, as shown in Figure 7-11.

FIGURE 7-11 The bird is being rotated around a defined fulcrum point.

Use More Transform Tools

The Rotate tool tearoff includes the Reflect tool. The Scale tool tearoff reveals the Shear and Reshape tools. All three of these tools provide more options for warping, stretching, and basically mangling any selected object(s). These tools work much as the Rotate tool does, but they produce different effects.

In the dialog boxes for the Reflect and Shear tools, the Preview check box shows your changes before you click OK or press ENTER. The Objects and Patterns check boxes, when available, determine whether objects and/or pattern fills are transformed.

The Reflect, Shear, and Reshape tools are demonstrated in Figure 7-12.

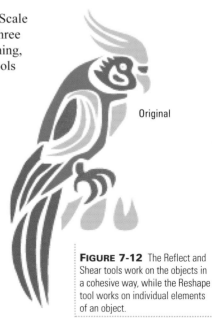

Original

FIGURE 7-12 The Reflect and Shear tools work on the objects in a cohesive way, while the Reshape tool works on individual elements of an object.

The Reflect tool (in the Rotate tool tearoff) allows you to mirror selected objects precisely by using a dialog box. You can flip an object upside down by choosing the Horizontal button. Choosing Vertical mirrors an object without changing the top/bottom relationship. Or you can rotate both horizontally and vertically by choosing the Value button and entering an angle in the Angle box.

The Shear tool (in the Scale tool tearoff) skews selected objects. The shearing (skewing) takes place around the center point of the object unless you first click to set an anchor point. In that case, the anchor point is fixed while the rest of the object shears. You can also define shearing for a selected object by double-clicking the Shear tool to open a dialog box similar to the Rotate dialog box.

The Reshape tool (also in the Scale tool tearoff) interactively works on selected objects to stretch and distort them. Click first to set a fixed anchor point, and then drag on another point to distort the object. The Reshape tool is not associated with a dialog box.

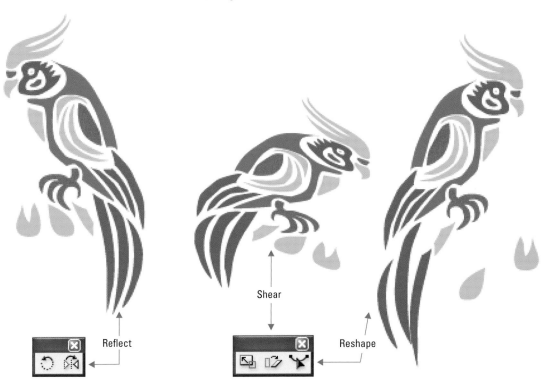

Reflect

Shear

Reshape

Part III Add Type

Chapter 8

Create and Edit Text

How to...

- Use type in Illustrator
- Create text in Illustrator
- Get text from somewhere else
- Edit text
- Check spelling in Illustrator
- Choose fonts and characters
- Insert glyphs
- Work with OpenType
- Use alternate glyphs

Illustrator provides an elaborate set of features that give you incredible control over the appearance of type. You can shape text along a path, package it inside an object, align text vertically (instead of the usual left to right), and generally cast text like molten metal to flow into your illustration.

Illustrator CS integrates several helpful new features for managing type. Most dramatic is the ability to easily access *thousands* of characters from a single set of extended fonts called OpenType fonts. In addition, Illustrator CS supports type and paragraph styles (explored in Chapter 9) that allow you to save and apply sets of formatting features to selected text or paragraphs.

Other Illustrator tools allow it to function as a scaled-down word processing utility, letting you perform basic editing, formatting, and even spell checking on your text.

On the downside, the folks at Adobe have been careful not to copy and paste *too* many text formatting features from their InDesign desktop publishing program. If you want to design and lay out a multipage brochure, or access relatively basic features such as easy drop-cap formatting, you'll bump up against the limits of Illustrator.

Create Text

FIGURE 8-1 Creating text in Illustrator

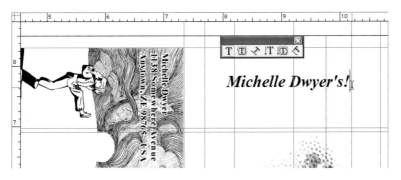

To start creating text in Illustrator, select the Type tool in the Toolbox and start typing. As you do, the cursor displays as an I-beam text cursor. A vertical line that is larger (its size depends on text size) indicates where the insertion point is set, as shown in Figure 8-1.

If you want to constrain your text within a set width and height as you type, select the Type tool and draw a text box first. Then click inside the text box (with the Type tool still selected) and type. Lines of text will wrap at the edge of the defined Type text box, as shown in Figure 8-2.

FIGURE 8-2 Creating text constrained by a predefined text box

As you type, you can change the location of the insertion point by pointing and clicking with your mouse or by using keyboard cursor movement keys. Some standard word processing rules apply in Illustrator: END moves the insertion point to the end of the block of text, HOME moves it to the beginning of the block, and COMMAND- (CTRL-) UP ARROW or DOWN ARROW moves it up or down a paragraph.

Note *If you first define a text box and then type, your text may not all fit in the text box. I'll show you how to resolve this problem by linking text boxes in the section entitled "Link Text Boxes," in Chapter 10. Another option is to resize the text box. You'll learn to do that in Chapter 10 as well.*

Get Text from Somewhere Else

If you want to copy text from a word processor or other source outside of Illustrator, you can copy text into your clipboard, and paste it into Illustrator. To do that, you can click and drag with the Type tool to create a text box, and then select Edit | Paste. When you do that, the text will be constrained within the defined text box. Or, you can simply click on the Artboard with the Type tool and select Edit | Paste. With this option, the text in your clipboard will be pasted with paragraph breaks preserved. The first option, drawing a text box before you paste, preserves more formatting from the original text.

To paste text while preserving text formatting, don't select the Type tool first. Just choose the Selection tool and then select Edit | Paste. When you copy text in this way, font, text size, attributes such as boldfacing, and text box width will be preserved from the original text.

Edit Text

Regardless if you created text in your document (pasting or typing), the type in your document becomes a text box after you select another tool. To edit text in an existing text box, you can double-click the text with the Selection tool. The Type tool automatically becomes selected, along with the block of text. You can select text by clicking and dragging or by holding down SHIFT as you use the navigation keys on your keyboard.

You can use the Edit menu to select Cut, Copy, Paste, or Clear (which is the same as Cut, but the text is not saved to the clipboard).

To view non-printing symbols such as paragraph marks, blank spaces, or forced line breaks (use SHIFT-ENTER to create these), select Type | Show Hidden Characters.

Use Illustrator's Proofing Tools

Illustrator's spell checking capability was beefed up a bit for CS, making it easier to edit a custom dictionary, among other things. You'll find that it offers enough basic word processing tools to keep bad spellers from making fools of ourselves. You can also convert the case of selected text, and automatically generate quotation marks for the beginning and end of quotes.

In earlier versions of Illustrator, the spell check features were found on the Type menu. In CS they've been moved to the Edit menu.

To check spelling, it's not necessary (or worthwhile) to select a text box first. The spelling checker will check all the text in your document. Just select Edit | Check Spelling. The Check Spelling dialog box will prompt you to correct spellings not found in Illustrator's dictionary. If you click the Options button in the Spelling dialog box, you can elect to find or ignore repeated words and a few other handy potential typos you might want to check for.

FIGURE 8-3 Replacing dashes (but not ellipses) with smart characters for selected text only

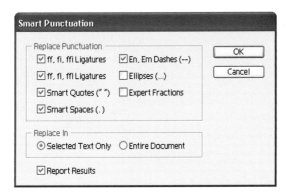

To use Illustrator's smart punctuation tools, select text within a text box by clicking and dragging with the Type tool. You'll then have the option of applying smart punctuation changes to just the selected text or to your entire document. Choose Type | Smart Punctuation to open the Smart Punctuation dialog box, as shown in Figure 8-3.

Use the available check boxes to make the optional conversions, for instance, from two hyphens (--) to an em dash (—), or from standard quotes (") to smart open (") and close (") quotes. After you click OK in the dialog box, you'll see a Report dialog box summarizing the changes that were made to your text.

As always in Illustrator, you can select Edit | Undo if the results are undesirable.

You can apply the Change Case feature only to selected text. First, select text by clicking and dragging with the Type tool, and then select Type | Change Text to open the Change Text dialog box. You can convert selected text to UPPERCASE, lowercase, Title Case, or Sentence case.

The find and replace option in Illustrator works only on an entire open document. Select Edit | Find and Replace to open a standard Find and Replace dialog box and either find text or replace text throughout a document. Find and replace options allow you to match case, find a whole word, and search

FIGURE 8-4 Skipping text in locked and hidden layers

backwards—or not. New options in Illustrator CS also allow you to check hidden layers and/or check locked layers. By default, these options are *off*, and searching and replacing will not corrupt content on hidden or locked layers. The Find and Replace dialog box in Figure 8-4 will skip any text in a locked or hidden layer.

Tip   *You'll learn to lock and hide layers in Chapter 20. If you find you're bumping into locked layers in a project you are working on, or if you want to know right away how to prevent a section of your document from being edited, jump up to Chapter 20.*

Choose Fonts and Characters

In Chapter 9, you'll explore how to assign formatting to text. By default, the last font you selected is the font used next time you type. To select a new font for selected type or for text you are about to type, choose Type | Font. Illustrator's list of fonts is cool enough to demonstrate how each font looks, so if you don't have a specific font in mind, you can browse through the options. Some fonts also have boldface versions, italic versions, or both—as shown in Figure 8-5.

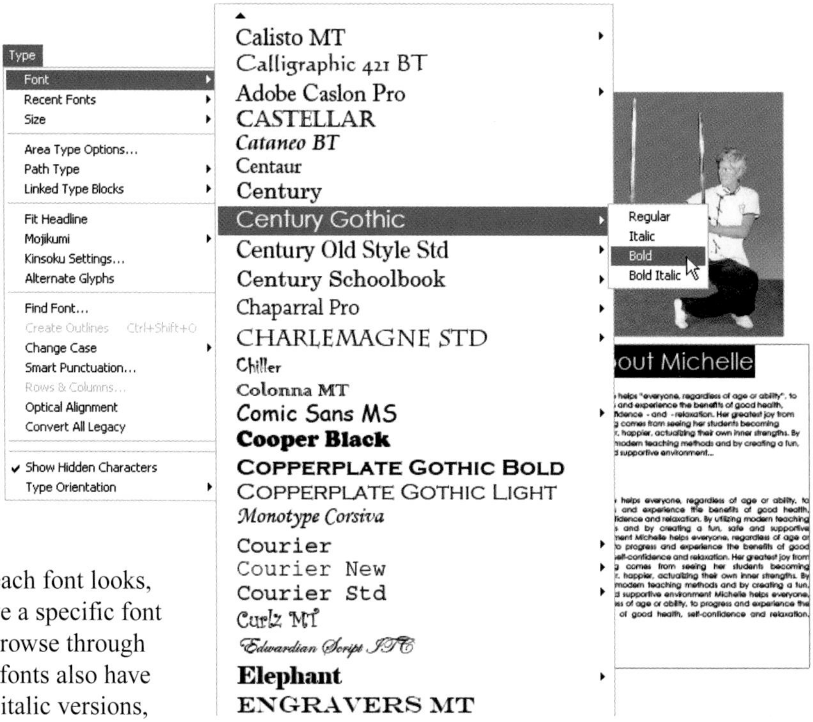

You can also use the Type | Size menu to select a font size for selected type or for text you are about to type.

Because you are likely to have dozens if not hundreds of fonts installed on your computer, Illustrator provides some tools for quickly finding a font in the Find Font dialog box. Select Type | Find Font to display this dialog box and use it to find or replace fonts in your document. If you want to replace a font in your document with another one in your document, choose Document in the Replace with Font From drop-down list. But if you want to access all the fonts on your system, choose System from the drop-down list, as shown in Figure 8-6.

FIGURE 8-5 Selecting a boldface font

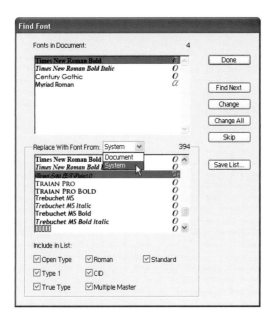

FIGURE 8-6 Viewing a full range of available fonts to replace an existing font

Many characters in font sets are available from your computer's keyboard. But, interestingly, *most of them are not.* In the remainder of this chapter, you'll learn to view, select, and insert additional characters that are useful but not immediately accessible from your keyboard.

Insert Glyphs

Glyph is a term that encompasses both normal characters (such as A through Z, 1, 2, 3…, and so on) as well as non-character symbols such as ©, ®, ™, and so on. Each glyph in traditional font sets has a defined three-digit number associated with it. For instance, you can quickly insert the Spanish ñ character by entering OPTION-164 (ALT-164) on your keyboard.

Illustrator makes it much easier to find these glyphs—so you don't need to memorize keystroke combinations of character values. Just choose Type | Glyphs to display the Glyphs palette. The glyphs associated with your character set will display in an easy-to-use character map. Double-click on any glyph to insert it at the insertion point in your text, as shown in Figure 8-7.

Most typeface sets include hundreds of glyphs in addition to standard characters. Some sets of fonts, such as Symbols, Wingdings, and Webdings, include sets of frequently used symbols. For handy reference, the entire set of popular Webdings symbols is displayed in Figure 8-8.

New fonts that utilize OpenType technology have not hundreds but *thousands* of alternate glyphs. You'll explore those fonts next.

About Michelle™

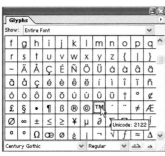

FIGURE 8-7 Inserting a glyph

…e, regardless of age or ability", to … the benefits of good health, …relaxation. Her greatest joy from …eing her students becoming …lizing their own inner strengths. By … methods and by creating a fun, …ronment…

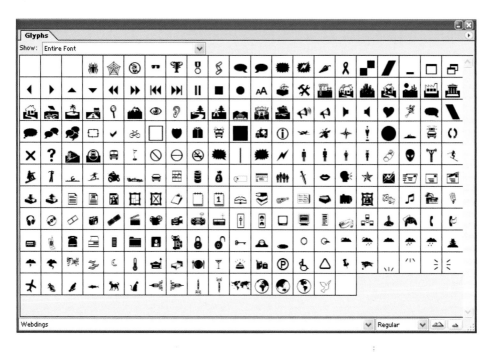

Work with OpenType

FIGURE 8-8 The Webdings symbol set has frequently used symbols.

One of the more dramatic improvements in Illustrator CS is the ability to utilize OpenType fonts. These font sets include as many as thousands of glyphs, including characters and symbols.

In many cases, this additional character capacity is used to create multilingual font types. These multilingual fonts allow you, for example, to design a brochure with text in Korean, English, Dutch, Vietnamese, Chinese, and Russian *without changing font.*

Tip *How much does it add to the aesthetic structure of a multilingual document to use the same font for Chinese, English, and Russian characters? Certainly, very few readers will look closely at the typeface of languages they don't read. And font differences between characters as disparate as English and Korean, Chinese, or Japanese tend to overshadow similarities imbued by using the same font for all content. All this is true. But it is still the case that when they display multilingual content in a unified font, documents* do—*on one level or another—take on a more cohesive and coherent look. And we can expect that, as the world continues to shrink and multilingual documents become even more prevalent, typeface designers will work to develop style attributes that "translate" from one character set to another.*

Beyond providing multilingual font support, OpenType font sets often provide *alternate glyph* options. For example, you might want to use one uppercase *M* in a font set at the beginning of paragraphs, another at the beginning of sentences, and a third version for capitalized words not at the beginning of a paragraph or sentence. Or you might take advantage of OpenType alternate glyphs to choose from a set of options for symbols such as ™, @, or ®. OpenType fonts also offer a vast array of non-character glyphs.

FIGURE 8-9 Consistency in appearance can be maintained even in multilingual documents by assigning the same OpenType font to all text.

Create Multilingual Documents with OpenType Fonts

If you create or import (copy and paste) type in multiple languages, you can use an OpenType font to assign uniform font characteristics to all your text. Or if you are typing on a western keyboard, you can quickly and (relatively) easily insert some Korean or Cyrillic characters.

In either scenario, you can take advantage of multilingual OpenType font sets. To apply a multilingual font to selected text, simply select text (from many language character sets if you wish) and apply a multilingual OpenType font. Figure 8-9 shows a single font being applied to text content in English, Korean, and Portuguese.

To (relatively) quickly insert characters from different language character sets, choose Type | Glyphs from the menu. Scroll down the

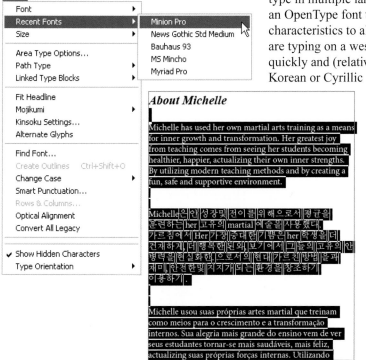

Glyphs palette and find your character, as shown in Figure 8-10.

the opponent. The 12 animal practice   combin
Elements to cre[...] beautiful fighting t
based on the s[...]imal. In addition t[...]
forms there ar[...]ts and Fighting An
Person Forms [...]eople are pitted ag[...]
other in an excit[...]hed battle.

¥ リ Five Element and [...]e Animal Forms
¥ Five Elements Fighting Form

FIGURE 8-10 Inserting a glyph from the Kozuka Minchu Pro font set

Use Alternate Glyphs

OpenType font sets often include many variations for standard (and non-standard) characters. In addition to the example at the beginning of the section (using many versions of an uppercase *M*), you can also access other sets of alternative characters such as fractions, scientific notation, or superscript characters.

    To access these sets of glyphs, choose Type | Glyphs from the menu. In the Glyphs palette, use the Show menu to narrow down the set of characters that is displayed. If you have a character selected, you can use the Show menu to display only alternatives to that selected character, as shown in Figure 8-11. Double-click on a glyph to insert it at the insertion point in a selected text box.

FIGURE 8-11 Choosing between alternative options for the @ symbol

If the Glyphs palette is displaying characters for a different font set than the one you want, you can choose the font you wish to display from the Font drop-down list at the bottom of the Glyphs palette.

Chapter 9

Format Type

How to...

- Format characters
- Define stroke and fill for type
- Format paragraphs
- Align paragraphs
- Set tabs
- Define type styles
- Create and apply character and paragraph styles
- Embed fonts for sharing files
- Convert text to outlines

In Chapter 8 you learned to define text type (font) and size from the Type menu, but the Character, Paragraph, and Tabs palettes provide even more control over character and paragraph formatting.

In addition, many graphical tools such as stroke and fill attributes are applicable to text. You'll learn high-powered text formatting techniques in this chapter.

Format Characters

As demonstrated in Chapter 8, you can assign font and size to type from the Type menu, either before or after creating the text. To define the font before you type, select Type | Font and select a font from the menu. Where supported, additional attributes such as italic or boldface can also be selected here. To define type size, select Type | Size and select a font size in points. You can assign size and font to existing type by first selecting the text and then using the menu to define font and size.

The Character palette provides additional options for formatting text. Select Window | Type | Character to display the palette, and choose Show Options from the palette menu to display all the formatting options. The expanded palette is shown in Figure 9-1.

The following options in the Character palette provide detailed control over how characters are spaced horizontally and vertically:

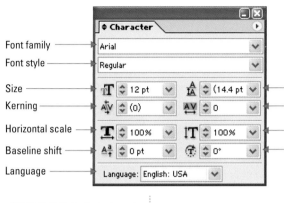

Font family
Font style
Size
Kerning
Horizontal scale
Baseline shift
Language
Leading
Tracking
Vertical scale
Rotation

FIGURE 9-1 Assigning type size in the Character palette

- **Font Family**   This is the font set, like Arial, Times Roman, Myriad, and so on.

- **Font Style**   Many font families include boldface, italic, or bold and italic formatting, selected here.

- **Size**   This measures font size in points. You can enter size with another unit of measurement (for example, by typing **0.25 inches**) and it will be converted, by default, to points.

- **Leading**   Leading is so named for the olden days when printers used extra shims of lead to separate lines of text. Combining 18-point leading with 12-point text, for example, produces 1 1/2 line spacing, while combining 12-point text with 24-point leading produces the equivalent of double-spacing, as shown in Figure 9-2.

FIGURE 9-2 Double-spacing is created by setting leading at twice the font size.

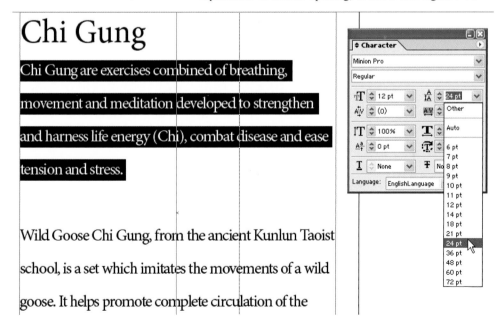

Chi Gung

Chi Gung are exercises combined of breathing, movement and meditation developed to strengthen and harness life energy (Chi), combat disease and ease tension and stress.

Wild Goose Chi Gung, from the ancient Kunlun Taoist school, is a set which imitates the movements of a wild goose. It helps promote complete circulation of the

■ **Kerning** This option controls spacing between two selected characters. The default value is 0. The unit of measurement is the *em*—about the size of the letter *m*—and values are defined in units of 1/1000th of an em. Positive kerning values add spacing. More frequently, negative kerning is used to move characters closer together, as shown in Figure 9-3.

FIGURE 9-3 100 percent kerning pushes the *r* back next to the *B*

Kerning is only applied to two characters and can only be assigned when the Type insertion cursor is between two characters.

■ **Tracking** This selection controls horizontal spacing between characters and words. Measured in ems, like kerning, positive tracking values increase space while negative values crunch type together. Tracking is illustrated in Figure 9-4.

FIGURE 9-4 Positive and negative tracking regulate horizontal spacing. Negative tracking is much more frequently used and tends to make type more readable.

Push Hands, Tai Chi's highly developed sport requiring two people to exercise together creating an element of confrontation as they try to upset each other's balance. It gives one deep insight into the solo form, and is fun and demanding , including one's relaxation and self-defense awareness

Positive tracking ——————

Tai Chi training with swords is a beautiful and int form as well as sport, self-defense and social activ strong upper body muscles, and rotates the should wrist joints. This practice helps one extend natural energy outside the body for fighting and healing. └————— Negative tracking

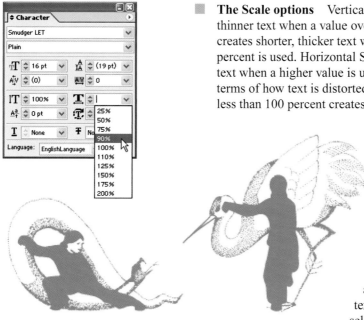

■ **The Scale options**   Vertical Scale creates taller, thinner text when a value over 100 percent is used; it creates shorter, thicker text when a value less than 100 percent is used. Horizontal Scale creates shorter, thicker text when a higher value is used. Proportionally, in terms of how text is distorted, vertical scaling set to less than 100 percent creates the same shape of text as horizontal scaling set to over 100 percent. Both are demonstrated in Figure 9-5.

■ **Baseline Shift**   When the baseline shift is positive, it raises any selected character(s) above the baseline of the text; negative values move selected characters below the text baseline. This treatment is usually reserved for individual superscript or subscript characters.

■ **Rotation**   Character rotation rotates a character or symbol, as illustrated in Figure 9-6.

↞ Normal

← Over 100 percent vertical scale

← Less than 100 percent vertical scale

← Over 100 percent horizontal scale

← Less than 100 percent horizontal scale

FIGURE 9-5 Horizontal and vertical scaling compresses or stretches type

Note   *You set default values for hyphenation language in the Preferences dialog box. To adjust them, select Illustrator (Edit) | Preferences | Hyphenation.*

■ **Language**   Language settings determine what spell check and hyphenation dictionaries are applied to selected text.

Define Stroke and Fill for Type

By default, type has a fill color but no stroke color. If you add a visible stroke, type becomes thick and sometimes a bit ugly. But you can experiment with different stroke and fill colors and attributes to create some interesting text effects. If you assign a stroke but no fill to text, the text appears outlined, as shown in Figure 9-7.

You can assign stroke and fill attributes to type just as you would to any path, using the Eyedropper or Paint Bucket tool.

Format Paragraphs

The Paragraph palette is where you find tools to align type. Illustrator CS allows you to align paragraph type to the right, left, or center. There are also four alignment options for full justification. The

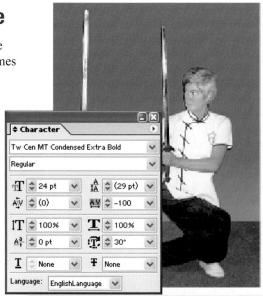

FIGURE 9-6 Rotated text is combined here with extreme negative tracking and kerning to push together letters that have been separated by rotation.

FIGURE 9-7 The effect of outlining on the Impact font is enhanced with a high horizontal scale value (of 200%).

Chi Gung

Chi Gung are exercises combined of breathing, movement and meditation developed to strengthen and harness life energy (Chi), combat disease and ease tension and stress.

Wild Goose Chi Gung, from the ancient Kunlun Taoist school, is a set which imitates the movements of a wild goose. It helps promote complete circulation of the blood and clears the passages through which the Chi flows.

full justification feature lets you decide how to align the *last* line of a full-justified paragraph (left, center, right, or full justified).

The Paragraph palette also defines indenting for a paragraph. You can set indentation from the left, right (or both), and also first line indenting. These features work like those in your word processor or desktop publishing program, and you'll pick them up quickly on your own.

Select Window | Type | Paragraph to view the Paragraph palette. To align or indent text, first select a specific paragraph within a text box. You can perform this task easily by triple-clicking on a paragraph with the Type tool. With a paragraph selected, you're ready to apply formatting.

FIGURE 9-8 Paragraph alignment options allow for justification with left, right, or center alignment (not shown) for the last line in a paragraph.

Align Paragraphs

With a paragraph selected, use the self-evident alignment buttons in the Paragraph palette to left-, center-, or right-align the text. Use the Justify Last Left, Centered, or Right option to justify every line but the last in a paragraph with the right and left edges of the text box, and use the Justify All button to stretch all of the lines to the left and right borders of the text box, including the last. This last option will create very large spacing in short lines of text.

Full justification often creates awkward looking spacing in the final line of a paragraph. For instance, if the line only has a few characters, the spacing required to stretch that text across the entire width of a column looks just plain ugly. To help resolve this, Illustrator CS introduces some helpful new alignment options. The Justify Last Left, Justify Last Centered, and Justify Last Right options all assign full justification *except* to the last line, which is aligned at the left, center, or right. Figure 9-8 identifies the paragraph alignment tools and demonstrates a couple of the new alignment options.

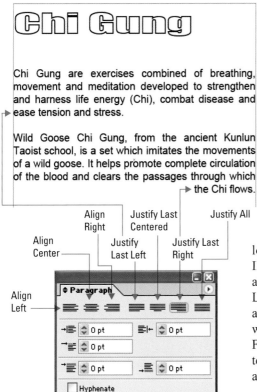

The other boxes in the Paragraph palette (except for the last one) define horizontal indentation and spacing around paragraphs (in points):

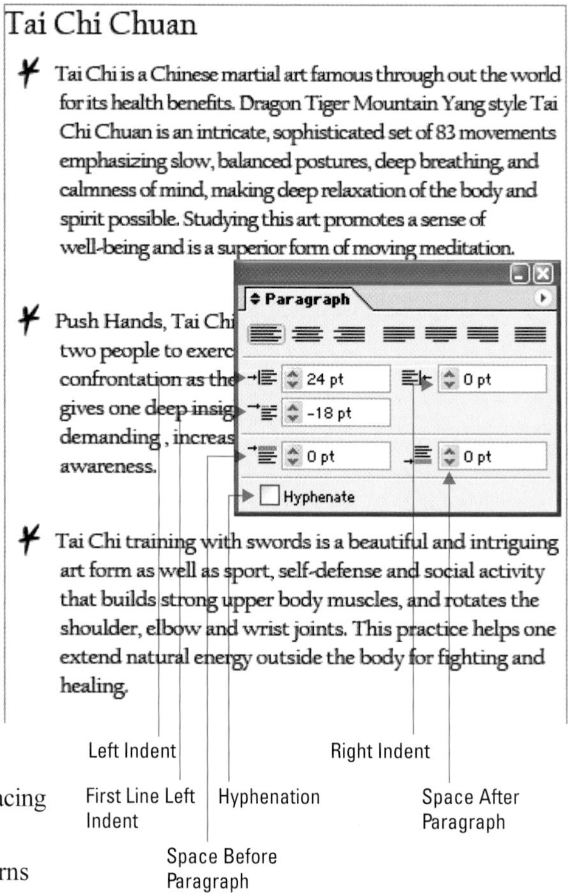

FIGURE 9-9 A positive Indent Left Margin setting is combined with a negative Indent First Line value to create the bulleted list paragraph format.

- **Indent Left Margin**   This box defines how far to indent the entire selected paragraph from the left edge of the text box.

- **Indent First Line**   In this box you can define how far to indent (or outdent) the first line of the paragraph in relation to the rest of the paragraph. A positive value indents the first line of the paragraph. A negative value outdents the first line of the paragraph, which is useful, for example, for numbered or bulleted lists where a number or bullet extends out to the left of the text, as shown in Figure 9-9.

- **Indent Right Margin**   This box defines the space between the right edge of the text and the right edge of the text box.

- **Space Before Paragraph** You can use this box to define line spacing before the selected paragraph(s).

- **Space After Paragraph** In this box you can define line spacing after the selected paragraph(s).

- **Hyphenation**   This checkbox turns on automatic hyphenation.

Tai Chi Chuan

Tai Chi is a Chinese martial art famous through out the world for its health benefits. Dragon Tiger Mountain Yang style Tai Chi Chuan is an intricate, sophisticated set of 83 movements emphasizing slow, balanced postures, deep breathing, and calmness of mind, making deep relaxation of the body and spirit possible. Studying this art promotes a sense of well-being and is a superior form of moving meditation.

Push Hands, Tai Chi [...] two people to exerc[...] confrontation as the [...] gives one deep insig[...] demanding, increas[...] awareness.

Tai Chi training with swords is a beautiful and intriguing art form as well as sport, self-defense and social activity that builds strong upper body muscles, and rotates the shoulder, elbow and wrist joints. This practice helps one extend natural energy outside the body for fighting and healing.

Left Indent   Right Indent

First Line Left Indent   Hyphenation   Space After Paragraph

Space Before Paragraph

Display Hidden Characters

As you add more character and paragraph spacing attributes to type, it can get confusing as to where spacing is coming from. For instance, did you add double-spacing between paragraphs?

Spaces

Tai·Chi·Chuan¶

›→   →   Tai·Chi·is·a·Chinese·martial·art·famous·through·out·the·
world·for·its·health·benefits.····|Dragon·Tiger·Mountain·Yang·
style·Tai·Chi·Chuan·is·an·intricate,·sophisticated·set·of·83·
movements·emphasizing·slow,·balanced·postures,·deep·
breathing,·and·calmness·of·mind,·making·deep·relaxation·of·
the·body·and·spirit·possible.·Studying·this·art·promotes·a·
sense·of·well-being·and·is·a·superior·form·of·moving·
meditation.·¶

Tab   Paragraph

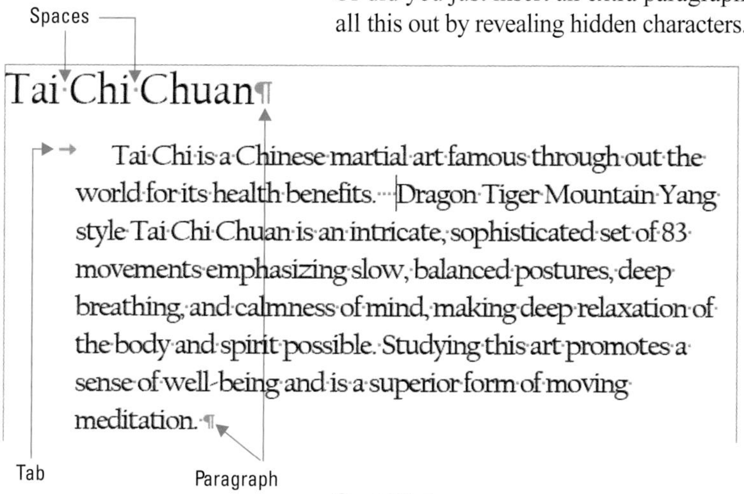

FIGURE 9-10 In this text box,
hidden characters are displayed to
make it easier to manage spacing.

Or did you just insert an extra paragraph break? You can sort
all this out by revealing hidden characters. Do that by choosing
Type | Show Hidden Characters. If all the hidden characters
become confusing, turn it off the same way (by deselecting
Show Hidden Characters from the Type menu). The space, paragraph,
and tab characters are identified in Figure 9-10.

Set Tabs

You set tabs and indentation with the Tabs palette (Window |
Type | Tabs). Working with tabs in Illustrator is similar to
working with them in word processors such as Microsoft
Word. First you select some text, and then you define the tab
settings. By default, tabs are set as left-aligned tabs and spaced
every 0.5 inch.

Use the Tabs palette to resize tabs. The palette is resizable
and can be aligned with selected text by clicking the Position
Palette Above Text button on the right edge of the tab ruler.

The Tabs palette has four buttons that allow you to select
the type of tab you want to define: left-, center-, right-, or
decimal-justified. After you select a type of tab (usually
left-aligned), either click the ruler to define the tab or enter
a value in the X box in the palette.

If you select a Decimal-Justified tab, you can define a
character other than the default period character in the Align
On box. The character you define in that box will be the one
used to line up your tabbed breaks.

The Leader box allows you to define a character that
will repeat to fill the tab space. Figure 9-11 shows text with
a left-aligned tab set at 0.25 inches, with a period used as a
tab leader.

You can also use the movable markers on the left edge of
the ruler to define first line (the top marker) or paragraph
indentation. These options provide a graphical alternative to
defining indentation in the Paragraph palette.

9

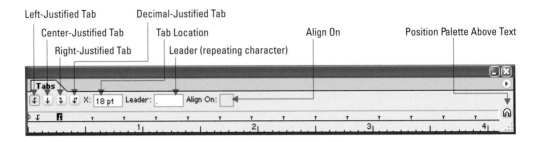

 *The unit of measurement for the Tabs palette is determined by the selected unit in the Preferences dialog box. To change this unit, choose Illustrator (Edit) | Preferences | Units & Display Performance. Choose a unit of measurement (such as inches) in the General drop-down list to set the ruler increments for the Tabs palette. Or, if you wish, you can enter a unit of measurement in the tab ruler (such as **0.25 in** to enter a value in inches) and it will be converted to the assigned unit of measurement (in the case of 0.25 inches, the conversion is to 18 points).*

FIGURE 9-11 Setting a tab with a leader

Define Type Styles

Both characters and paragraphs can have assigned styles. This new feature in Illustrator CS incorporates a level of type management heretofore reserved for desktop publishing.

Character styles might, for example, include font type, font size, font color, rotation, and spacing. A single style will save all the attributes applied to a character and allow you to apply those attributes to other characters.

Similarly, paragraph styles can be stored and used to apply a whole set of paragraph formatting settings—such as before-and-after spacing, indenting, and alignment.

FIGURE 9-12 Defining a character style

Use Character Styles

The easiest way to create a character style is to apply all the formatting you want to preserve to a character. Once you've formatted that character, select it. Then choose the Character Styles palette (Window | Type | Character Styles).

With your "model" character selected, and the Character Styles palette open, choose New Character Style from the Character Styles palette menu, as shown in Figure 9-12.

In the Style Name area of the New Character Style dialog box, type a name for your style (spaces and special characters like "-" or "!" are fine). Then click OK to preserve the style.

To apply a named character style, select some

FIGURE 9-13 Applying a character style

By utilizing modern teaching methods and by creating a fun, safe and supportive environment Michelle helps everyone, regardless of age or ability, to progress and experience the benefits of good health, self-confidence and relaxation.

Her greatest joy from teaching comes from seeing her students becoming healthier, happier, actualizing their own inner strengths.

By utilizing modern teaching methods and by creating a fun, safe and supportive environment Michelle helps everyone, regardless of age or ability, to progress and experience the benefits of good health, self-confidence and relaxation.

characters and click on the named style in the Character Styles palette, as shown in Figure 9-13.

9

You can revise a style—and apply the new formatting to all characters to which that style was applied. Do this by double-clicking on a style in the Character Styles palette. That opens the Character Style Options dialog box. Choose from the categories of attributes on the left of the dialog box—General, Basic Character Formats, Advanced Character Formats, Character Color, and OpenType Features. Within these categories, you'll find options for changing any formatting applied to the character style.

After you change formatting options for the selected character style, click OK. The new formatting attributes will be applied to all the text associated with the edited character style.

Use Paragraph Styles

Just as with character styles, the best way to define a paragraph style is to first format a paragraph with attributes such as before-and-after spacing and indentation. Then view the Paragraph Styles palette (Window | Type | Paragraph Styles).

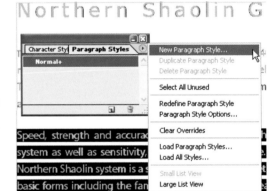

With your paragraph still selected, choose New Paragraph Style from the Paragraph Styles palette menu. In the Style Name area of the New Paragraph Style dialog box, enter a name for your style. (As with character style names, spaces and special characters work fine). Then click OK to preserve the style.

To apply a paragraph style, click anywhere in a paragraph and then click on the named style in the Paragraph Styles palette.

As with character styles, you can revise a paragraph style and apply the revised formatting to paragraphs to which that style is associated. Double-click on a paragraph style in the Paragraph Styles palette to open the Paragraph Style Options dialog box.

Choose from categories of attributes on the left of the dialog box—the names of these categories (such as Tabs or Justification) are helpful, but if you don't find the formatting feature you want, keep looking. Change formatting options for the selected style and click OK. The new formatting attributes will be applied to all the paragraphs to which the paragraph style has been attached.

Embed Fonts

The fonts available for assignment in Illustrator depend on the fonts installed on your system. And those fonts can be viewed on another computer only if the person looking at your Illustrator file has those same fonts installed on his or her system. That presents a problem when sharing Illustrator files or when sending illustrations to a printer.

If the person viewing your file does not have the fonts you used in your illustration, his or her system will substitute a different font, or worse yet, have trouble opening your file. If you've ever opened an Illustrator file from a collaborator and been prompted to OK a replacement font, you've seen this process in action from the receiving end. You can include (embed) required font types when you save a file, making them available to the person who opens that file.

Most typeface license agreements allow this. If they don't, the typeface is not good for much because only you can see the fonts you assign. But you should check on what rights you have to embed fonts if you have purchased custom fonts.

To embed fonts when you save your file, click the Embed All Fonts check box or radio button that appears in the Save dialog box for your selected format. The various Save dialog boxes (they differ depending on which format you are saving to) also provide options for you to restrict file size by saving only those characters (or font subsets) used in your illustration.

9

Convert Text to Outlines

The safest way to preserve the look of your formatted text is to convert it to *outlines*—regular Illustrator paths that can no longer be edited with Type tools. And with text converted to outlines, you can apply all of the effects and path editing techniques available for any other outline.

The downside of converting text to outlines—and it is a significant downside—is that the text is no longer editable, and you cannot use any of the Type tools with it. Therefore, you might want to save your text first as type, and then create a copy that you convert to an outline.

To convert text to an outline, select the text box and choose Type | Create Outlines. The resulting object will consist of a group of paths. To move or edit individual letters, ungroup the characters. Converting text to outlines is especially useful for text destined for the Web. Because the "text" is actually a graphic image, all formatting characteristics are preserved, regardless of which fonts are supported by a viewer's system.

Figure 9-14 shows characters that have been converted to outlines and that are being manipulated as graphical objects—no longer editable as text.

FIGURE 9-14 Outlined text can be edited like any path or shape—but not with Type tools

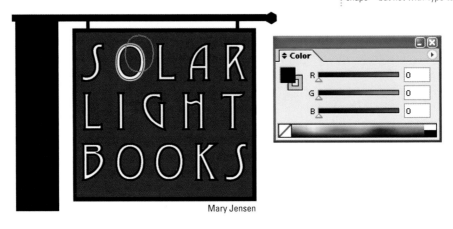

Mary Jensen

Chapter 10

Flow Text

How to...

- Flow text from one box to another
- Lay out with type in columns
- Shape type
- Align type to a path
- Create vertical type

In Chapter 8 you learned to use Illustrator's text editing tools, and in Chapter 9 you learned to apply pretty intense levels of formatting to text. But the real fun comes next, when you use Illustrator to control the flow of type around objects, to fill objects with text, and to create text that runs vertically or along the path of an object.

Flowing text around objects allows detailed control over layout for brochures, white papers, print ads, and text-heavy illustrations. Filling an object with text can be an effective technique for combining media and message, as illustrated in Figure 10-1.

In this chapter, you'll also learn to flow vertical text along a path for effect, as shown in Figure 10-2 .

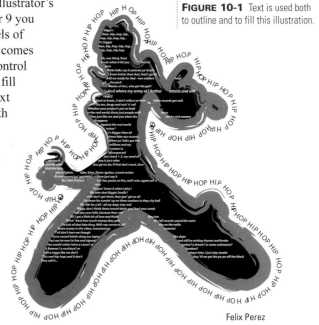

FIGURE 10-1 Text is used both to outline and to fill this illustration.

Felix Perez

The text warp in Figure 10-2 was created by selecting the type, choosing Object | Envelope Distort | Make with Warp, and then applying a vertical arc warp.

Link Text Boxes

Susan Steinhauer

FIGURE 10-2 Flowing vertical text along an arc

FIGURE 10-3 The overflow text icon indicates that there is more text than fits in the text box.

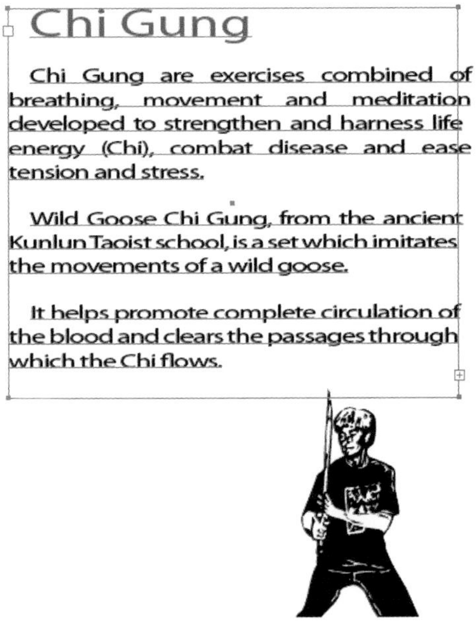

If you type more text than will fit in a defined text box, an almost impossibly tiny plus (+) sign appears in the lower-right corner of the text box, as shown in Figure 10-3. Overflow text can be continued in linked text boxes.

The basic routine for linking text boxes is to select both the original (overflowing) text box and another shape (any shape), and link the two objects. You can then flow text from one shape into another. The following steps will walk you through that process.

To link two text boxes, follow these steps:

1. Start by using the Type tool to draw a text box about 1 inch square. After you draw the box, type enough text to fill the square.

2. Keep typing. As you enter more text than the text box can hold, you won't see the text, but Illustrator will store it and it will be available for a linked text box.

3. After you've typed more text than your text box will hold, you'll notice the tiny plus sign on the right side of the text box.

4. Use any tool to create an additional closed path or shape, as shown in Figure 10-4.

5. Use the Selection tool to select both the original text box and the new shape.

6. Select Type | Threaded Text | Create. Text will flow from the text box into the new shape, as shown in Figure 10-5.

You can unlink text boxes by selected them and choosing Type | Threaded Text | Release Selection. Or choose Type | Threaded Text | Remove Threading to break the link between the text blocks. The Release option can be used when type is flowed into several shapes, and releases only the selected object from the flow

10

of type. The Remove Threading option breaks the linkage between shapes, but does not affect the type in objects.

When you link text in multiple objects, the text flows from the earliest created object into the objects created later. Or, if you change the stacking order of objects that are linked text boxes (by selecting Object | Arrange and choosing a stacking option), text will flow from the top object into lower objects within the stacking order.

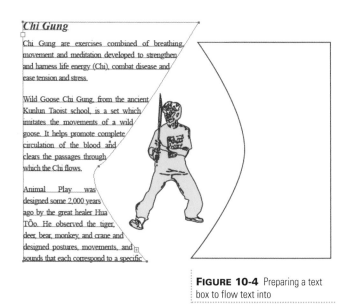

FIGURE 10-4 Preparing a text box to flow text into

Shortcut *You can flow text into a newly created object without using the commands available on the Type menu. To do this, click on the plus sign with a selection tool to change the pointer to a text icon. Then you can either click on another object to establish the link or click (or drag) on the artboard to create a new object to flow text into.*

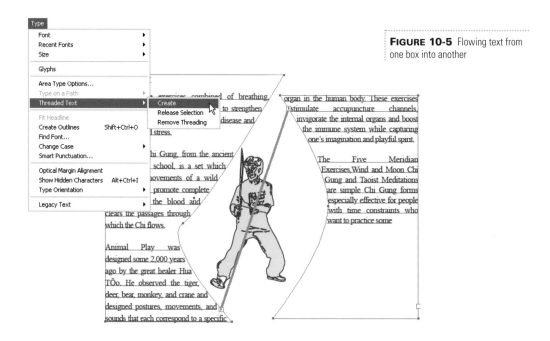

FIGURE 10-5 Flowing text from one box into another

Automatically Lay Out Type

As mentioned in Chapter 8, Illustrator is slowly adding desktop publishing features as it evolves. Among these are features that allow you to automatically wrap text around an image, automatically lay text out in columns, and instantly expand a headline to fill the width of a text box.

None of these features will inspire you to lay out a book in Illustrator—that's a job for InDesign (or its rival, Quark). But Illustrator's quasi-desktop publishing features can simplify and speed up the process of designing a text-heavy poster, flyer, postcard, or brochure.

FIGURE 10-6 Preparing to wrap text around an object

Wrap Type

You can manually wrap text around an object (such as an illustration) by simply creating a text box that fits around the object. You can also make this process even easier (if less exact) by using Illustrator's Text Wrapping feature to automatically wrap text around an object. To have text automatically wrapped around it, the object must be *on top of* the text. You can move an object in front of another one by selecting the object to move forward and choosing Object | Arrange | Bring to Front.

Select both the text block and the object around which the text will be wrapped. Then select Object | Text Wrap | Make Text Wrap, as shown in Figure 10-6.

After you apply a text wrap, the Text Wrap Options dialog box appears. The Bumper box allows you to define how much space you want to leave between the object and the text. As you

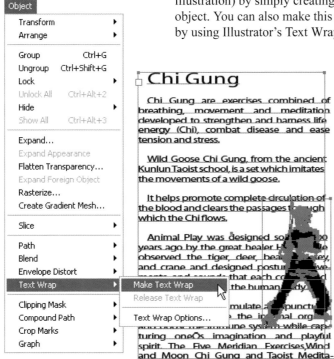

set a value, if you have checked the Preview check box in the dialog box you can see how the text will flow around the object.

The Invert Wrap check box in the Text Wrap Options dialog box flows text *through* the wrapped object, instead of *around* the object—which is what you usually want to do. After you tweak your wrap settings, click OK to create a text wrap like the one in Figure 10-7.

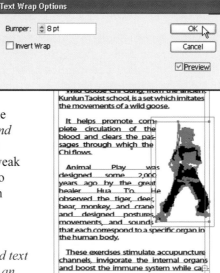

Tip *Automatically wrapped text does not flow around an object with the same accuracy and detail as text that flows into a box you design yourself. If automatic wrapping doesn't produce a close enough flow, use the technique described in the "Link Text Boxes" section earlier in this chapter to customize a precise text flow by drawing a text box with the exact text flow you need.*

FIGURE 10-7
Automatically wrapped text flows around an object.

Lay Out with Columns

Illustrator allows you to lay out type in sequential rows or columns. The most useful application of this feature is to format text in columns. To lay out type in a text box in columns, select the text box and select Type | Area Type Options. In the Rows box or Columns box, choose a number of columns or rows.

You can also define text flow options using the two buttons at the bottom of the dialog box. If you are flowing text from one row to the next, click the button on the right. To flow text from one column to the next, you will want to click the one on the left.

Fit Headlines

You can quickly and easily expand the width of a headline to fill the entire width of the text box. To do this, simply click anywhere in the text of a headline and choose Type | Fit Headline.

Northern Shaolin Gung Fu

The Northern Shaolin Gung Fu system originated 1400 years ago in northern China and traces its roots back to the celebrated Shaolin Temple. The trademark of this style is large, flowing movements, leaps and flying kicks.

Speed, strength and accuracy are developed through training in this system as well as sensitivity, reactions and endurance. The core of the Northern Shaolin system is a series of 10 empty hand sets supported by 4 basic forms including the famous Tom Tuei, various weapons forms and two person fighting forms.

Both elegant and demanding, this style is replete with many practical fighting techniques designed specifically for cultivation of the power of the whole body. The system includes an abundance of traditional

When you apply the Fit Headline feature, you actually increase tracking for your headline, as shown in Figure 10-8.

Shape Text

Once you create a text box, you can reshape the text box and the text within it using the path editing tools that are explained in Chapter 6. Or you can start with a shape and then either align the text to a path or place the text within the path.

You can reshape any text box using path editing tools such as the Pen, Pencil, or Selection tool. As you do, text flows to fill the changed path. If you reshape or resize a text box so that text no longer fits inside it, the oh-so-tiny overflow icon (the plus sign) appears on the right edge of the text box. The following steps illustrate just one technique for converting a standard rectangular text box into a shaped text box.

Follow these steps to reshape a text box:

1. Select an existing rectangular text box, or create one.

2. Use the Add Anchor Point tool (in the Pen tool tearoff in the Toolbox) to add a few new anchor points to the text box.

3. Use the Convert Anchor Point tool to change anchor points into smooth points.

4. Manipulate the anchor control points to change the contours of the text box. Figure 10-9 shows the outline of a text box being edited to match the shape of the hip-hop illustration so that text will flow within the drawing.

By changing the location and curve attributes of the anchors in your text box, you can create text that smoothly flows around an adjacent shape.

FIGURE 10-8 The tracking for the expanded headline has been increased to 189 percent, almost doubling the spacing between words and characters to fill the text box.

FIGURE 10-9 Editing a path to alter the flow of text within it

To review how to edit paths, refer to the discussion of the Pen tearoff tools in Chapter 6.

When you edit anchor points with the Direct Selection tool to change the path of an object filled with text, you change the path but you don't alter the font size, leading, or other attributes of the text itself.

You *can* also interactively resize text *as you resize the text box*. To resize text as you resize a text box, you can use either the Scale tool or the Free Transform tool. Sometimes the Free Transform tool is more effective, because it's a better choice for controlling sizing interactively and it can also be used to rotate or even mirror text (for special effects).

As you resize a text box with the Scale tool or the Free Transform tool, you'll see the text get wider and/or higher depending on how you resize the text box. Text spacing (both line spacing and word and letter spacing) adjusts proportionally as you resize the text box. Figure 10-10 shows an example of text and the text box being resized to make both longer.

FIGURE 10-10 Resizing a text box with the Free Transform tool transforms *both* the size and shape of the text box *and* the size and shape of the text.

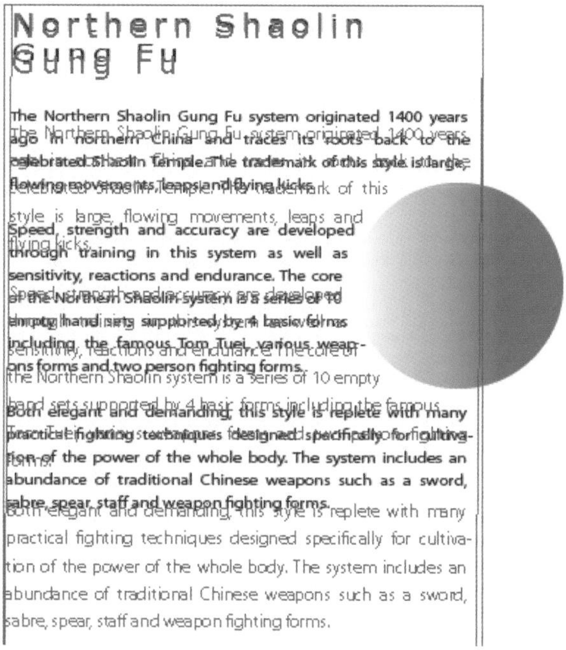

Place Text in a Shape

Rather than starting with a text box and reshaping it, you can start with an existing drawing and simply fill it with text. To fill an existing path with text, you use the Area Type tool in the Type tool tearoff. Follow these steps to fill a path with text:

1. Create a path with any drawing tool, or use an existing path. It doesn't have to be a closed path.

2. Choose the Area Type tool from the Type tool tearoff in the Toolbox.

3. Click the outline of the path.

4. Start typing. The text will appear inside the path, as shown in Figure 10-11.

Tip

When you use a path as a holder for Area Type, the fill and stroke properties of that object are removed, and the only role the shape plays is to form a container for the type. If you want to preserve the fill and stroke attributes of a shape and use it as an envelope for Area Type, you need to first duplicate the object, and then sacrifice one of the two copies of the shape to serve as a type container.

FIGURE 10-11 Using the Area Type tool to enter type in an object

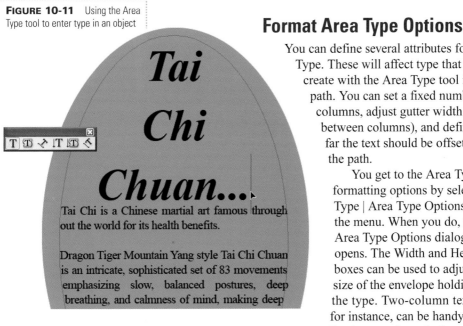

Format Area Type Options

You can define several attributes for Area Type. These will affect type that you create with the Area Type tool inside a path. You can set a fixed number of columns, adjust gutter width (space between columns), and define how far the text should be offset from the path.

You get to the Area Type formatting options by selecting Type | Area Type Options from the menu. When you do, the Area Type Options dialog box opens. The Width and Height boxes can be used to adjust the size of the envelope holding the type. Two-column text, for instance, can be handy for flowing text through shapes such as the one in Figure 10-12.

10

FIGURE 10-12 Two-column text in a text area

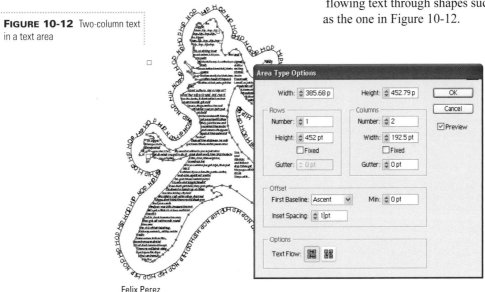

Felix Perez

The Insert Spacing box defines the amount of padding between the type and the shape outline. The other Offset options (available from the First Baseline and Min) drop-down menus define the type and amount of shifting of text within an area. You can use the Preview check box to test these features before clicking OK.

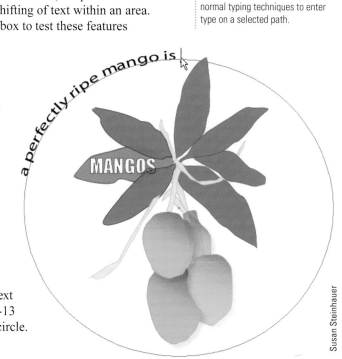

FIGURE 10-13 You can use normal typing techniques to enter type on a selected path.

Align Type to a Path

Aligning type along the outside of a path is similar to aligning it along the inside of a path. You just use a different tool: the Path Type tool.

To attach type to a path, first create the path or use an existing path. Then select the Path Type tool from the Type tool tearoff and click the path to which you want to align the text. You can then simply begin to type (or paste text from the clipboard). Figure 10-13 shows type being entered on a circle.

Susan Steinhauer

Tip

Try this to get comfortable flowing text: Use the Selection tool to select a text box with its text. When a text box is selected, you can move it (or delete it or copy it). You can select text within a text box by double-clicking the box with the Selection tool. This process automatically activates the Type tool. To select a portion of the text within a text box, click and drag (or hold down SHIFT while using the keyboard cursor keys). Triple-click with the Type tool to select an entire paragraph of text. With the Type tool and a text box selected, press COMMAND-A (CTRL-A) to select all text in a text box. To select either a text box or only the text, use the Direct Selection tool. This tool is useful for resizing a text box without changing the size of the type, but it's tricky to do because most text box outlines are not stroked (that is, they are invisible). Use Outline view to more easily select the text box outline with the Direct Selection tool.

When you attach type to a path, the path stroke changes to no stroke. Illustrator assumes that you created the path only to use as a guide for the text, and you don't want it to be visible.

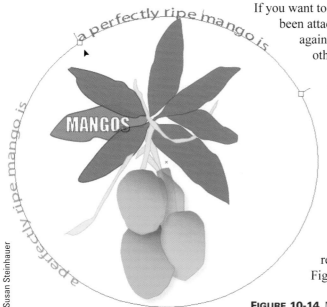

If you want to see the path to which the text has been attached, you can select that path again and assign a stroke color and other stroke attributes.

When you select text on a path, diamond-shaped icons define the beginning and end of the text. The second of these icons (the one that appears after the text) can be adjusted to enlarge or contract the text area. To adjust the location of the text along the path, use the Selection tool to select the I-beam cursor that appears at the beginning of the text, and drag along the path to reposition the text, as shown in Figure 10-14.

FIGURE 10-14 Moving text along a path

You can click and drag on the center I-beam that appears when the path text is selected to "flip" the orientation of the text on the path.

FIGURE 10-15 New path type effects in Illustrator CS

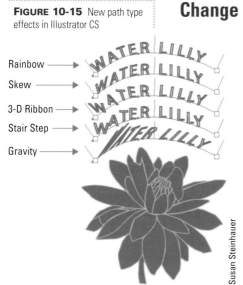

Rainbow
Skew
3-D Ribbon
Stair Step
Gravity

Change Path Type Options

Illustrator CS includes five new options for controlling the flow of text on a path. With Path type selected, you can access these options by selecting Type | Type on a Path, and choosing one of the five options from the submenu. The Rainbow, Skew, 3-D Ribbon, Stair Step, and Gravity effects are illustrated in Figure 10-15.

You can further tweak how text paths appear by opening the Path Type Options dialog box. You can access this by first selecting type on a path and then choosing Type | Path Type | Path Type Options from the menu.

The Effect drop-down menu in the Path Type Options dialog box allows you to change which type of type path effect to use. The Flip check box flips text both horizontally and vertically.

Susan Steinhauer

The Align menu lets you align text along the Ascender (top), Descender (bottom), Center, or Baseline of text.

The difference between descender alignment and baseline alignment is that descender alignment aligns using the bottom of characters, such as the lowercase g or j, that go below the baseline of text.

Create Vertical Type

The Vertical Type, Vertical Area Type, and Vertical Path Type tools work like their horizontal type cousins, except that text is presented vertically, usually from top to bottom.

For example, if you want to create vertical text, click the Vertical Type tool, click to create an insertion point on the artboard, and start typing. Text flows down vertically, as shown in Figure 10-16. After you adjust to the oddity of a horizontal text I-beam insertion point, you can enter, paste, and edit text just as if it were presented horizontally.

You can reverse the orientation of existing text from horizontal to vertical (or vice versa) by selecting the type and then choosing Type | Type Orientation and selecting either Horizontal or Vertical.

FIGURE 10-16 Entering vertical type

Part IV

Work with Drawings

Chapter 11

Combine and Arrange Objects

How to...

- Wield selection tools
- Use the Select menu to select
- Use Smart Guides
- Group objects
- Align objects
- Align with rulers and guides
- Snap to points
- Use the Align palette
- Arrange objects front and back

As your expertise with Illustrator grows and you begin to create more complex projects, you'll want to upgrade your skills for selecting and aligning objects. Relatively uncomplicated illustrations can be edited by selecting and moving paths with the Selection or Direct Selection tools. More sophisticated illustrations, with many intersecting and overlapping paths, are more easily managed if you are able to take advantage of Illustrator's many options for selecting and aligning objects.

In this chapter, you'll step back for a moment from the process of creating illustrations and focus on more advanced techniques for selecting and aligning objects.

Select Objects

During your tour of Illustrator in Chapter 1, you were introduced to the Selection and Direct Selection tools. The Selection tool is the basic—if sometimes rather crude—tool for selecting objects. The Direct Selection tool is probably used more often because it allows you to dissect an object and select more detailed elements—line segments and line anchor points.

Other selection techniques include the Group Selection tool, the Lasso tool, and a rather detailed array of menu options for selecting objects. When you've reached the point where you have bumped up against the limitations of just using the Selection and Direct Selection tools, you'll want to immerse yourself in the remainder of this chapter.

Wield the Selection Tools

Both the Selection and the Direct Selection tools can select objects in a number of ways. If you hold down the SHIFT key as you click on objects, these tools *add* new objects to the set of selected objects. You can also draw a marquee by clicking and dragging to mark a rectangular shape around a set of objects with either the Direct Selection or the Selection tool to select a set of objects. You can draw a marquee around an irregularly shaped collection of objects using the Lasso tool by clicking and drawing, as you would with the Pencil tool. An irregular marquee is shown in Figure 11-1.

FIGURE 11-1 Selecting all the objects in one of the birds with the Lasso tool

Another tool for selecting objects is the Group Selection tool on the Direct Selection tool tearoff. The Group Selection tool works like the Selection tool in that it selects objects (whereas the Direct Selection tool can select *elements* of an object—such as a line segment, an anchor point, or a control point). The difference between the Group Selection tool and the Selection tool is that you can use the Group Selection tool to select *entire objects within a group.* A bit later in this chapter, you'll explore grouping in some detail.

11

Select Objects with the Menu

The Select menu reveals several really handy features for selecting sets of objects. The Select | All choice instantly selects every object in your document—on or off the artboard. The Select | Deselect menu option is great for clearing the selection slate and often makes it easier to select that elusive line segment that the Direct Selection tool seems to be resisting.

Other helpful Select menu options are

- **Reselect**   Repeats the last selection made.

- **Inverse**   Selects everything that isn't currently selected and deselects everything that is currently selected.

- **Next Object Above**   Selects an object that is on top of the selected object.

- **Next Object Below**   Selects an object that is underneath the selected object.

- **Same**   Opens a submenu that allows you to instantly select objects that match one of a number of sets of attributes of the currently selected object, such as fill and stroke or fill color.

A quick way to select all objects with the same fill color is to use the Magic Wand tool, as shown in Figure 11-2.

- **Object**   Opens a submenu with two parts. The first two options (All on Same Layers and Direction Handles) work with an object already selected (choosing Selection Handles reveals control points and direction lines associated with the selected object). The last four options (Brush Strokes, Clipping Masks, Stray Points, and Text Objects) work without anything selected.

FIGURE 11-2 Selecting a set of objects with the same fill color with the Magic Wand tool

Sets of selected objects can be saved as named selections within a document. With a set of objects selected (using any tool or technique, including menu options), choose Select | Save Selection. The Save Selection dialog box opens and prompts you to name the selection to be saved. Named selections are added to the Select menu. After you save a selection, you can quickly reselect it at any time from the Select menu, as shown in Figure 11-3.

FIGURE 11-3 Selecting a saved selection

You can edit the name or content of any selection by choosing Select | Edit Selection.

Take Advantage of Smart Guides

The Smart Guides feature assists you in *selecting* objects and *moving and aligning* them. Smart Guides function as a selection aid because they tell you when you are hovering over a line anchor, line segment, or other object that can be tricky to zero in on without some help. To use Smart Guides, open the View menu and make sure Smart Guides is selected.

Smart Guides are especially useful with the Direct Selection tool, since you use that tool to select elements of an object instead of the whole object. Figure 11-4 shows Smart Guides assisting in the selection of an anchor within an illustration.

Smart Guides also help you move or copy existing objects while keeping them aligned. When you move an object with

Smart Guides turned on, the guides indicate when your object has been moved horizontally, vertically, or at a 45-degree angle. If you hold down SHIFT as you drag, you constrain your move to 45-degree increments.

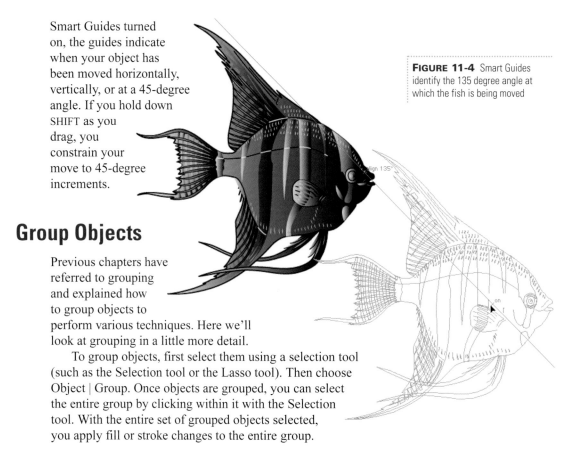

Group Objects

Previous chapters have referred to grouping and explained how to group objects to perform various techniques. Here we'll look at grouping in a little more detail.

To group objects, first select them using a selection tool (such as the Selection tool or the Lasso tool). Then choose Object | Group. Once objects are grouped, you can select the entire group by clicking within it with the Selection tool. With the entire set of grouped objects selected, you apply fill or stroke changes to the entire group.

 The keyboard shortcut for grouping is COMMAND-G *(*CTRL-G*). An alternate way to select several objects is to hold down* SHIFT *while clicking with the Selection tool.*

In a similar way, transforming tools such as the Scale, Rotation, and Free Transform tools work on a *group* of objects as if the group was a single object. If you want to change just one object within a group, you can ungroup the objects and then select an individual object within the group.

 Grouping, ungrouping, and regrouping can get tedious. If you want to quickly select an object within a group, remember to use the Group Selection tool found in the Selection tool tearoff.

To more-or-less permanently ungroup a set of objects, select the group and choose Object | Ungroup (or use the shortcut keys COMMAND-SHIFT-G [CTRL-SHIFT-G]). Groups can themselves be grouped again. However, if you're going to get into multiple levels of grouping, you'll probably be better served by organizing sets of objects into more powerful layers. You'll learn to use layers in Chapter 20.

Each level of grouping has to be ungrouped in turn. So if you've grouped a group within a group, you'll have to choose Object | Ungroup more than once to ungroup all the objects.

Align Objects

As is almost always the case with just about anything you want to do in Illustrator, there are multiple ways to align objects. You can rely on grids, guides, or rulers and snap objects to incremental points on the page. Or you can use the Align palette to line up sets of objects.

Align with Rulers and Guides

Rulers can be helpful in sizing and locating objects. To view rulers, select View | Show Rulers. Hide them by selecting View | Hide Rulers. To define the unit of measurement on the ruler, select Illustrator (Edit) | Preferences | Units & Display Performance. The General drop-down list in the Units area of the Preferences dialog box defines the unit that is displayed on the ruler.

FIGURE 11-5 Locating the fish exactly 2 inches from the left edge of the page using the x coordinate in the Info palette

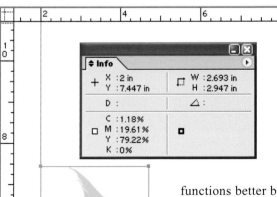

The easiest way to generate horizontal or vertical nonprinting guides on the artboard is to click and drag on either of the rulers, pulling a guide onto the artboard. These guides are locked, by default. So if you want to move or delete them, select View | Guides and deselect Lock Guides. With guides unlocked, you can click and drag on them to move them, or select them and press DELETE to remove them.

You can perform most of the ruler functions better by using other techniques. For example, if you want to precisely size an object, you can view the Info palette while you resize with the Scale tool. If you want to locate an object at an exact spot, you can view the Info palette and see the exact x coordinates (measured horizontally from the left edge of the page) and y coordinates (measured vertically from the bottom of the page) as you move a selected object, as shown in Figure 11-5.

Similarly, you can use guides to align objects, but the Align palette, which is discussed a bit later in this chapter (in the "Use the Align Palette" section), is usually an easier tool for this task. Rulers and guides can be rough layout tools for arranging objects on a page because they're simple and easy to use, and they provide an approximate idea of the size and alignment of objects as you rough out an illustration.

Snap to Grids

You can turn on an invisible set of horizontal and vertical lines called *grids* and use these lines to easily align or size objects. Grid lines are especially useful for creating technical drawings and maps, designing floor plans, and creating other illustrations that tend to be regular in shape and rely closely on measurements.

FIGURE 11-6 Defining grid spacing every 0.5 inch

To view grid lines, choose View | Show Grid. Hide the grid lines by choosing View | Hide Grid. Enable snapping to a grid by choosing View | Snap To Grid. Deselect Snap To Grid to turn off snapping. To change the increments (or units of measurement) of the grid, choose Illustrator (Edit) | Preferences | Guides & Grid. In the Preferences dialog box, use the Gridline Every box to define the spacing of grid lines, as shown in Figure 11-6.

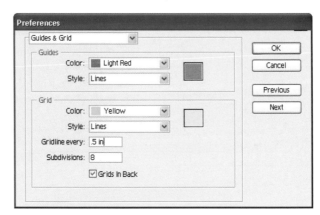

Snap to Points

Snapping to points is a handy trick for connecting two anchor points in the same or different curves. You can use this to close an open curve (making a curved object a contiguous outline). Choose View | Snap To Point to enable snapping to points. Then select an anchor point (use the Direct Selection tool) and drag it to another anchor point.

When the anchor points connect exactly, the mouse cursor changes from black to white, indicating that you have exactly connected the two points, as shown in Figure 11-7.

 The Preferences dialog box allows you to change the grid display from lines to dots, to change grid display color, or to move grid lines on top of (instead of behind) your displayed objects.

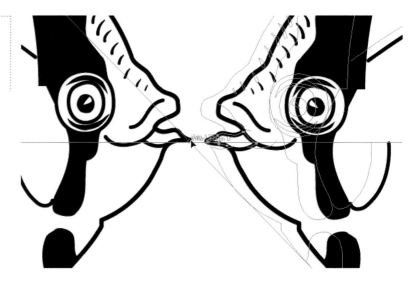

FIGURE 11-7 Smart Guides combine with the Snap To Point option to make it easy to align two anchors exactly.

FIGURE 11-8 Both alignment and distribution are used to line up and evenly space the onions.

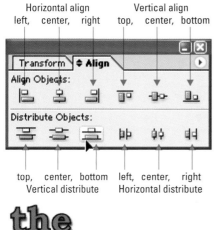

Horizontal align
left, center, right

Vertical align
top, center, bottom

top, center, bottom
Vertical distribute

left, center, right
Horizontal distribute

Use the Align Palette

You use the Align palette to align selected objects horizontally or vertically or to assign even spacing between selected objects. View the Align palette by choosing Window | Align.

The six buttons in the top row of the palette align selected objects left, horizontal center, right, top, vertical center, or bottom. The buttons in the bottom row distribute (space) objects using the top, vertical center, bottom, left, horizontal center, or right side of the selected objects. Figure 11-8 illustrates the use of vertical and horizontal alignment, as well as vertical and horizontal distribution, to align and evenly space objects.

Use the Align palette options (you can view them using the Align palette menu) to tweak how vertical or horizontal distribution is spaced. The Options area of the palette has a drop-down menu that allows you to define spacing increments in points. The alignment palette options are shown in Figure 11-9.

11

Arrange Objects Front and Back

You can move any object or group of selected objects in front of or behind other objects on the artboard. For complex illustrations, this job is managed powerfully with layers, which are explained in Chapter 20. But for simple illustrations, you can move any selected objects forward or backward by choosing Object | Arrange and then choosing Bring to Front, Bring Forward, Send Backward, or Send to Back.

Choosing Send Backward or Bring Forward moves the selected object(s) up or back one layer at a time. Choosing Send to Back or Bring to Front moves an object behind or in front of all objects on the artboard.

If you "lose" objects behind other objects and can't select them, switch to Outline view (View | Outline). Switch back to Preview view (View | Preview) to see objects as they will appear in your final output—in front of or behind each other. Figure 11-10 shows an illustration viewed in both Preview and Outline view.

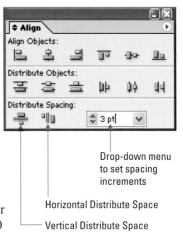

FIGURE 11-9 Defining spacing options

Drop-down menu to set spacing increments

Horizontal Distribute Space

Vertical Distribute Space

Note   *You can hold down* COMMAND *and click (or right-click on a PC) on any selected object(s) and then choose Arrange and one of the four arrange options from the menu. The menu also displays keyboard shortcuts for moving objects forward and backward, but because a couple of them require three keystrokes, they're a bit unwieldy.*

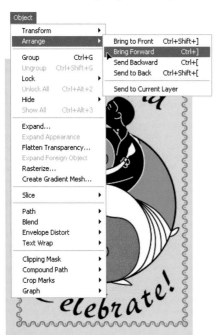

FIGURE 11-10 It's sometimes easier to select objects and bring them forward in Outline view.

Chapter 12

Create Blends

How to...

- Blend objects
- Set blend spacing
- Define blend orientation
- Create step blends
- Create smooth color blends
- Reverse and remove blends
- Blend between anchors
- Manage groups and blends

The Blend feature is one of the most powerful, versatile, and fun tools in Illustrator. You can use blends to create transitional images. Or you can create smooth color transitions to use for shadows, for tube-like results, or for other interesting effects. Blends take full advantage of Illustrator's underlying math-based curve logic.

Aesthetically, you can use blends to create a series of distinct transitions or to attach what appear to be effects such as shading or gradient blending to images. Figure 12-1 shows blending used for both purposes.

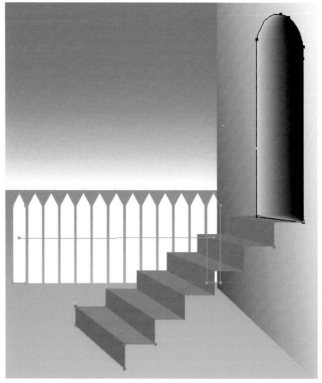

FIGURE 12-1 The fence and steps were generated with step blends, while the subtle shading on the door was created with a smooth blend.

Nathan Alan Whelchel

Tip *You can't apply blending to bitmaps that you place in an Illustrator drawing. You also can't assign blends to type. If you need to assign blending to text, you'll need to convert that text to outlines. (Select the type block and choose Type | Create Outlines.) For more on working with type, see Part III in this book.*

Set Blend Options

FIGURE 12-2 A smooth blend was generated between the larger, lighter-colored part of the door and the darker part to create a 3-D impression.

Blending is fun and easy. The tricky part is setting up blend options. So before you start up the blender, you'll need to do a little nitty-gritty preparation. You'll use the Blend Options dialog box (double-click on the Blend tool to open this box) to define the kind of blend you want to apply.

The main decision to make is what kind of spacing you want between the generated objects. A very small spacing creates a smooth, gradient-like result and it is often used for color gradation in effects such as shadows or 3-D illusion. Larger spacing creates a series of distinct images, with distinct steps visible. Figure 12-2 shows a smooth blend in detail.

Smooth blends use large numbers of very closely spaced iterations. A smooth blend is often employed to create the illusion of a 3-D shadow. On the other hand, step blends use fewer, more widely spaced steps to create animation-like transitions. Figure 12-3 shows a step blend in detail.

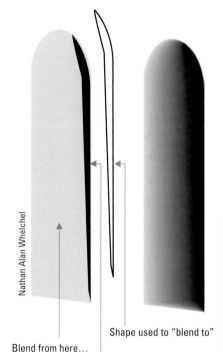

Nathan Alan Whelchel

Blend from here...

Shape used to "blend to"

...to here

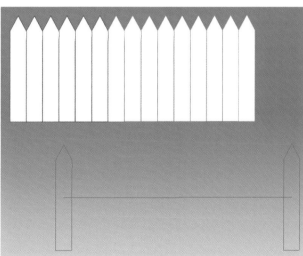

FIGURE 12-3 The fence is a 13-step blend.

You define blend options by double-clicking the Blend tool. You can either do this *before* you begin to generate a blend or you can click on an *existing* blend and open the Blend Options dialog box to alter the blend settings. The Blend Options dialog box is shown in Figure 12-4.

If you select an already-applied blend with the Selection tool and then double-click the Blend tool, you will edit the blend.

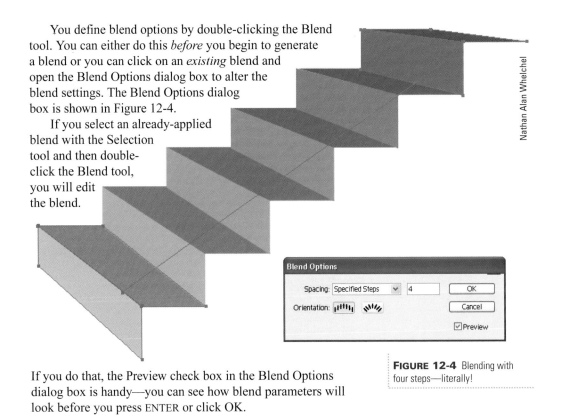

Nathan Alan Whelchel

FIGURE 12-4 Blending with four steps—literally!

If you do that, the Preview check box in the Blend Options dialog box is handy—you can see how blend parameters will look before you press ENTER or click OK.

Set Blend Spacing

There are two basic options for blend spacing: smooth or steps. But Illustrator also offers further fine-tuning options for applying a blend.

If you choose Smooth Color from the Spacing drop-down list in the Blend Options dialog box, Illustrator calculates the optimum number of steps to create a smooth, gradient-looking blend. If you elect to define a limited number of steps, you can either choose the number of generated intermediate shapes or you can define spacing in intervals.

To define a set number of steps, choose Specified Steps from the Spacing drop-down list and enter a value next to the Spacing box. If you want to define a set distance between steps, choose Specified Distance from the Spacing drop-down list and enter a value and a unit of measure. You can type **12 pixels** (or **12 px**, which is short for "pixels"), **.5 inches** (or **.5 in**), and so on.

Define Blend Orientation

If you define a specified blend (either specified steps or a specified distance), you can also define how objects rotate along a curve. This task is worth performing only if you create a curved path to define your blend. To help illustrate this, Figure 12-5 shows both kinds of orientation: aligned to the page and aligned to a path.

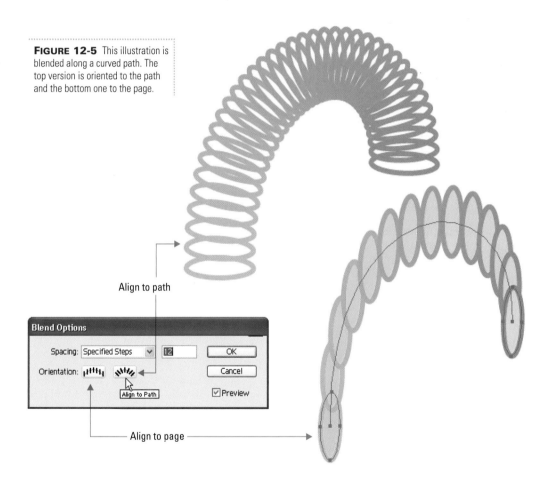

FIGURE 12-5 This illustration is blended along a curved path. The top version is oriented to the path and the bottom one to the page.

Align to path

Align to page

Orientation along an aligned path means that the intermediate objects in a blend will rotate in conformity with the path along which they are generated. Orientation to the page means that objects that are vertical to start with, for example, stay vertical throughout the blend.

Counting Steps

The value you enter after selecting Specified Steps from the Spacing drop-down menu in the Blend Options dialog box defines the number of *generated* shapes, not the *total* number of shapes. The total number of shapes is the number of generated shapes plus the original shapes. Also, if you are defining a Specified Distance for your steps, you can enter a value and a unit of measurement (like .25" or 1cm). Illustrator will convert the value and unit of measurement you enter into the Preferences dialog box for general units. To change your default unit of measurement, select Illustrator (Edit) | Preferences | Units & Display Performance.

To define how orientation will be applied (and again, this concept is relevant only if you will be blending along a path), click either the Align to Page button or the Align to Path button in the Blend Options dialog box. After you define blend options, close the dialog box by pressing ENTER or clicking OK. The options you defined will apply to each blend you create.

Generate a Blend

Blending can get rather complex—and fun! But before you explore the widest reaches of what you can do, you should get comfortable working with the two basic types of blend: smooth colors and steps.

To get some experience with blending, you can follow the steps in the exercises that follow. First you'll create a step blend with a defined number of steps. Then you'll use a blend to produce a smooth blend effect.

Create a Step Blend

To get some experience using step blends, try the instructions below to create a set of steps generated by blending two steps.

Follow these instructions to blend two steps of different sizes and shapes:

1. On a nice, clean artboard, use the Pen or Pencil tool to draw two steps. Use the grid lines, as shown in Figure 12-6, to help size and shape the steps. Group each step (select all the elements of each individual step and choose Object | Group).

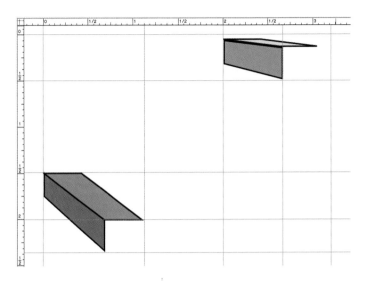

FIGURE 12-6 The two steps will be blended, creating intermediate steps that change size and location.

2. Double-click on the Blend tool to open the Blend Options dialog box. Select Specified Steps from the Spacing drop-down list, and enter **4** next to the Spacing box.

3. Choose Align to Page orientation.

4. Click OK in the Blend Options dialog box. The Blend tool is still selected.

5. Click once in the middle of the bottom step. Move the Blend tool over the top step. As you do, the cursor displays with a tiny plus (+) sign. Click in the middle of the top step to generate a blend. Your blend should look something like the one in Figure 12-7.

If your steps don't match up after the blend, you can fix that. After you generate your blend, select all the objects in one of the original steps with the Direct Selection tool. With all the objects in one of the two original steps selected, click and drag to move it closer to, or farther from, the other step to interactively reshape the blend, as shown in Figure 12-8.

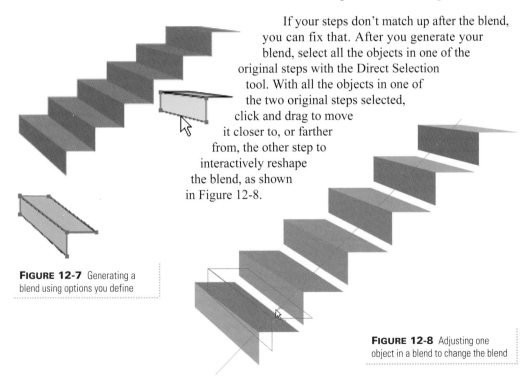

FIGURE 12-7 Generating a blend using options you define

FIGURE 12-8 Adjusting one object in a blend to change the blend

12

Create a Smooth Color Blend

Try this next set of steps to experiment with using a smooth blend to create a doorway that uses blending to create a shadow. This blend will use the Smooth Color blend option to transition from a light color to a dark color using two identical shapes of different sizes.

Follow these steps to assign a color blend:

1. You won't need precise drawings for this, just a doorway. Draw one doorway and duplicate it. Scale the second doorway to about one-fourth the size of the original.

2. Assign a light-colored fill to the original, full-sized doorway, and a darker color to the second, smaller version.

3. Place the smaller doorway in the upper-right corner of the larger version, as shown in Figure 12-9.

4. Double-click the Blend tool in the Toolbox to open the Blend Options dialog box.

5. In the Spacing drop-down list, choose Smooth Color. Click OK in the dialog box.

6. With the Blend tool still selected, click once on the large doorway and once on the small shape. The colors will blend, creating a 3-D-like shadow, something like the one in Figure 12-10.

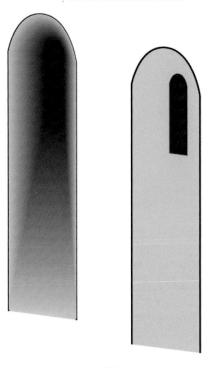

FIGURE 12-9 Preparing a smooth blend to create a shadow effect

Reverse, Change, or Remove a Blend

Sometimes you will want to modify a blend so that the object on the bottom of the blend moves to the top. This revises the whole blend and reverses the stacking order that was originally generated.

Reversing the stacking order is useful (and relevant) only if your intermediate objects overlap each other. To reverse the stacking order in a blend, select the entire blend using the Selection (not the Direct Selection) tool. Then select Object | Blend | Reverse Front to Back.

Finally, it's important to know how to undo a blend. To remove a blend, first select it. (You can select blends just as you do other objects. They aren't grouped—for purposes of the Selection tool, they are like a single

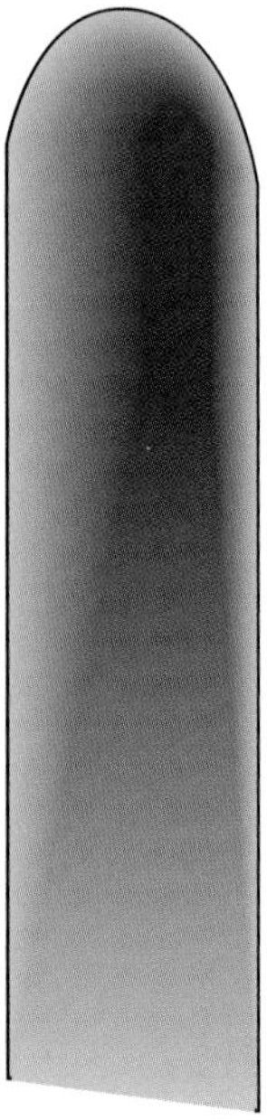

FIGURE 12-10
By blending a smaller, darker shape with the doorway you can create a shadow effect.

path.) You can use the Selection tool to select the whole blend. With the blend selected, choose Object | Blend | Release. Now the blend is gone.

Blend Between Defined Anchors

In the blends you've explored so far, you've learned to blend between two objects. You can fine-tune blends and create some interesting deviations on those blends by basing a blend on selected anchor points in the blended objects. The result of blending from anchor points instead of objects produces very complex and intriguing effects.

Tip   *You can use the Direct Selection tool to select individual objects within a blend. Stay away from that tool for now because the goal is to select the entire blend.*

FIGURE 12-11 Blending from one specific anchor to another

Anchor two

Anchor one

You can use anchor blends with either step or smooth blends. Often the most interesting and useful anchor point–based blends use smooth color transitions to tweak shading and 3-D effects.

Follow these steps to create a blend between anchor points on two different paths:

1. Double-click the Blend tool to open the Blend Options dialog box.

2. Choose Smooth Color in the Spacing drop-down list and click OK.

3. It's easier to define anchor point blends if you can see the anchor points. Use the Selection tool to select both objects involved in the blend—making their anchor points visible.

4. Now that you can see the anchor points in both selected objects, choose the Blend tool. The anchor points remain visible.

5. Click an anchor point in one of the objects.

6. Move the Blend cursor over an anchor point in the second object. As you do, the anchor point and the Blend cursor display together as a black square. Click to generate the blend, as shown in Figure 12-11.

The main "rule" for creating anchor point blends is to experiment! After a while, you will almost be able to anticipate the effect you'll produce with various anchor point blends. Keep the Undo option on the Edit menu handy as you experiment.

12

Bend a Blend

You can further stretch the blending envelope by defining a custom path along which to generate the blend. This custom path is called a *spine*, and you can create it with any drawing tool (such as the Pen or Pencil tool).

FIGURE 12-12 With the spine of the blend selected, the fence is being reshaped with the Pencil tool.

You can use blending along a spine to create a follow-the-path series of transitioning, blended objects. Or you can use a smooth blend combined with a custom spine to create interesting shadow or 3-D effects such as tubing or a snakelike blend. Figure 12-12 demonstrates the use of a smooth blend to "bend" a fence.

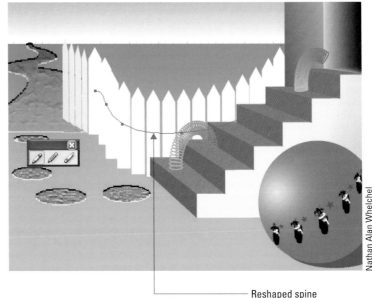

Reshaped spine

Follow these steps to create a blend that uses a defined spine:

1. Draw a small ellipse at the top of your artboard. Assign a dark fill and no outline to the shape.

 Refer to Chapter 5 for help drawing shapes and to Chapter 4 to review how to assign fill and stroke color.

2. Create a second ellipse at the bottom of the artboard. Make it about 12 times as large as the original circle. Assign a lighter fill and a black outline to the second ellipse.

3. Draw a curving line, like the one in Figure 12-13.

4. Double-click the Blend tool and set Spacing to Smooth Color. Click on the Align to Path button in the Orientation area of the dialog box.

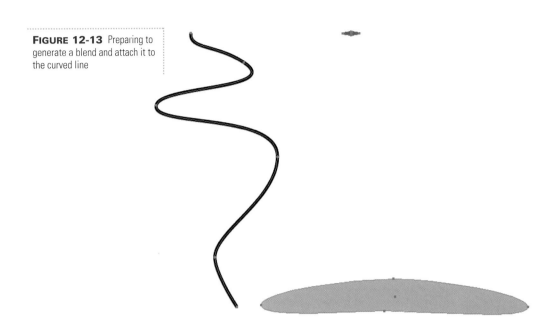

FIGURE 12-13 Preparing to generate a blend and attach it to the curved line

5. With the Blend tool, click on the edge of one ellipse and then again on the edge of the second ellipse to generate a blend.

6. Select both the generated blend and the curve. Choose Object | Blend | Replace Spine to align the blend along the path defined by the wavelike curve.

After you append the blend to the path, you can experiment with changing blend options. (Try both Align to Path and Align to Page, for instance.) You can use the Direct Selection tool to select and move either the first circle, the second circle, or the spine path. And you can use editing tools such as the Scale and Free Transform tools to alter either of the three elements of the blend.

You can reverse the direction of a blend along a spine by selecting Object | Blend | Reverse Spine. And you can select an entire blend—including a blend along a spine—and edit it with tools such as the Free Transform and Scale tools.

12

Blend Groups

Blending between two or more grouped objects can get ugly. In general, blends work well between simple shapes or shapes that are not that different (such as resized objects). But blends can get scary when you start to blend complex shapes.

Bad blends can happen when you try to blend grouped objects. In general, the results are kind of a mushy mess. For example, in the top set of flowers in Figure 12-14, two grouped flowers were blended, with not-very-pretty results.

A nicer blend results when the flowers in Figure 12-14 are ungrouped and separate blends are assigned to each object within the group.

Tweak Blends

As you've seen, blending is a very versatile technique that you can use for everything from seamlessly smooth color blends to animation-style sets of objects that transition from one shape to another. Although you can do a lot to control blends—both in the Blend Options dialog box and by adhering a blend to a spine—sometimes you will want to *tweak* (adjust) the result of a blend.

For example, Figure 12-15 was created with a blend, augmented by some significant altering of the generated transitional blend objects.

You can't do this level of fine-tuning using only a blend. *Expanding* a blend converts each of the generated transitional shapes into a distinct, editable shape. To expand a blend, first select the blend. Then select Objects | Blend | Expand. The result will be a set of paths that you can edit. When you first expand a blend, the objects that made up the blend will be grouped, so ungroup them (Object | Ungroup) before you start editing individual objects.

Once you expand a blend, of course, it loses all its blend properties. You can no longer adjust the blend options or work with a spine path.

FIGURE 12-14 Sometimes blending works best when you ungroup objects and blend each individual component of a drawing.

Grouped and blended all at once

Ungrouped and blended one element at a time

FIGURE 12-15 The flowers were generated by a blend that was then expanded so that the middle flower could be resized.

Chapter 13

Clip with Masks

How to...

- ▨ Make a clipping mask
- ▨ Edit a clipping mask
- ▨ Use type as a mask
- ▨ Release a mask
- ▨ Crop a bitmap with a mask

Clipping masks play an essential role in cropping artwork in Illustrator. This is one of those concepts that can be a bit disorienting for designers migrating from Photoshop or other bitmap graphics software.

Artists coming from a bitmap background to Illustrator often ask, "Where's the eraser?" There is an Eraser tool (found on the Pencil tool tearoff and discussed in Chapter 4), but it's not really what you need to crop objects in Illustrator. Instead, Illustrator crops objects by imposing a clipping mask over the object and then trimming away everything not covered by the clipping mask.

In Figure 13-1, the rectangle is the mask, and the streets are masked objects. As you can see, the only part of the label that is visible after masking is the part within the rectangle.

FIGURE 13-1 The rectangle acts as a clipping mask over the map to constrain it to the proper size.

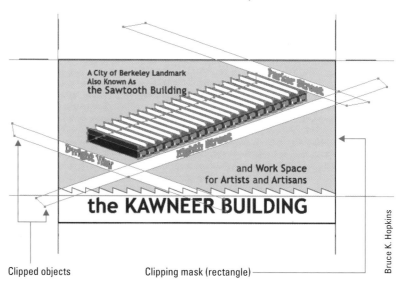

A City of Berkeley Landmark
Also Known As
the Sawtooth Building

and Work Space
for Artists and Artisans

the KAWNEER BUILDING

Bruce K. Hopkins

Clipped objects   Clipping mask (rectangle)

Make a Clipping Mask

There are two basic steps in clipping (trimming) an object with a mask. The first is to create the masking object, which can be any vector image (not a bitmap). Your masking object can also be text. The second step is to trim an object with the mask.

It doesn't matter which fill or outline you apply to an object that will be used as a masking object. The outline will disappear when the object is used as a mask, and the mask's fill will become the section of the masked object that lies underneath the masking object.

Follow these steps to create a masking object and use it to clip an underlying object:

1. Start with any illustration. (Either vector or bitmap will work.)

2. To make it easier to work with your illustration, group it. (Select all objects and choose Object | Group.)

3. Draw a shape using any of the tools in the Rectangle tool tearoff. At this point, you should have both an illustration and another object you plan to use to crop the object, as shown in Figure 13-2.

4. Move the shape on top of the illustration. If the mask ends up behind the illustration, choose Object | Arrange and move objects forward or backward until the clipping object is on top, as shown in Figure 13-3.

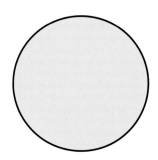

FIGURE 13-2 The circle will be used as a clipping mask on the flower.

Susan Steinhauer

13

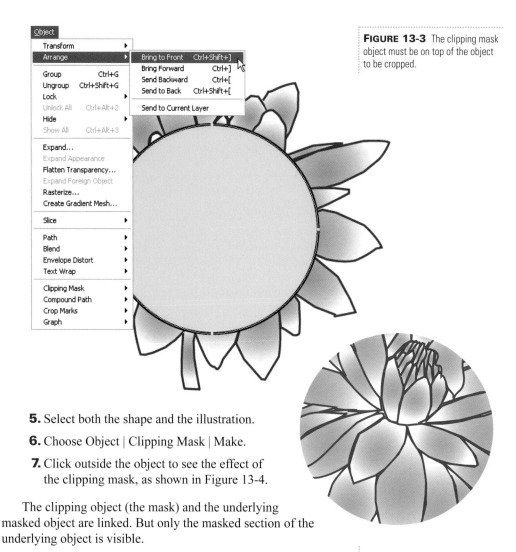

FIGURE 13-3 The clipping mask object must be on top of the object to be cropped.

5. Select both the shape and the illustration.

6. Choose Object | Clipping Mask | Make.

7. Click outside the object to see the effect of the clipping mask, as shown in Figure 13-4.

The clipping object (the mask) and the underlying masked object are linked. But only the masked section of the underlying object is visible.

FIGURE 13-4 The masking object loses all fill and stroke characteristics and simply acts to constrain the display of the masked object.

Edit a Mask

Once you have created a masked object, you can edit the shape and location of the mask. Editing a mask is pretty much like editing any other object, except that your illustration is complex and it's tricky to select the mask object. Use the Direct Selection tool to edit the path of a masking object.

FIGURE 13-5 Editing a mask interactively

Be careful to select the masking object, and not the hidden, underlying object. Click and drag with the Direct Selection tool on mask object handles to change the area that is revealed, as shown in Figure 13-5.

You can also move a masking object to different locations over the masked object. Do this by choosing the Group Selection tool and dragging the masking object to a different location. Here again, be careful not to select elements of your underlying illustration with the Group Selection tool.

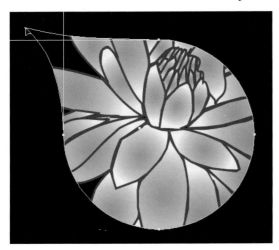

FIGURE 13-5 Editing a mask interactively

Use Type as a Mask

When you use type as a mask, you can adhere the pattern of the underlying masked object to your text. Chapter 18 explores fill options in detail, but for now it's worth noting that the fill options available for type are not as versatile as fill options for other paths. For instance, you can't assign a gradient fill to type. But you can work around the constraints on type fills by using type as a mask over patterns of illustrations.

Follow these steps to use a mask to apply a gradient fill to type:

1. Create some text.

2. Create a rectangle about the size of your text, and apply a gradient fill, as shown in Figure 13-6. Gradient fills are covered in more detail in Chapter 16, but for now simply click the default gradient fill in the Toolbox.

FIGURE 13-6 The gradient-filled rectangle will eventually provide a fill for the text.

3. Move the type on top of the filled rectangle. Make sure the type is on top. (Choose Object | Arrange | Bring to Front if necessary.)

4. Select both the type and the rectangle.

5. Choose Object | Clipping Mask | Make.

13

6. Click outside your type to see the effect. Figure 13-7 shows type with a gradient fill.

Release a Mask

When you use an object as a mask, you permanently wipe out any fill and/or outline you applied to that object before you applied it as a mask. You can unlink the masking object and the masked object so that the masked object will resume its original appearance. But the masking object will become a path with no outline or fill.

To remove a mask from an object, select the combined masked object. Choose Object | Clipping Mask | Release, as shown in Figure 13-8. After you detach the masking object from the previously masked object, you can create a new fill and outline for the object that was the masking object.

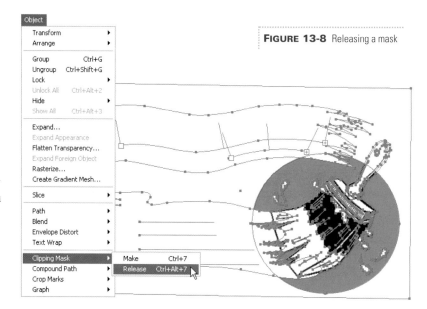

Crop Bitmaps with Masks

Bitmap images—either placed from other sources (such as Photoshop) or created in Illustrator—can be cropped with masks. A photo or any bitmap illustration can be cropped using a vector object as a mask.

The basic routine for creating a mask for a bitmap is to first place a bitmap on your artboard and then place a vector image on top of the bitmap.

FIGURE 13-9 Using a bitmap image (the onions) as a clipping mask fill for text

With both the masking vector object and the underlying bitmap selected, choose Object | Clipping Mask | Make to generate a mask, as shown in Figure 13-9.

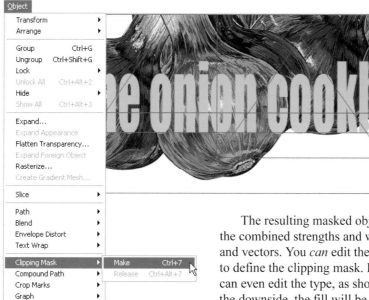

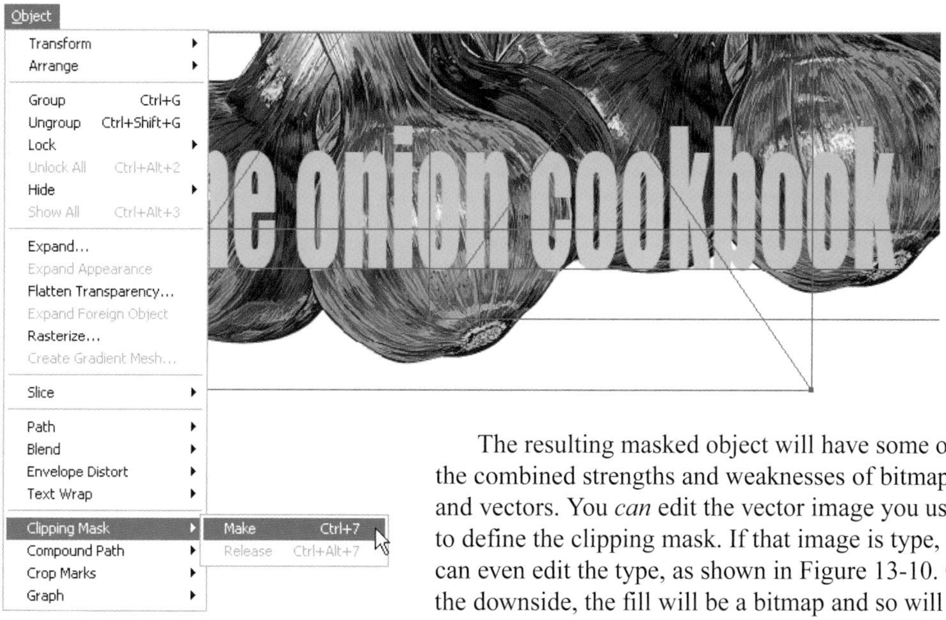

The resulting masked object will have some of the combined strengths and weaknesses of bitmaps and vectors. You *can* edit the vector image you used to define the clipping mask. If that image is type, you can even edit the type, as shown in Figure 13-10. On the downside, the fill will be a bitmap and so will not be scalable.

  For more on working with bitmaps, see Chapter 19.

13

FIGURE 13-10 Editing type filled with a clipped bitmap

What About Other Kinds of Masking?

Illustrator offers other tools that do some form of masking. Most of those tools are explored in other chapters of this book in detail, but it will be helpful to quickly note them here and explain their relationship to clipping masks.

Opacity masks work like clipping masks except that in addition to clipping a section of an object, they also apply various definable filters or effects. For instance, you can use an opacity mask to both crop a section of a drawing *and* assign a blue tint to that section of the illustration. Or you can use an opacity mask to crop a section of an illustration and make that section semi-transparent. Chapter 17 explains how to create and apply opacity masks.

Printers' crop marks are used to tell printers where to trim (cut) an illustration. You can create printers' crop marks by drawing a rectangle over an illustration and selecting Object | Crop Area | Make, as shown in Figure 13-11.

Crop marks appear on the printed page and are often included in helpful templates available from print shops for designing CD covers, business cards, postcards, and other designs. You remove crop marks by choosing Object | Crop Area | Release. Working with print shops is examined in more detail in Chapter 22.

Finally, *layers* can be used as clipping masks. Chapter 21 explains how to use layers to automate and manage complex illustration procedures.

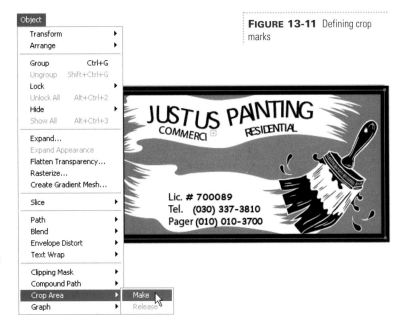

FIGURE 13-11 Defining crop marks

Chapter 14

Trip Out with Effects and Filters

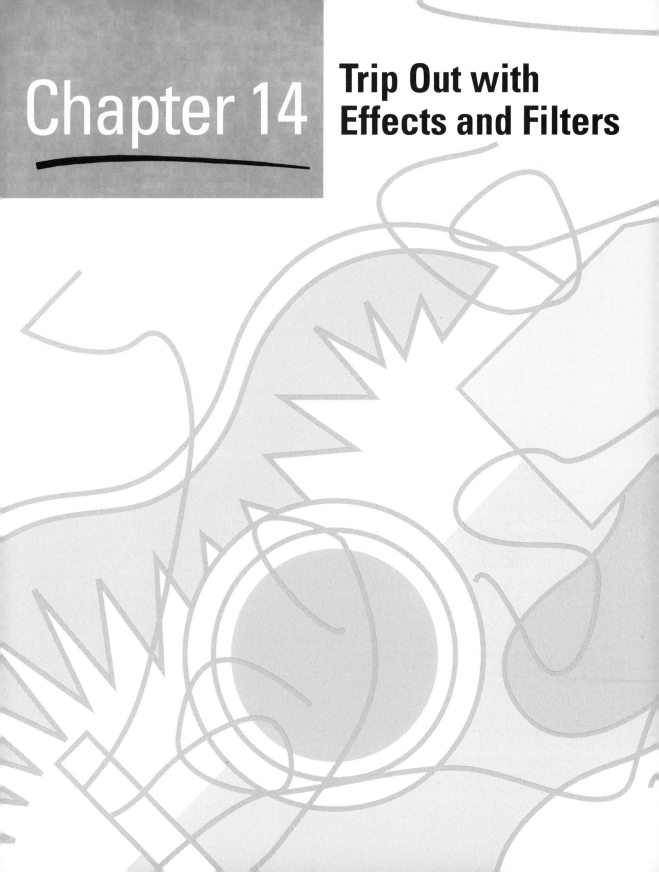

How to…

- Apply effects and filters
- Apply Convert to Shape effects
- Distort and transform objects
- Create Path, Pathfinder, and Rasterize effects
- Assign drop shadows and arrowheads
- Use Warp effects
- Remove or edit effects
- Generate 3-D objects
- Apply filters

Illustrator's Filter and Effect menus provide similar sets of fun ways to distort your illustrations. There's nothing magical about effects and filters; they are simply sets of changes to an object's path and fill. But by packaging groups of stroke and fill changes, Illustrator provides a kind of one-stop shopping for altering your images.

Some effects and filters are pretty esoteric, but others—such as drop shadows or arrowheads—are on an illustrator's "most wanted" list. Other effects and filters are great for warping, distorting, stylizing, and generally having fun with shapes.

Understand Effects

The main difference between filters and effects is how they affect an object's path. Effects do not change an object's path but simply alter the image based on the original path. Filters, on the other hand, do change the object's path. Effects have an advantage over filters in that the underlying paths are not changed when they are applied. Therefore, after you apply an effect, you can still edit the original path.

Illustrator CS has incorporated limited 3-D–generating features, which are available from the Effect | 3D menu. You'll explore this significant new feature in this chapter as well.

Apply Effects

In a way, applying one or more effects allows you to transform an object while keeping the original path intact. Think of looking at yourself in a funhouse mirror. You still have the same shape (fortunately!), but the image in the mirror is distorted. As you move, crouch down, or change your stance, the distorted image in the mirror transforms as well. That's how effects work. You apply them, and they appear in any output (printed or digital). But the underlying outline is unchanged by the effect.

You can apply effects to selected paths. If you want to apply an effect to a group of paths, make sure to select all the paths to which you want to apply the transformation. Or you can apply an effect to a grouped object. With the object(s) selected, choose an effect from the Effect menu. Different effects display different dialog boxes with options for defining the applied effect. For example, choosing the Drop Shadow option displays the dialog box in Figure 14-1.

FIGURE 14-1 Applying the drop shadow effect

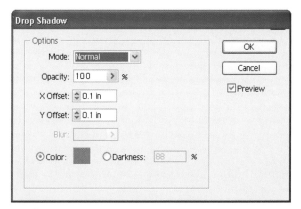

Note *Options in the Styles and Appearances palettes provide other methods for altering how a path looks without altering the underlying path itself. The features in these palettes are relatively complex, advanced ways of assigning transformations to objects. In Chapter 21, you'll learn to save time by applying sets of transformations using the Graphic Styles palette. Also, the Effect menu includes Pathfinder palette options, which are explained in Chapter 5.*

14

Change or Delete Effects

After you apply an effect, that effect and the settings you defined for it appear at the top of the Effect menu for easy reapplication to additional objects on the artboard. Illustrator remembers your last Effect selection even after you close a document.

To edit or remove an effect, select an object to which the effect was applied, and view the Appearance palette (choose Window | Appearance). Applied effects and filters are listed in the Appearance palette. You can double-click on an effect in the Appearance palette to reopen the associated dialog box and change the effect.

In some cases, you can "turn off" an assigned effect by changing the settings in the effect's dialog box. For instance, you can "remove" a drop shadow effect by changing the opacity of the shadow to 0.

A more definitive way to remove an effect is to choose the Reduce to Basic Appearance menu option in the Appearance palette menu for a selected effect, as shown in Figure 14-2.

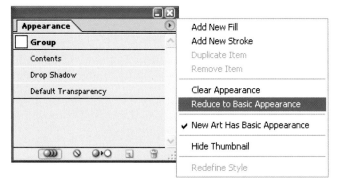

FIGURE 14-2 Removing the drop shadow from the type

Expand Effects

As emphasized earlier, objects to which effects have been applied *maintain their original path structure.* So you can "undo" an effect by reducing the path to its basic appearance, as explained in the previous section.

That's nice if you really need to be able to work with the shape in its original form. But if you want to edit the shape in its *new* form—with the effect(s) applied—you'll want to generate a new object that *abandons* the original paths and is simply an editable object.

To convert an object with applied effects into a plain old regular object, select the object and choose Object | Expand Appearance.

Expanding an object that has effects applied to it "finalizes" the applied effects, replacing the original object with the new object.

Use Illustrator's Effects

As you explore and experiment with Illustrator's wide-ranging set of effects, keep a few "cautions" in mind. First, be aware

Original

Transform

that effects can add vast numbers of anchors to your object or make drastic changes in fills. Using effects is like using a shotgun, not a rifle, to make changes to your illustrations. For this reason, many hard-core professional designers don't use effects much, preferring instead to rely on their skills with the Pen tool.

Beyond making radical changes to your illustration, some effects—3-D effects in particular—require tremendous processor resources and can multiply your file size.

With these cautions in mind, you'll certainly have fun experimenting with Illustrator's effects and filters.

Chapter 19 focuses on Illustrator's limited bitmap editing features and explores filters in more detail.

Use Convert to Shape Effects

The effects on the Convert to Shape menu convert a path to a rectangle, a rounded rectangle, or an ellipse. One use of this feature is to create a rectangular or elliptical shape to use as a layout guide for old-fashioned pasteup.

The effect is simple to apply. Just select an object, choose Effect | Convert to Shape, and then choose either Rectangle, Rounded Rectangle, or Ellipse from the submenu. Each menu choice opens a Shape Options dialog box in which you can define the shape and size of the generated shape.

FIGURE 14-3 Adding effects from the Distort & Transform menu

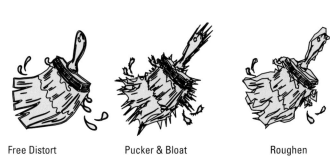

Free Distort

Pucker & Bloat

Roughen

Tweak

Twist

Zig Zag

Apply Distort and Transform Effects

The effects on this menu offer a zany set of hypertransformations. The Distort & Transform effects are illustrated in Figure 14-3.

The Free Distort menu option opens an interactive dialog box for a selected

14

image. You can click and drag on the corner handles in the dialog box to transform the selected object, as shown in Figure 14-4.

You use the Free Distort effect to alter the perspective on an object. The four corner handles function as vanishing points—dragging them creates the illusion of an object emerging or fading from front to back or from left to right.

The popular Pucker & Bloat effect was known as "Punk & Bloat" in earlier versions of Illustrator, and it creates a pointy or puffy distortion of your original image. The slider in the dialog box allows you to assign relatively more pucker (pointiness) or bloat (puffiness), as shown in Figure 14-5.

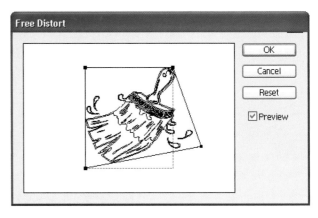

FIGURE 14-4 Stretching the paintbrush with the interactive Free Distort effect

The Roughen effect is kind of the opposite of the Simplify menu command (Object | Path | Simplify) discussed earlier in Chapter 6. Instead of smoothing a path, this command roughens up a path by adding anchors. The Roughen dialog box allows you to choose either smooth or corner anchors. The Size slider defines how much the paths will be distorted either by percent (if you choose the Relative option) or in pixels or another unit of measurement (if you use the Absolute option). The Detail slider defines how many new anchors will be added. Lower settings produce less distortion.

FIGURE 14-5 Assigning pucker to generate a star

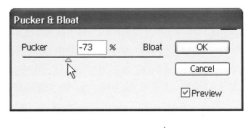

The Transform effect allows you to rescale, move, or rotate selected objects. You expand or contract vertical and horizontal scaling by using sliders. The Move sliders move selected objects right or left, up or down—but remember, these changes are applied to your illustration as *effects,* so the basic path of the object is unchanged. The Rotation dial allows you to change the angle of your objects. The Copies box lets you generate additional copies as you transform your selected objects. The Reflect boxes let you flip your object horizontally (reversing left and right [Reflect X]) or vertically (reversing up and down [Reflect Y]).

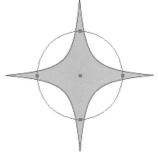

Using the Tweak effect is a little like throwing your object against a wall to see what happens! Lower Horizontal and Vertical slider settings produce less distortion. The Relative option assigns distortion levels relative to the object size, while

the Absolute option defines the distortion in your selected unit of measurement. The Anchor Points, In Control Points, and Out Control Points check boxes in the Modify area of the dialog box allow you to change anchor points or alter only the control points (either the In or the Out control points).

In defining "Tweak," Illustrator uses the phrase "control point" to refer to control points and their direction lines. See Chapter 6 for an explanation of how to use anchor point control points and direction lines to alter curves.

The Twist effect is something like twirling an object and watching the shape and fill appear as if they are spinning around. You can increase the intensity of the effect by selecting an angle of a higher degree in the dialog box.

The Zig Zag effect literally applies zig zags or a curvy distortion to paths in a selected object. The Size slider determines how large the zig zags or curves are. The Relative options define curves or zig zags relative to the size of the object. The Absolute options let you use a unit of measurement such as pixels to define zig zag or curve size. The Ridges Per Segment slider defines how many curves or zig zags to create. The Smooth option generates curves, and the Corner option generates zig zags.

Explore Path Effects

When you select Effect | Path, you can choose from three effects that allow you to duplicate or transform an object's outline: Offset Path, Outline Object, and Outline Path. The Offset Path effect allows you to create a new path that is offset from the original. You can determine the offset distance by changing the value in the Offset area of the Offset Path dialog box.

You can also change join types and miter values for those joins. You use the Outline Object and Outline Stroke effects to convert complex objects—such as those imported from a multilayer Photoshop file—into simpler paths. You use Outline Stroke to convert strokes, while you use Outline Object to simplify fills and strokes.

Try Pathfinder Effects

The Pathfinder effects (selected from the Effect | Pathfinder menu) are very similar to the tools available from the Pathfinder palette discussed in Chapter 5. Like the tools in the Pathfinder

14

palette, Pathfinder effects combine or divide intersecting paths, and the object on the bottom usually assumes the fill and stroke attributes of the object on top.

Before you apply any Pathfinder effect, you will want to arrange objects front to back (choose Object | Arrange). Pathfinder effects don't work with bitmaps, but they do work with type and vector objects.

Rasterize

You can apply many of the transformations available from the Effect menu *only* to raster (bitmap) images. However, Illustrator provides a unique option for applying these effects without permanently destroying the vector object to which you want to apply the bitmap filter. That option is to create a raster *version* of your vector object, while preserving the underlying vector paths and anchors. This method is called *rasterizing* an object.

When you rasterize an object, you get the best of both the vector and bitmap worlds. You can still edit paths and anchors, and your objects are still easily rescalable. But you can also apply effects that work only on raster images. After you rasterize an image, it will appear as a bitmap on the artboard—jaggy lines, coarse resolution, and all those other attributes associated with bitmaps. If you want to see the paths and anchors, choose View | Outline to view your object without the bitmap attributes.

To rasterize a selected object, choose Effect | Rasterize.The Rasterize dialog box opens, as shown in Figure 14-6.

If your graphic is destined for a web site, choose 72 ppi from the set of Resolution options. If your graphic is going to be used with print output, select a higher resolution. The Color Model options are those available for digital or web graphics: RGB (best for web graphics), Bitmap, or Grayscale. In the Background section of the dialog box, choose the Transparent option for web graphics when you want the web page background or background color to show through behind uncolored portions of the image.

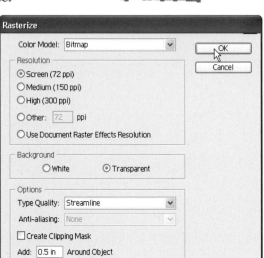

FIGURE 14-6 Rasterizing a vector object

Stylize

Somewhat buried in Illustrator's vast Effect and Filter menus are the very useful Stylize effects. They include such popular appearance changes as arrowheads, drop shadows, and cool color tinting.

To add arrowheads to a path, first select the path and then choose Effect | Stylize | Add Arrowheads. The intuitive Add Arrowheads dialog box appears, as shown in Figure 14-7.

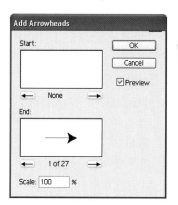

FIGURE 14-7 Defining an arrowhead at the endpoint of a path

You can define an arrowhead for the start and/or for the end of a path. The Scale area allows you to adjust the size of the arrowhead relative to the size of the path stroke. Clicking on the arrows scrolls through a set of symbols to use as arrowheads. Use the Preview check box to watch changes interactively on the artboard.

The other Stylize effects alter path or fill effects. With the Preview box checked, experiment with different options in the dialog boxes to see changes on the artboard before you finalize effect settings.

The Inner Glow and Outer Glow effects add subtle glowing tints to colors, moving either toward the center (Inner Glow) or beyond the edges (Outer Glow) of a selected object. Inner Glow is illustrated in Figure 14-8.

FIGURE 14-8 The Inner Glow effect is added to the inside of the selected mango path.

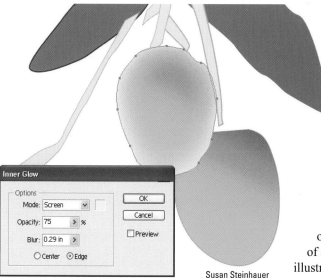

Susan Steinhauer

14

The Drop Shadow effect is great for quick shadows. The Feather effect creates a transitional fade at the edges of an object, and the Round Corners option produces some interesting distortions of your original image.

Apply SVG Filters

Adobe is promoting Scalable Vector Graphics (SVG) format for web browsers. The SVG filter set provides interesting vector-based mutations of the fill for a selected object. If you are saving your illustration to SVG format, you'll be able to preserve and display these effects in web graphics.

Unlike other vector-based effects, SVG filter effects don't have dialog boxes, much less a preview option. You can try 'em, like 'em, or undo 'em. For an explanation of SVG graphics, how to use them, when they work, and their limitations, see Chapter 23.

Warp

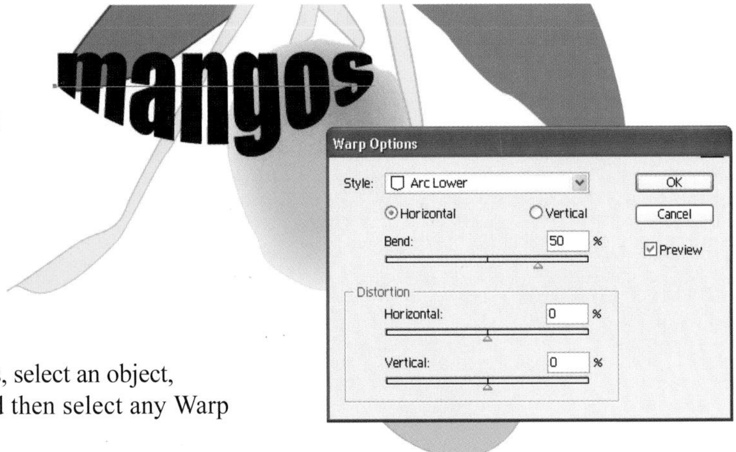

FIGURE 14-9 Distorting text with a lower arc effect

You can use Warp effects to make waving flags or surf on water or to create distortion-like bulges and arcs in selected objects. Illustrator makes it easy to experiment with Warp effects because they are all available in the dialog box of any warp you select. To experiment with warps, select an object, choose Effect | Warp, and then select any Warp effect.

The resulting dialog box allows you to choose from the entire array of warps. And by activating the Preview check box, you can try on any warp from the same dialog box, as shown in Figure 14-9.

Create 3-D Effects

Illustrator CS introduces two basic types of 3-D effects. The Extrude & Bevel effect adds perspective to an object. The Revolve effect generates 3-D objects by "spinning" an object

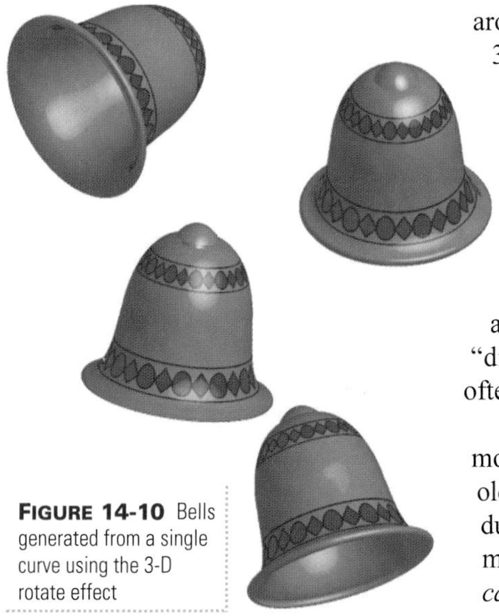

FIGURE 14-10 Bells generated from a single curve using the 3-D rotate effect

Bruce K. Hopkins

around a pivot point to generate an object. The third 3-D effect, Rotate, can be applied to rotate objects in any direction. To take a simple example, you can use 3-D effects to transform an angled line into a cone. Figure 14-10 shows bells generated from a single curve. You'll learn how those bells were created in this section.

Extrusion applies 3-D effects by reshaping an object using an imaginary *vanishing point*— a point into which the object would eventually "disappear into the distance." Extrusion effects are often applied to text for a flashy, 3-D look.

The 3-D effects in Illustrator do not give you 3-D modeling capability, even on the level of those in the old Adobe Dimensions program. And they are far from duplicating the features of powerful full-scale 3-D modeling software such as 3D Studio Max. But you *can* use Illustrator's effects to create basic 3-D objects.

Caution *Generating 3-D objects draws tremendous processing resources from your computer. You'll need at least 1GB of RAM to utilize Illustrator's 3-D effects.*

Generate a Revolved 3-D Object

The first step in generating a 3-D illustration is to create a curve that will be revolved and duplicated to generate the 3-D object. The curve in Figure 14-11 is the basis for the bells illustrated in Figure 14-10.

To generate a 3-D look, the artist converted the curve in Figure 14-11 into an outline stroke. (With a path selected, choose Object | Path | Outline Stroke.)

If you want to include a pattern that will wrap around your generated 3-D object, you must add that pattern object to the Symbols palette. Draw a pattern, like the one in Figure 14-12, and drag it into the Symbols palette in preparation for revolving it to generate your 3-D object.

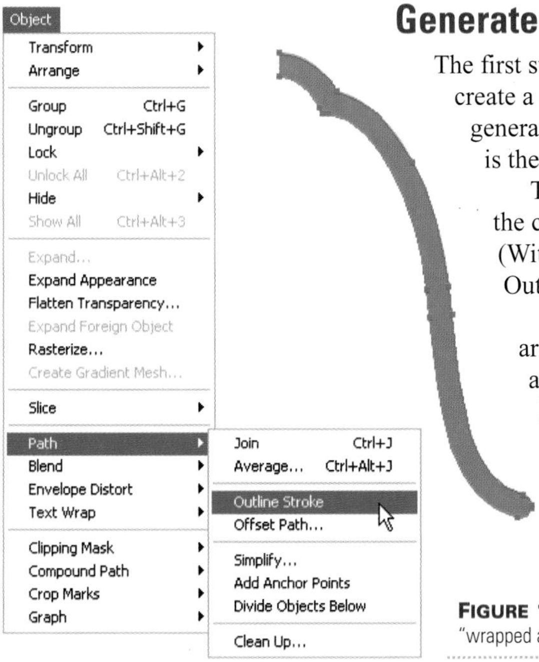

FIGURE 14-11 his curve will be "wrapped around" to generate a bell.

14

Note *It isn't necessary to save the pattern you convert into a symbol. You'll explore Symbols in more detail in Chapter 21.*

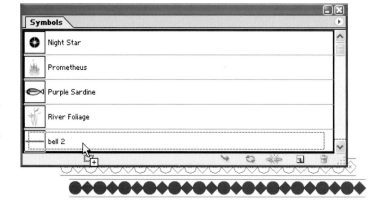

With *just* your curve selected, choose Effect | 3D | Revolve to open the 3D Revolve Options dialog box. If you click the More Options button, you'll see a rather mind boggling array of options. This discussion will not explore every option in depth, but it will explain how to use the main features of the 3D Revolve Options dialog box to generate objects.

In the Revolve area of this dialog box, leave Angle set to the default value of 360 degrees to generate a full (360-degree) revolved object.

It's easiest to choose Custom Rotation from the Position drop-down list at the top of the dialog box and experiment with settings for the X (horizontal), Y (vertical), and Z (front to back) rotation settings simply by clicking and dragging on the cube in the dialog box. If you click the Preview check box, you'll see your generated 3-D object in the document window, outside of the 3D Revolve Options dialog box, as shown in Figure 14-13.

You can add a symbol to your generated 3-D object by clicking the Map Art button in the 3D Revolve Options dialog box. Depending on the size and shape of your object, the Map Art dialog box will give you the option of adding a *mapped symbol* (applied pattern) to one of a number of *surfaces* (bands) on the generated object.

Use the arrows next to the Surface list to choose a surface, and use the Symbol drop-down list to select a symbol to apply, as shown in Figure 14-14.

FIGURE 14-12 Converting a pattern into a symbol in preparation for integrating it into a 3-D object

FIGURE 14-13 Revolving the curve generates a bell. This object is rotated on three axes as well.

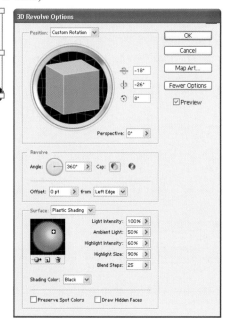

Caution *Remember, you need to save a pattern as a symbol by dragging it into the Symbols palette before you can apply it to your generated 3-D object as a mapped symbol.*

Again, if you leave the Preview check box checked, you can see the impact of your mapped symbol on your generated object.

The options for revolved 3-D objects in the bottom half of the 3D Revolve Options dialog box affect the surface and lighting source for the object. Use the Surface drop-down list to experiment with different surface textures. (Start with Plastic Shading; you'll probably want to use that.) Depending on the surface you select, options become active to allow you to tweak the surface appearance.

Use the lighting sphere to click and drag on the interactive square and define a lighting source for your illustration. The three buttons to the right of the lighting sphere allow you to move the light source, or add or delete lighting sources—the first button moves the light source behind the generated object. The second button adds a light source, while the button on the right deletes a selected lighting source.

After you define a 3-D object, click OK to generate the object.

It is *not* advisable to use standard Illustrator editing tools (such as the Scale, Free Transform, or Rotate tool) to edit objects generated with 3-D effects. Attempting to use regular editing tools will be frustrating and unpredictable. Instead, reopen the 3-D Revolve dialog box by selecting the object and viewing the Appearance palette. Double-click on the 3-D Revolve effect in the Appearance palette to reopen the 3D Revolve dialog box, as shown in Figure 14-15.

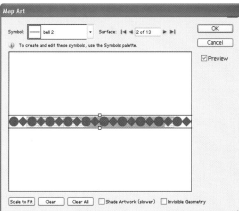

FIGURE 14-14 Adding a mapped symbol to a 3-D object

FIGURE 14-15 Selecting a 3-D effect for editing in the Appearance palette

Extrude and Bevel

Extrusion and beveling add 3-D effects using an imaginary vanishing point towards which the object shrinks. Figure 14-16 shows extruded text.

Rotation, lighting source, and other 3-D options for extrusion and beveling are similar to the ones for revolved 3-D effects, so you can refer to the previous section to experiment with those options.

14

To generate a 3-D object by extruding a shape, follow these steps:

1. Select the object.

2. Choose Effect | 3D | Extrude & Bevel.

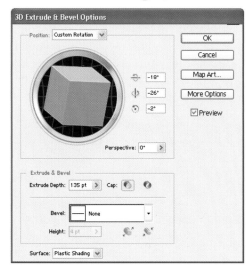

FIGURE 14-16 Extruded type "vanishes" toward a point above and to the left of the text.

Tip   *Rotation, Surface, and Lighting options are similar to those for revolved 3-D effects—they are available if you click the More Options button in the Extrude and Bevel Options dialog box. You can refer back to the previous section in this chapter for advice on setting these values.*

FIGURE 14-17 Experimenting with extrusion depth

3. Experiment with various depths of extrusion by changing the value in the Extrude Depth box. Click on Preview to see how the extrusion will look, as shown in Figure 14-17.

4. Click OK when you have defined your extrusion setting.

Beveling is similar to extrusion but is usually applied to shapes or curves to transform them into 3-D objects. Select an object, and then choose Effect | 3D | Extrude & Bevel to open the 3D Extrude & Bevel Options dialog box.

In the dialog box, you can adjust the rotation, surface, and lighting attributes. Adjust rotation using the rotation cube. Lighting attributes are accessible if you click the More Options button in the dialog box. You can refer back to the discussion of these attributes in the "Generate a Revolved 3-D Object" section of this chapter.

Use the Bevel drop-down menu to choose from a variety of beveling options. You can test these as you go by clicking the Preview check box, as shown in Figure 14-18.

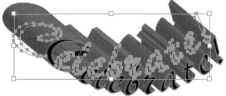

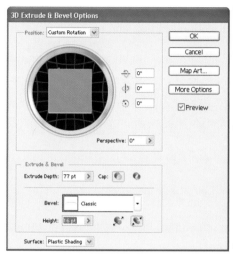

When you have selected a bevel, click OK to apply it to the selected object.

Unlike objects to which 3-D Revolve effects have been applied, objects to which beveling or extrusion have been applied can be effectively edited with standard editing tools. Experiment with changing the size, rotation, and fill and stroke properties of your extruded or beveled object to alter the effects.

FIGURE 14-18 Experimenting with beveling options

Filter drop shadow

Effect drop shadow

FIGURE 14-19 Applying drop shadows to an image—filter vs. effect

Apply Filters

The options available from the Filter menu are similar to those available from the Effect menu. However, as mentioned at the beginning of this chapter, after you apply a filter, you can no longer edit the original underlying structure of the object's path.

The good side of this is that you *can* edit the new path that the filter generates. Figure 14-19 shows a drop shadow effect from the Filter menu (top) and a drop shadow effect from the Effect menu (bottom), with similar option settings. As you can see, the results are similar.

Now take a look at the underlying paths, as revealed in Outline view. As you can see in Figure 14-20, the paths and anchors of the object with the filter-generated drop shadow are entirely changed, while the paths and anchors of the object with an effect-generated drop shadow are unchanged—the drop shadow isn't visible when the path is revealed.

14

Apply Filters for Vectors

Both the Effect and Filter menu are divided into two sets of filters. The filters that apply to vector paths are *mostly* (but not entirely) listed in the top section of the menu, and the filters that apply to bitmap objects are organized on the bottom part of the menu. Since bitmaps aren't defined by vector paths, there's little advantage in using an effect on a bitmap instead of a filter, so we'll explore bitmap effects and filters in their Filter menu versions.

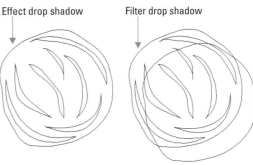

Effect drop shadow   Filter drop shadow

FIGURE 14-20 The filter and effect drop shadows look similar; the real difference is in how the underlying path is handled.

The options available from the Filter | Distort and Filter | Stylize submenus are very similar to those available from the Effect | Distort & Transform and Effect | Stylize menus.

The Filter | Colors menu has several options for adjusting the coloring of single objects or groups of objects. Filter | Colors | Adjust Colors opens the Adjust Colors dialog box, which can be used to change the fill color, stroke color, or both colors of selected objects, as shown in Figure 14-21.

Other options in the Filter | Colors submenu apply to groups of three or more selected objects. The various blend options take two objects and generate colors for objects in between them. This works something like a gradient blend—merging from the starting color to the ending color. Figure 14-22 shows the Filter | Colors | Blend Horizontally option being used to generate colors starting from the green on the left and ending with the red on the right.

FIGURE 14-21 Adjusting a set of colors

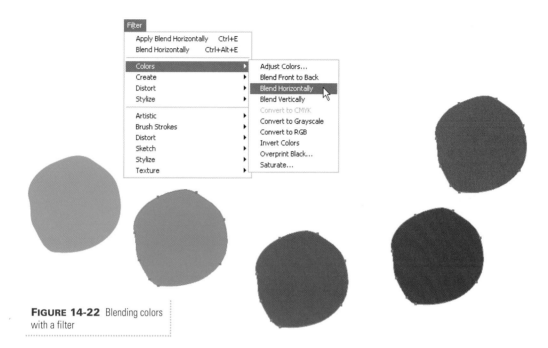

FIGURE 14-22 Blending colors with a filter

  The options accessible in the Filter | Colors submenu are similar to options available for combining overlapping colors in the Transparency palette. Chapter 17 explores how overlapping colors interact in the Transparency palette.

The Filter | Create | Object Mosaic menu option transforms a *bitmap* image into a mosaic (large squares of color). Filter | Create | Crop Marks generates printer crop marks around *any* selected object(s)—vector or bitmap.

Apply Filters for Bitmaps

The bitmap effects on the bottom part of the Filter menu can be applied only to raster images. These raster objects can either be placed (using File | Place) or converted (using Object | Rasterize).

Objects using Effect | Rasterize to display as bitmaps cannot be used with bitmap filters. They aren't really raster objects; they just display that way.

14

The sets of effects available in the bottom half of the Filter menu are very truncated versions of effects available in Photoshop. They're used for applying effects to bitmaps— again, if this is the terrain you are entering, you'll want to use Photoshop or another bitmap editor for anything more complicated than very basic effects.

Different effects provide different option sliders, but you can always preview the changes in the small preview area right in the dialog box. Use the plus (+) and minus (−) buttons to zoom in and out. Zooming out shows more of your image, while zooming in displays the details of the effect. Each of these bitmap filters can be previewed in a dialog box, as shown in Figure 14-23.

Experiment with settings in the dialog box and watch the filter effect appear on the artboard. Then click OK to assign the filter.

FIGURE 14-23 Checking out a bitmap filter

Chapter 15

Bend with Envelopes and the Liquify Tools

How to...

- Distort with envelopes
- Apply an envelope
- Apply a gradient mesh
- Warp with the liquify tools

In this chapter, you'll explore different ways of quickly applying major transformations to illustrations using envelopes, gradient meshes, and the liquify tools.

An *envelope* is a shortcut for reshaping an object so that the original shape is warped and reshaped into a different shape but still maintains its original path structure. Envelopes can be selected from a set of preset shapes, they can be created from shapes you make, or they can be defined by applying a grid-like mesh to an object. Related to this last option, *gradient* meshes not only warp objects, but allow a very high level of control over blending colors within an object.

The *liquify tools* make rather drastic changes to objects and aren't so easily controllable. They come as close as any set of tools in Illustrator to giving credence to the misconception that "computer art" is "generated"—that is, that digital artists simply push some buttons and "art" happens. But they can be fun, and there is a role for experimentation and even chance in art, so the liquify tools have their function.

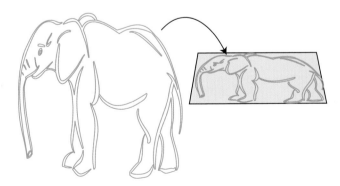

FIGURE 15-1 Cramming an elephant into an envelope shape

Distort with Envelopes

Imagine an elephant stuffed into an envelope. Having trouble? Figure 15-1 might help. It's a painful image to evoke, but the vision helps demonstrate how Illustrator uses the *envelope* metaphor.

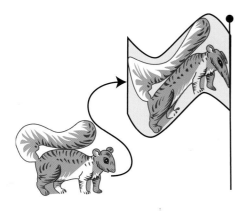

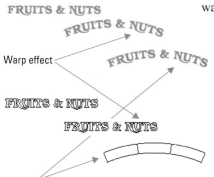

FIGURE 15-2 No real animals were harmed or mistreated in warping the squirrel into a flag.

FIGURE 15-3 Using an Envelope Distort menu option generates a new path, while a warp effect does not transform the underlying path.

Figure 15-1 is an example of stuffing an object into a custom-defined shape (in this case, an elephant into an envelope). You can also *warp* an object into a predefined path (such as an arc or a waving flag). Figure 15-2 shows a squirrel enshrined painfully in a waving flag warp.

There is a third type of envelope option available. You can impose a *mesh* on an object. Meshes, and their more powerful cousins—gradient meshes— are quite different in their use, you'll explore them separately in the next section of this chapter. First you'll learn to work with the more conventional envelope tools—warps and shapes.

Many Ways to Distort Objects

Illustrator provides at least three ways to apply envelopes or warps to objects. All three produce similar results—but with some significant differences.

Envelope and Warp options available from the Object | Envelope Distort menu each generate a new shape that serves as a container for the old object.

In contrast, warp *effects* (applied from the Effect | Warp menu) work like all effects; transformations you make using warp effects *do not change the underlying path structure of your object.* So after you apply a warp effect, your object's path is not easily editable. Figure 15-3 shows an arc warp applied twice to the same object, once as an effect from the Effect menu, and once as an envelope from the Object menu. The Outline view in the lower part of this figure shows the different effects of the options on the paths.

The *liquify tools* (on the Warp tool tearoff in the Toolbox) provide yet another way to distort objects. The liquify tools work *interactively*—you click and drag to distort objects. Figure 15-4 shows the fish's nose being distorted with the Warp tool.

In the following sections of this chapter, you'll first explore the options available from the Object | Envelope Distort submenu. Then you'll discover the complex and finely-tuned potential of

15

distorting objects and fills with gradient meshes. Finally, you'll learn to use the interactive warping (liquify) tools available in the Toolbox.

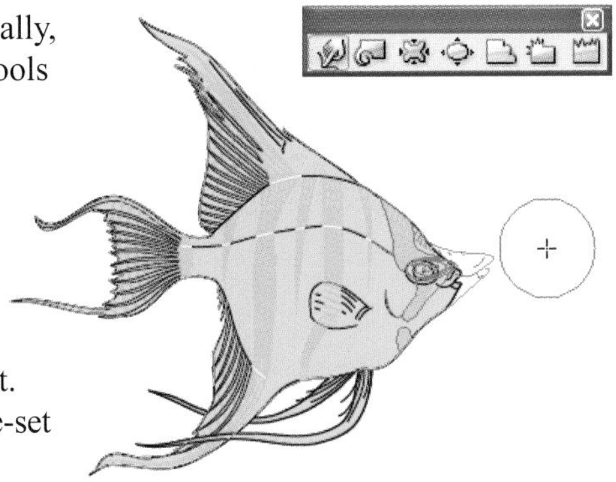

Use an Envelope to Distort an Object

The Object | Envelope Distort submenu allows you to assign three types of distortion to a selected object. You can select Make with Warp to choose a warp (pre-set shape) into which you can *envelope* (stuff) your selected object. The second option is to choose Make with Top Object to distort one object by squeezing it into a second shape that you have created on the artboard. The third option, meshes, are grids with editable anchors. (You'll dive into these in the next section.)

FIGURE 15-4 Distorting a section of the fish interactively with the Warp tool—part of the liquify set of tools

When you apply a warp or second-shape warp, you are actually combining two objects—the first object is the one you are distorting, and the second object is the "envelope" into which you are stuffing the first object. If you choose one of the warp options, the second envelope shape is created for you. If you use a Make with Top Object to "envelope" one shape into another, you create both shapes before you apply an envelope distortion. In either case, you can release your resulting warp into its two components by choosing Object | Envelope Distort | Release. For example, if the squirrel in Figure 15-2 is *released* from the envelope shape, the result is the two shapes displayed in Figure 15-5.

FIGURE 15-5 Animal rights activists release the squirrel from the warping shape.

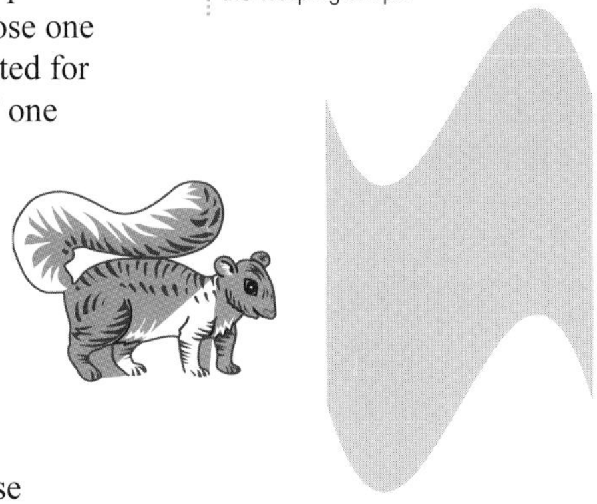

To convert a selected, enveloped object into a single object (shaped like the applied envelope), choose Object | Envelope Distort | Expand. You can also easily edit the content of the *original* (pre-distortion) object by choosing Object | Envelope Distort | Edit Contents. This displays the anchors and paths of the original object. Figure 15-6 shows an original path being edited for an enveloped object.

You can edit envelope options by choosing Object | Envelope Distort | Options and opening the Envelope Options dialog box. The top options are

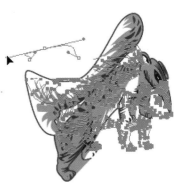

FIGURE 15-6 Editing the path of the original squirrel shape. The warped squirrel shape is still visible in the background while the paths and anchors of the original are edited.

applicable to raster (bitmap) objects only. The Anti-Alias check box automatically smoothes out jagged edges produced by envelope distortion. The Clipping Mask and Transparency option buttons provide two ways to save the resulting object as a bitmap.

The Fidelity slider determines how accurately the enveloped object will match the envelope shape. Higher values create larger files and more complex paths. The Distort Appearance, Distort Linear Gradients, and Distort Pattern Fills check boxes do not affect the outline shape of the distorted object—they define only whether or not a gradient fill or pattern fill *inside* the object will be stretched and distorted along with the object shape.

Unless you are distorting a vector object with a linear gradient fill or a pattern fill, you probably won't need to alter the default settings in the Envelope Options dialog box.

Now that you're familiar with the concepts involved in envelope distortion, it's time to dive into the details of how different envelope options work.

Warp

Illustrator CS provides 15 customizable warping shapes. To access them, select an object and choose Object | Envelope Distort | Make with Warp. The Warp Options dialog box appears.

Use the Style drop-down menu to choose from the various warping options. The dialog box options are the same for each of the styles of warp. The horizontal or vertical option buttons define which way your object will be stretched. The Bend slider determines the intensity of the warp. In the Distortion area, the Horizontal slider allows you to skew the impact of the distortion to the left (negative) or right (positive) side of the object. The Vertical slider adjusts how distortion is applied to the top or bottom of the selected object.

FIGURE 15-7 Experimenting with warp options

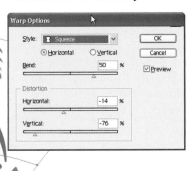

In reality, you'll play with the various sliders and use the Preview check box to see how your object appears with various distortion settings, as shown in Figure 15-7.

After you find a distortion setting you like, click OK to apply the envelope.

15

Reshape with a Second Object

Reshaping with a second object requires two objects—the original artwork, and the second object that will serve as a container or envelope to reshape the first object. For instance, in Figure 15-8, the circle will serve as the envelope into which the bird will be squished.

Before you stuff one object into another, you need to make sure the two objects are set up correctly. The object *to be reshaped* should be grouped. And, most importantly, the object that will serve as the envelope must be *on top of* (in front of) the object to be reshaped. You can move the envelope object in front of the object to be reshaped by selecting it and choosing Object | Arrange | Bring to Front.

When everything is all set, select both the object and the envelope and choose Object | Envelope Distort | Make with Top Object.

Reshape with a Mesh

Meshes are a tricky way to distort an object. They generate a grid—a set of horizontal and vertical lines connected by movable points that work something like normal anchor points. Meshes generated from the Object | Envelope Distort | Make with Mesh option are movable, but there's a better and more powerful way to create Meshes.

Gradient meshes have the same power to reshape an object, but they *also* allow you to edit the *color* of the mesh points. So, it will be more productive to explore meshes in detail later in this chapter, in the section "Apply a Gradient Mesh."

FIGURE 15-8 Preparing to use the circle as an envelope for the bird

FIGURE 15-9 Applying envelope distortion to type

Distort Type

Envelope distortion also works with type. Just select some type and choose any warp distortion. Or you can select type and a shape object and then choose Object | Envelope Distortion | Make with Top Object to squeeze the type into a shape, as shown in Figure 15-9.

Tip

Remember, if you are distorting type into a shape, the shape must be in front of *the type.*

The options, release, and expand features of envelope distortion work the same with type as they do with any other object. However, you *cannot* edit type while it is distorted into an envelope.

Apply a Gradient Mesh

A gradient mesh is an envelope with intersecting horizontal and vertical grid lines that is imposed on an object. The intersection of mesh grid lines creates editable anchors. Mesh anchors and paths can be edited to create subtle shifts in an object's shape *or color.*

FIGURE 15-10 Mesh point color blending is even more powerful than gradient fills.

You click and drag on mesh points with the Direct Selection tool to alter an object's shape. Just as intriguing, you can assign a *different* color to any mesh point. In Figure 15-10, a mesh grid has been created within an object, and a color has been applied to a mesh point. Manipulating the mesh point control lines adjusts how the mesh point color blends into the surrounding color.

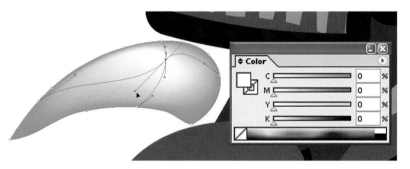

One way to create individual gradient mesh points is to click within an object using the Mesh tool in the Toolbox. Each click within an object generates one set of intersecting mesh grid lines.

You can also automatically generate a gradient mesh that envelopes a selected object by choosing Object | Envelope Distort | Make with Mesh. That command opens the Envelope Mesh dialog box, in which you can select the number of rows and columns you want to generate in the mesh. The drawback here, as noted earlier, is that you can't edit the *coloring* of the

15

mesh points generated this way. Use the Preview check box to see how the mesh will be applied, as shown in Figure 15-11.

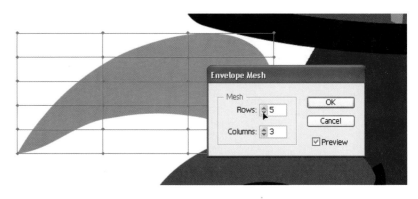

Once you have created mesh points on an object—either with the Object | Envelope Distort | Make with Mesh command or with the Mesh tool, you can select distinct mesh points using the Direct Selection tool. However, with a mesh point selected, you can assign a new color to the mesh point from the Color palette *only if you created the Mesh point with the Mesh tool.*

FIGURE 15-11 Generating a mesh with the Make with Mesh menu command

In addition to assigning colors to a mesh point, you can click and drag on a mesh point with the Direct Selection tool to warp or distort the object's shape, as shown in Figure 15-12.

Tip *The toughest part of working with mesh points is selecting them! Remember to use the* Direct Selection *tool, not the Selection tool, when hunting around for these hard-to-click-on points. Also, you'll find it easier to select a mesh point with Smart Guides turned on (choose View | Smart Guides if they're not already on). To make it easier to select a mesh point, zoom way in (click the Zoom tool and draw a marquee around just the area of the mesh point).*

Technically speaking, when you apply either a warp or an object envelope from the Object | Envelope Distort submenu, you are actually *generating a mesh* to shape that object. The difference between using those enveloping options and applying a gradient mesh is that in the second case you will interactively distort the object yourself by manipulating the gradient mesh as opposed to having a gradient mesh generated for you.

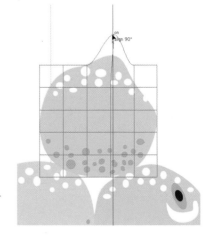

FIGURE 15-12 Dragging on a mesh point to reshape the lemon

Warp with the Liquify Tools

The Warp, Twirl, Pucker, Bloat, Scallop, Crystallize, and Wrinkle tools have been dubbed the "liquify" tools because they allow you to reshape objects with fluidity. Some professional illustrators look down their noses at these fun-loving tools because the results tend to be something of a crapshoot. On the other hand, if you're up for a bit of experimenting and seeing what happens, fire away with these tools and see if you come up with a result you can use.

FIGURE 15-13 The liquify tools

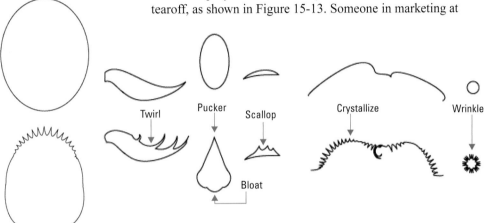

The liquify tools are actually the tools on the Warp tool tearoff, as shown in Figure 15-13. Someone in marketing at

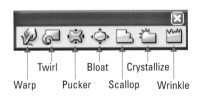

Adobe thought "liquify" expressed the fluidity with which they affect objects, and Adobe has promoted this nickname for the Warp tools. You apply them interactively to selected objects, so first select an object using any of the selection tools. Then click on one of the liquify tools and click and drag to distort the selected object(s).

Each liquify tool has a set of options. Double-click on any of the tools to open its respective options dialog box. While the options vary somewhat for different liquify tools, they all have definable brush sizes and shapes. Larger brush sizes produce more dramatic effects on objetcs, while smaller sizes produce more manageable results. Different tools have different value box options as well as different combinations of complexity, detail, and simplification sliders. In general, more detail and complexity create more anchors and paths.

15

 In addition to being unpredictable, the liquify tools also put quite a strain on system resources, quickly generating huge numbers of anchor points.

Figure 15-14 illustrates all seven of the liquify tools in action. Take a look and pique your imagination.

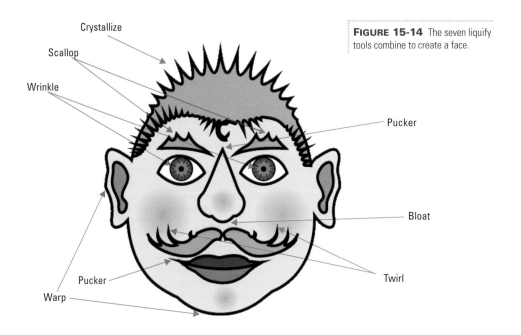

FIGURE 15-14 The seven liquify tools combine to create a face.

Part V

Manage Fills

Chapter 16

Manage Colors and Gradients

How to...

- Manage Color palette options
- Choose and change colors
- Change color palettes
- Use pre-set gradient fills
- Create a two-color gradient fill
- Define multicolor gradients
- Save gradients as swatches

Manage Color Palette Options

There are many ways to choose colors for fills and strokes. You can pick colors from the Color palette or the Swatches palette, or you can mix up gradient fills in the Gradient palette.

Before we dig further into all these sources of color, it will probably be helpful to summarize ways of *applying* color to objects. When you draw an object using any tool (such as the Pen tool, any shape tool, the Pencil tool, and so on), that object will be created with the stroke and fill colors that are displayed in the Fill and Stroke buttons at the bottom of the Toolbox. You can *change* the stroke or fill color of a selected object by clicking on either the Stroke or Fill buttons in the Toolbox, which opens the Color palette. You can quickly change the color of the object's stroke or fill by clicking on a color in the Color palette.

You can also define a color by selecting either the Stroke or Fill button in the Toolbox, choosing the Eyedropper tool, and clicking anywhere on your workspace. The Stroke or Fill button (depending on which one you selected) takes on the color you clicked with the Eyedropper tool. The Eyedropper tool can also be used to "sample" a color from one object and apply it to another. To do this, select the object to be recolored and click on the Eyedropper tool. Hold down the SHIFT key and click on another object from which you want to copy the fill or stroke. In Figure 16-1, the fill color of the rooster's beak is being applied to the fill color of the eye.

FIGURE 16-1 Sampling a color with the Eyedropper tool

You can quickly apply the selected Fill and Stroke colors to any object by clicking on that object with the Paint Bucket tool, as shown in Figure 16-2.

FIGURE 16-2 Applying the selected fill color using the Paint Bucket tool

FIGURE 16-3 Selecting all tiles with a fill and stroke color matching one tile

One technique that is useful for large-scale recoloring in an illustration is to use the Select menu to choose all objects of a similar fill, stroke, or fill and stroke. Do this by clicking on one object that has the fill and stroke colors you wish to change. Then choose Select | Same. From the Select | Same submenu, you can choose Fill & Stroke (as shown in Figure 16-3), Fill Color, or Stroke Color.

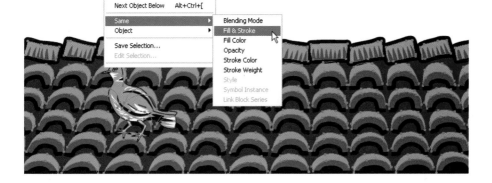

Once you have used the Select menu to select all matching objects, you can recolor them simply by choosing a new fill and/or stroke color from the Color palette.

Select, Change, and Use Color Palettes

Now that we've reviewed a few quick and easy ways to apply colors, let's dig more into how to mix up and access colors. The Color palette offers five basic sets of colors—you'll investigate all five in this section of this chapter. But there are also all kinds of special color palettes available with useful sets of colors for various purposes. Or you can make your own color palettes.

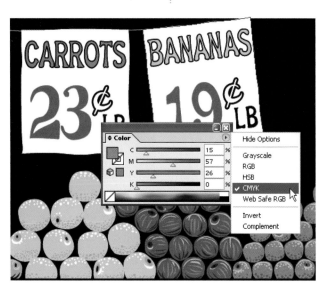

FIGURE 16-4 Choosing the CMYK color palette for an object that will be printed on an ink jet printer

There are five basic color palettes available from the Color palette menu. They are Grayscale, RGB, HSB, CMYK, and Web Safe RGB—as shown in Figure 16-4. These five palettes can be divided into three basic sets: those used for black-and-white printing, those used for color printing, and those used for digital output (including the Web).

In addition to these basic palettes available from the Color palette, there are many more palettes available from the swatch libraries. (Choose Window | Swatch Libraries to access a list of available color sets.)

The CMYK palette creates colors by mixing cyan, magenta, yellow, and black to make different colors. Since cyan and magenta aren't everyday household colors, this set of colors is illustrated in Figure 16-5.

The RGB palette defines colors by combining red, green, and blue. The HSB model essentially generates RGB colors but uses a set of values for hue, saturation, and brightness. The value of having the HSB option is that if you've been given color settings—for example, if a client provides you with a color scheme defined with HSB values—you can translate these colors to the RGB model

FIGURE 16-5 Cyan, magenta, yellow, and black combine to make up the colors on the CMYK color palette.

by defining colors with the HSB palette. The Web Safe RGB palette restricts you to the 216 colors that reproduce with the most reliability and stability on a variety of web browsers and operating systems.

Exactly how and when to use each of these palettes depends mainly on how your artwork will eventually be displayed. Print and web color are discussed in more detail in Chapters 22 (print) and 23 (web). If you know that your artwork is going to be printed in black and white, you'll want to restrict yourself to the Grayscale palette. If you're printing in four-color output (frequently used in commercial printing and in many printers), choose CMYK. If your artwork is going to be displayed digitally (in a Flash presentation, in a PowerPoint slideshow, or on a web site), use either the RGB, HSB, or Web Safe RGB palette.

 Another method for selecting Web-safe colors is to use the Web Colors swatch palette—choose Window | Swatch Libraries | Web.

Finally, if you are printing with defined spot colors, you'll want to apply colors using a swatch palette custom designed with those colors. For instance, if your printer is going to be using one of the Pantone Process colors, choose an appropriate color palette (there are several Pantone palettes available from the Window | Swatch Libraries menu) and apply that color, as shown in Figure 16-6.

You can use the Swatch palette as a temporary storage closet for colors you use most frequently. Choose Window | Swatches to view this palette. Simply drag a color swatch from any other palette (such as the Color palette) to save it as part of your Swatch palette. Chapter 18 goes into detail about how to use the Swatch palette to save colors, gradients, and other fills.

FIGURE 16-6 Applying spot colors from a Pantone Process color set

16

Create Gradient Fills

Gradient fills create transitions between two or more colors. The most basic gradient fills merge from one color to another. Gradient transitions can be linear (top to bottom or right to left) or radial (from the outside of an object to the inside or vice-versa). Figure 16-7 illustrates both a linear and a radial gradient fill. The flowers have radial fills, while the leaves use linear fills that blend from one side of the leaf to the other.

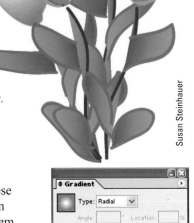

Susan Steinhauer

Note *You can't assign gradients to paths or strokes the same way you can assign them to other objects. To apply a gradient to a stroke, you first have to convert the stroke to a filled object (select Object | Path | Outline Stroke) and then assign the gradient.*

Gradient fill is one of the coolest Illustrator features. These fills add depth, subtlety, and either realism or surrealism to an illustration. But before you get too excited about applying them to your artwork, be warned that gradients often don't do well on the Web. The main reason gradients tend to *band*—or break down into streaky bands instead of smooth transitions—is that the set of web-safe colors is limited to 216 colors, and that set of colors is not sufficient to maintain a smooth gradation between colors.

Furthermore, the low resolution of monitors (usually 72 or 96 dots per inch) as opposed to printing (600 dots per inch, even on desktop printers) reduces the attractiveness of gradients. Chapter 23 explains some techniques for maximizing the appearance of gradients on web sites, but in general, it's something you'll want to avoid.

FIGURE 16-7 The radial fill emanates from the inside of the flower and blends into a red on the outside of the flower.

FIGURE 16-8 Viewing pre-set gradient swatches

Use Pre-set Gradients

Illustrator comes with several preconfigured gradient fills. To view them, choose Window | Swatches. Depending on your previous docking or undocking activity, the Swatch palette might be docked with other palettes. To view existing defined gradients, click the Show Gradient Swatches button on the bottom of the Swatches palette, as shown in Figure 16-8.

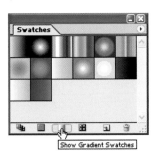

Susan Steinhauer

FIGURE 16-9 Assigning a selected gradient to the flower

Once the existing gradients in the Swatches palette are visible, you can assign any one of them as the default fill simply by clicking on it. You can then assign the selected gradient to an object using the Paint Bucket tool, as shown in Figure 16-9.

 Tip   *Alternatively, you can use the Eyedropper tool to point to any gradient swatch and apply that fill to any selected object(s).*

Create a Two-Color Gradient Fill

The pre-set gradients provide a nice selection, but the real fun is in defining your own gradients. The basic routine for creating a two-color gradient involves selecting the two colors, defining how they will transition into each other, and defining a radial or linear fill.

The processes for defining a linear fill and a radial fill are slightly different. To define a linear fill, you have to define a fill angle that determines whether your fill transitions from top to bottom, from right to left, or something in between. The angle setting does not apply to radial fills (because the fill goes from inside an object to outside or vice-versa).

Follow these steps to define a linear two-color gradient fill:

1. Open the Gradient palette by selecting Window | Gradient, by pressing F9, or by double-clicking the Gradient tool in the Toolbox.

2. From the Type drop-down list, choose Linear.

3. Select Window | Color (or press F6) so that the Color palette is accessible; you'll need it to define colors for your gradient fill.

4. Click on the first (left) gradient slider, as shown in Figure 16-10.

5. With the first gradient slider selected, click a color in the Color palette. This assigns the first gradient fill color.

16

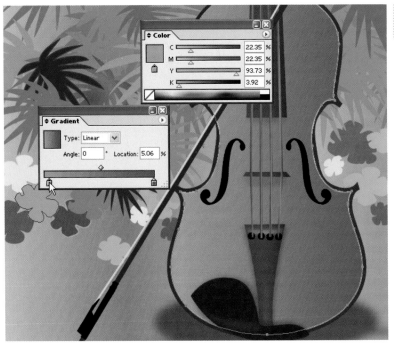

FIGURE 16-10
Selecting a gradient color

Mieko Mochizuki Swartz

6. Click the second (right) gradient slider and select a second color from the Color palette. The fill is previewed in the bar that runs between the two gradient sliders.

7. Slide the diamond-shaped midpoint to the right or left on the slider bar to change the rate at which the first color merges into the second color. As you do this, the Location percentage box in the Gradient palette will display a changing percentage, and the slider bar will preview the changes in your gradient fill.

8. Use the Angle box in the Gradient palette to rotate the fill. A setting of –90 degrees (enter **–90** in the Angle box) will tilt your fill so that the first color is at the top instead of on the left. A setting of 180 degrees will switch the direction of your fill and move the right color to the left edge of the fill.

Gradient angles are not previewed in the slider bar; you have to apply them to see how they look.

As you define your fill, it becomes the default fill in the Fill button in the Toolbox. Use the Paint Bucket tool to apply the fill

FIGURE 16-11 Tweaking a gradient fill interactively with the Gradient tool

Interactive line drawn with Gradient tool starts here...   ...and ends here

to any object in your workspace. You can interactively change the angle of a gradient fill by selecting an object to which the fill has been applied and then selecting the Gradient tool in the Toolbox. Click and drag with the Gradient tool cursor to change the direction, starting point, and ending point of a gradient fill, as shown in Figure 16-11.

Define Multicolor Gradients

In most cases, you need only two colors to create a complex and subtle gradient fill. Sometimes, however, you might want to add more colors (for example, if you are creating a rainbow fill). You can add more colors by clicking below the Gradient slider bar. Each time you click below the slider bar, you add another slider.

Or, if you want to start with an existing color slider, simply drag an existing slider to a new location on the Gradient slider bar. Assign colors to a new slider by selecting the slider and then clicking a color in the Color palette.

Each color transition will have its own diamond-shaped midpoint slider that you can use to define the location for the

16

fill. However, a single linear gradient fill can have only one angle setting—and that applies to the entire fill. Figure 16-12 shows a gradient fill with several different color sliders, creating an alternating background pattern.

FIGURE 16-12 A multicolored background gradient

Mieko Mochizuki Swartz

Save Gradients as Swatches

If you've gone to considerable work to create a custom gradient fill, you'll probably want to save it for future use. You do this by saving the gradient as a swatch in the Swatches palette.

Follow these steps to save a gradient fill as a swatch:

1. Define a gradient fill. (See the instructions earlier in this chapter, under "Create a Two-Color Gradient Fill.")

2. With the gradient fill defined in the Gradient palette, open the Swatches palette.

3. From the Swatches palette menu, choose New Swatch. The New Swatch dialog box opens.

4. In the Swatch Name box of the New Swatch dialog box, type a descriptive name for your gradient fill, as shown in Figure 16-13.

5. Click OK. Your fill appears in the Swatches palette. Remember, you can view only the gradient swatches by clicking the Show Gradient Swatches button on the bottom of the Swatches palette.

FIGURE 16-13 Generating a defined swatch from the selected gradient fill

You can delete a swatch from the Swatches palette by selecting it and then choosing Delete Swatch from the Swatches palette menu. Swatches are saved as part of your open Illustrator file. When you save the file and reopen it, the swatches are available.

Chapter 17

Adjust Transparency

How to...

- Understand transparency
- Assign transparency to objects
- Apply transparency to groups
- Filter transparency with blending modes
- Create opacity masks
- Print projects with transparency

A fully *transparent* object is one that is completely "see-through," like a clean, untinted window. At the other end of the scale, a fully *opaque* object is one that you cannot see through at all. *Partial transparency* (also called "partial opacity") allows an object to be made *partially* transparent, like a tinted lens. In common usage, applying "transparency" in Illustrator really means applying *partial transparency,* a filter that alters the density or color of an object.

In Illustrator, transparency is applied in degrees, ranging from 1 percent (almost completely opaque) to 99 percent (almost completely invisible). An object with 0-percent transparency is opaque, and an object with 100-percent transparency is invisible.

Transparency is used for objects that cover other objects. For instance, a tinted "plastic" sheet in Figure 17-1 tints the fruits it covers. However, the pricing signs are on top of the transparency object, and are therefore not affected.

FIGURE 17-1 The screen covering some of the fruits has partial transparency.

Bruce K. Hopkins

Objects with partial transparency affect objects stacked *below* them. An object stacked *beneath* a transparent object will be partially visible.

Make an Object Partially Transparent

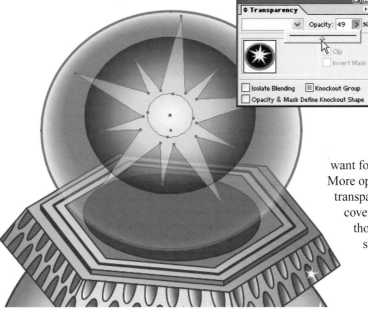

FIGURE 17-2 A 49-percent opacity is being applied to the circles and the star.

Bruce K. Hopkins

To apply transparency to a selected object, activate the Transparency palette (choose Window | Transparency). Use the Opacity area in the palette to define how much transparency you want for the selected object. More opacity means less transparency—it means that the covering layer covers more thoroughly. Figure 17-2 shows transparency being applied to several selected objects in an illustration.

Apply Transparency to Groups

When you apply transparency to a number of objects, the transparency is *cumulative*. For instance, in Figure 17-2, the section of the ring covered by *both* circles is covered more completely by the blue coloring than the section of the ring covered by only one of the circles.

On the other hand, if you *group* the objects that are being used to apply transparency, the transparency is not multiplied in the same way. In Figure 17-3, the circles have been grouped before the transparency application, and the effect is that the underlying ring is less affected by the overlaying transparent objects.

FIGURE 17-3 Grouping objects mitigates the impact of several transparent objects.

17

Layers (discussed in Chapter 20) act differently with respect to transparency. As mentioned earlier, transparency that is applied to an object affects how that *object partially obscures or tints an object* below *that object. You arrange objects by selecting them, choosing Object | Arrange, and then selecting a direction to move the object from the Object | Arrange submenu. However, if your project is organized into layers, the transparency of objects on a top layer will affect objects on a lower layer, and this supercedes the order that objects are arranged in on any particular layer. For a full explanation of how this works, see Chapter 20.*

Apply Transparency to Just Stroke or Fill

When you apply transparency from the Transparency palette, the level of transparency you define is applied to all selected objects. And it is applied to *both* the stroke and the fill of an object.

Often you'll want to apply transparency to *only* the fill of an object. Or sometimes you might want to apply transparency settings to only the stroke of an object. Or you might even want to assign different levels of transparency to the stroke and fill of a selected object. This can be done.

To apply transparency settings to only the stroke or fill of a selected object, select the object to which you want to apply transparency and view the Appearance palette. Click on Stroke in the Appearance palette, and adjust the transparency for the selected stroke in the Transparency palette. Similarly, click on Fill in the Appearance palette, and adjust the transparency for the fill separately. Figure 17-4 shows different transparency settings being applied to the stroke and fill of an object.

FIGURE 17-4 Opacity for the selected stroke is 86 percent, while opacity for the fill is 38 percent.

Stroke opacity at 86 percent

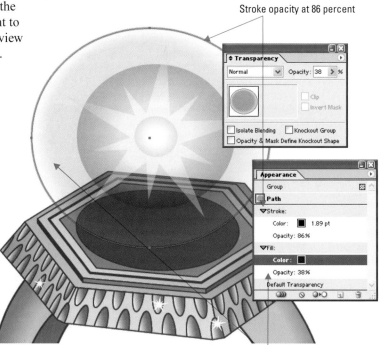

Fill opacity at 38 percent

Use Blending Modes

In addition to plain, plastic-wrap transparency, Illustrator's Transparency palette provides blending modes that transform colors in the underlying layer. These blending modes work something like sunglasses or a colored piece of glass—tinting, distorting, or enhancing the effect of a transparent overlay.

Just to make the concept of transparency a bit more confusing, you may apply an opacity setting of 100 percent when you use a transparency filter without completely obscuring the underlying object. You'll do this when you work with blending modes, which create a variety of color changes to objects by *combining* the transparency filter color with the color of the underlying object.

Blending modes were briefly touched on in Chapter 14, as part of an overview of all of Illustrator's effects and filters. Here you'll explore their role in generating transparency.

The following blending effects are available from the blending mode drop-down list in the Transparency palette.

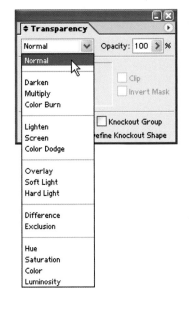

- **Normal**   This selection provides just transparency, no distortion of color.
- **Darken**   Darken changes any underlying colors that are lighter than the overlay color to the overlay color.
- **Multiply**   This darkens the resulting color.
- **Color Burn**   This option darkens the underlying object.
- **Lighten**   This selection lightens underlying colors that are darker than the overlay.
- **Screen**   This selection lightens the resulting color.
- **Color Dodge**   Color Dodge brightens the underlying object.
- **Overlay**   Overlay sharpens the contrast of a color (or pattern) filter by intensifying contrast.
- **Soft Light**   This option lightens the underlying object if the filtering object color is lighter than 50-percent gray. Otherwise, the underlying object is made darker.
- **Hard Light**   The Hard Light selection simulates shining a bright light on the underlying object.

 For the Darken and Lighten blending modes, Illustrator first determines whether the overlay color or the base color is darker (in the case of Darken) or lighter (Lighten). It is this color that is applied in the blend.

- **Difference** Difference calculates a new color based on the difference between the brightness values of the overlapping colors.

- **Exclusion** This option changes color using the same kind of calculation as the Difference effect, but the contrast between the original color and the changed color is muted and less dramatic than the Difference effect.

- **Hue** The Hue option retains the color of the top filtering object(s) while assuming the saturation (intensity) and brightness of the bottom object(s).

- **Saturation** This selection retains the saturation (intensity) of the top filtering object(s) while assuming the brightness and color of the bottom object(s).

- **Color** The Color selection retains the hue and saturation of the top filtering object(s) while assuming the brightness of the bottom object(s).

- **Luminosity** The Luminosity option retains the brightness quantity (intensity) of the top filtering object(s) while assuming the saturation (intensity) of the bottom object(s).

FIGURE 17-5 Transparency blends work like color lenses, tinting affected objects.

All 16 blending modes are on display in Figure 17-5.

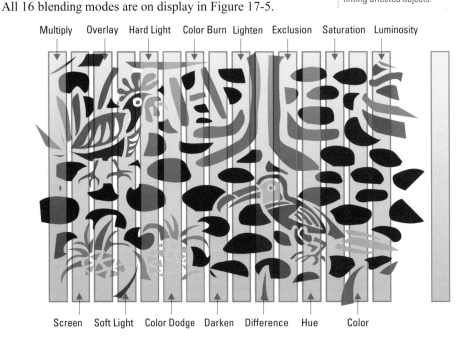

Many of the blending modes are determined by calculations based on hue, saturation, or brightness values. This tends to produce somewhat unintuitive results. You can look up color hue, saturation, or brightness values by choosing the HSB palette from the Color palette menu. As you experiment with different blending modes, you'll develop your ability to anticipate the effect they will have when used as filters.

Caution *If your output is destined for hardcopy that will use spot color printing, avoid the Difference, Exclusion, Hue, Saturation, Color, and Luminosity blending modes. They're not supported by spot colors. For more on spot color printing, see Chapter 22.*

FIGURE 17-6 Preparing an object to serve as an opacity mask

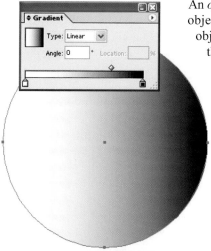

Clip with Opacity Masks

An *opacity mask* reveals part (and only part) of an underlying object. But, though it reveals a section of the underlying object, it does it through an *opacity lens;* that is, it distorts the brightness of the section of the underlying image that it masks.

Opacity masks are a little confusing because they combine two concepts (transparency and masking) that are both kind of confusing themselves. But you can create some of my favorite effects by using them, and you'll see how it's done in the steps in this section.

You can get a better handle on the impact of the opacity mask effect if you use a gradient fill in your mask object. Though fill doesn't matter when you apply a regular mask, it does matter when you apply an opacity mask. The lighter the fill, the more the masked illustration shows through the opacity mask. The darker the fill of the opacity mask, the less the underlying illustration shows through.

Follow these steps to apply a gradient fill as an opacity mask:

1. Create or open an illustration that you will use as a masked object. It will be easier to keep track of your masked object and your masking object if you group the underlying masked object.

2. Create a circle to use as an opacity mask, and fill it with a black-to-white gradient fill, like the one shown in Figure 17-6.

Nathan Alan Whelchel

17

3. Move the masking object (the circle with the gradient fill) over the illustration.

4. Open the Transparency palette.

5. Select both the mask object (the circle) and the underlying illustration.

6. From the menu in the Transparency palette, choose Make Opacity Mask, as shown in Figure 17-7.

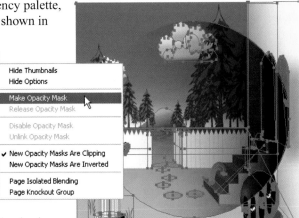

FIGURE 17-7 Applying an opacity mask

7. Click outside the masked set to reveal the results of the opacity mask. By default the Clip check box in the Transparency palette is selected when you apply an opacity mask. Figure 17-8 shows the result of applying an opacity mask to an image.

If you deselect the Clip check box in the Transparency palette after you apply an opacity mask, the mask functions like a regular transparency, not a mask. If you select the Invert Mask check box, you reverse the effect that dark and light colors have on the underlying image. If you reduce the opacity of the masking object, the resulting mask is more transparent.

You can click on the Link button in the Transparency palette—it's visible when an opacity mask is selected—to unlink the opacity mask from the underlying image. When you unlink the opacity mask from the underlying image, you can move either the underlying (masked) image or the opacity mask to change the area that is revealed through the mask.

Nathan Alan Whelchel

FIGURE 17-8 The overlaying object both masks and applies transparency to the underlying object.

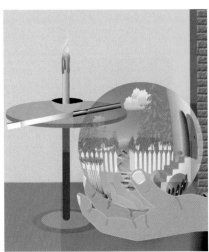

Nathan Alan Whelchel

Set Transparency Options

Transparency presents interesting challenges when you send illustrations to a printer or to a web-compatible graphic format. The problems involved in printing Illustrator documents with transparency will be returned to in Chapter 22, and the options for creating web-compatible graphics are focused on in Chapter 23. Here you'll learn how to manage your Illustrator files to minimize the hassles and quality issues that you'll have to face when you send your files to print or web.

The basic problem you'll confront when you send a transparent object to a printer is that printers put ink on paper (or other surfaces), and ink is never, in reality, transparent. Therefore, your illustration will be *flattened* in some form—the *effect produced by transparency will be preserved,* but the actual transparent character of color fills and strokes will not. Those properties *will* be saved as part of your Illustrator (AI) file or Illustrator EPS file.

Web graphics do support a form of transparency, but it's quite different from the transparency that you manage in Illustrator. Transparency has two meanings in digital graphic design. Web graphics that have one color "knocked out" so that the web page background shows through are called "transparent images." This feature can be applied to GIF- or PNG-format bitmap images. You'll see how this works in Chapter 23.

The second meaning is the one we've been using in this chapter. This type of transparency is partial opacity, where an underlying image is partially visible. And, as a matter of fact, you can use this kind of transparency with printed output, but it is very difficult to transfer to images destined for the Web. Therefore, you should avoid it if you are designing web graphics.

Set Background View Options

You can configure Illustrator to make it easier to anticipate what your transparent objects will look like when printed on colored paper. Do this by assigning a checkerboard background, and use the paper color you'll be printing on as one of the checkerboard squares.

To take one example of a fairly economical transparency project, you can "simulate" two-color printing by using black ink on a colored paper background. And, by having some of your objects semi-transparent, you can "mix" black with the paper background.

On the other hand, if you want to simulate what your project—including semi-transparent objects—will look like when printed on colored paper, you can select the same background color for both checkerboard squares using the two available color swatches, as shown in Figure 17-9. Check the Simulate Colored Paper check box to display the background color.

To configure your document settings to display transparency options, select File | Document Setup. Select Transparency from the drop-down menu at the top of the dialog box to configure transparency settings.

If you want to have a background that makes it easy to distinguish the white of the artboard from the color white, you can simply accept the default settings to place a gray and white checkerboard as a background grid.

FIGURE 17-9 Defining a background color simulates the results of printing on colored paper.

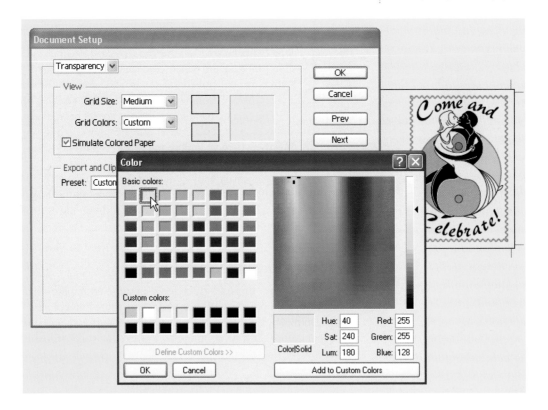

Print Illustrations with Transparency

As mentioned, the ink your printer (or your printer's press) uses can't really have semi-transparent attributes. Instead, the effects of applied transparency are translated for printing. There are two basic methods of performing this operation—creating printable vector objects to "fill in" for semi-transparent objects, or creating printable raster (bitmap) objects. In general, bitmaps are faster and easier for printers to handle, while vectors are more accurate but slower for printers to handle.

You define the basic way that Illustrator will handle these options in the bottom half of the Document Setup dialog box. The Export and Clipboard Transparency Flattener Settings drop-down list provides three options: High Resolution, Medium Resolution, and Low Resolution. You can fine-tune and have more control over these options if you click the Custom button in the Document Setup dialog box. Doing that opens the Custom Transparency Flattener Options dialog box.

The Raster/Vector balance slider defines how much rasterization (conversion to bitmap) you want to do. Remember, more rasterizastion = lower quality and faster printing. The Line Art and Text Resolution drop-down list allows you to set resolution for vector objects that are converted to bitmaps. The Gradient and Mesh Color Resolution drop-down list allows you to set resolution for gradients and mesh objects that will be converted to bitmaps for printing or export. Higher values produce better quality, along with slower printing and larger files.

 Gradient fills were covered in Chapter 16, and gradient meshes were explored in Chapter 15. Gradient fills and mesh objects present challenges similar to those presented by transparency when they need to be printed or exported to different file formats.

Other options in the Document Setup dialog box define printing and export options not specific to documents with transparency.

Chapter 18

Use Brushes and Pattern Fills

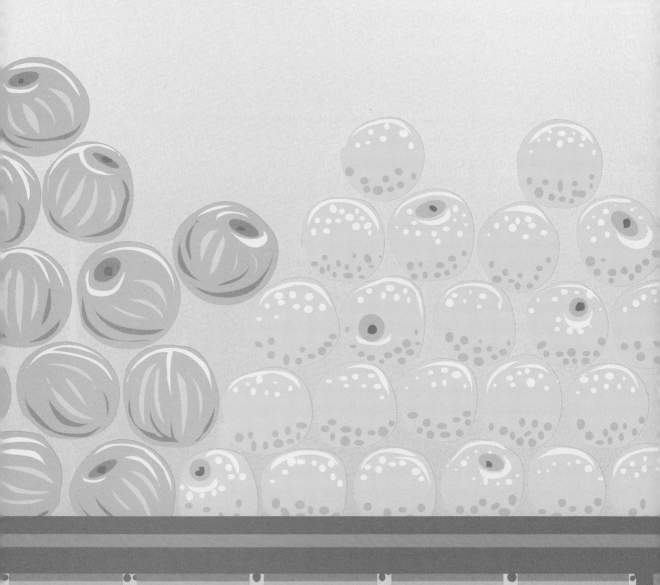

How to...

- Apply pattern swatches
- Create pattern swatches
- Use text as a pattern fill
- Create tiling fills
- Create a fill with a bounding box
- Use brush patterns
- Apply a brush pattern
- Use brush pattern libraries
- Create your own brush patterns
- Create calligraphic brush strokes
- Create a scatter brush
- Create an art brush
- Create brushes from scratch
- Share custom fills and brushes

Illustrator's pattern fills and brush strokes allow you to define a pattern or brush stroke and then use and re-use them in illustrations. Pattern fills and brush strokes are vector-based, so they have all the advantages of other vector graphics. They demand little memory, and you can easily rescale them without the graininess that results when you resize bitmap fills. Pattern fills also keep file size small because they consist of illustrations that tile (repeat) to fill an object.

A pattern fill is a single, repeating, small illustration that fills a path to which it is applied. If you have designed or observed patterns that repeat to form the background of a web page, you've observed this concept. The process of repeating a single illustration to fill a path is called *tiling*—a metaphor evoking the tiles laid end to end on a kitchen floor. The brick pattern in Figure 18-1 illustrates a repeating, tiled pattern.

In Figure 18-1, a single fill is applied to a large area, and tiling is used to fill the space with repeating fills. Another possible approach to this project would be to create a brick pattern that is sized to fill a *single* brick without tiling. This approach is illustrated in Figure 18-2.

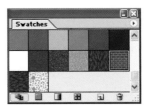

FIGURE 18-1 The small brick pattern *tiles* throughout the object to which it was applied.

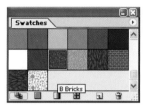

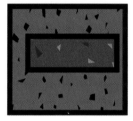

FIGURE 18-2 Each brick uses a single pattern fill. The concrete pattern is tiled in the background.

A similar kind of repeating image can be used to generate a *brush stroke* pattern. Stroke patterns tend to get a little more complicated, because you often want the shape of a stroke pattern to "bend" as it goes around corners. Therefore, some stroke patterns are actually composed of more than one illustration. You access stroke patterns from the Brushes palette, and you access pattern fills from the Swatches palette. Illustrator comes with a starter set of brush and swatch patterns, but the real fun is in creating your own patterns and applying them to achieve unique effects in your artwork. You'll learn to create pattern fills like the one in Figure 18-3 later in this chapter.

Brian Miyamoto

FIGURE 18-3 This pattern fill "adapts" as it goes around corners.

Apply Pattern Swatches

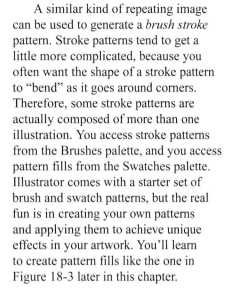

You can whet your appetite for designing unique pattern swatches by checking out the prefab ones that come with Illustrator. Do that by choosing Window | Swatches to display the Swatches palette. The first four icons at the bottom of the Swatches palette allow you to display all swatches or just color swatches, gradient swatches, or pattern swatches.

Figure 18-4 illustrates the swatch icons. The fifth icon in the Swatches palette—New Swatch—copies a selected pattern fill, and the final icon is Delete Swatch. You can drag existing swatches onto this icon to remove them from the palette.

Delete Swatch
New Swatch
Show Pattern Swatches
Show Gradient Swatches
Show Color Swatches
Show All Swatches

 Color and gradient swatches provide easy access to colors or gradient fills that you use frequently.

18

FIGURE 18-4 The Swatches palette

You can change the way these swatches are displayed by choosing Small Thumbnail View, Large Thumbnail View, or List View from the Swatches palette menu. Figure 18-5 shows the available fill swatch colors as a list.

When you select the Show Pattern Swatches button, you'll see the pre-set patterns that come with Illustrator. To experiment with the pre-set pattern fills, create a quick path or shape (or use an existing one). Select the path or shape with the Selection tool and click one of the pattern fills. Try moving your pattern fill within the path by holding down the tilde (~) key as you click and drag within the object. The object itself doesn't move (as long as you hold down the tilde key), but if you look closely, you'll see that the pattern fill has scrolled to a different position behind the path. Figure 18-6 shows two bricks with the same pattern fill applied, but with the fill "moved" within the shape.

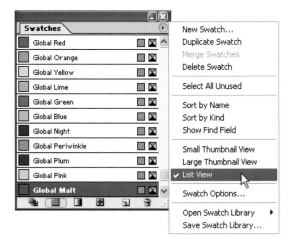

FIGURE 18-5 Viewing swatches as a list

 Technically speaking, the key you hold down as you move a pattern fill within a shape should be referred to as the key on your keyboard that would produce a tilde (~) if the SHIFT key was held down. However, nobody knows the name of the character under the tilde (few enough folks know what a tilde is!), so the key is usually referred to as the tilde key.

You can switch pattern fills by simply clicking a different one in the Swatches palette. Or choose a color from the Color palette to replace your pattern fill with a solid fill color.

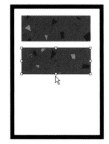

FIGURE 18-6 Each brick uses the same fill, but the location of the fill has been moved.

Create Pattern Swatches

Now that you've seen how much fun pattern fills can be, you're ready to create *your own* custom fills. Pattern fills are no more than Illustrator objects—repeated over and over to fill a path. They can be composed of strokes, fills, text, and/or shapes. Unfortunately, you can't use gradients, blends, many filters and effects, or bitmap images in pattern fills. Nor can you include objects to which a mask has been applied in a pattern fill.

Organize and Edit Swatches

After you have created a swatch, you can name that swatch by double-clicking on it in the Swatches palette. This opens the Swatch Options dialog box. Swatch options vary depending on the type of swatch you are creating, but all swatches allow you to assign a custom name in the Swatch Name area of the dialog box.

To delete a swatch from the palette, select the swatch and choose Delete Swatch from the Swatches palette menu. You can also edit a pattern after you create it. To edit a pattern swatch, drag the swatch onto the artboard and edit it as you would any object.

Use Text as a Pattern Fill

FIGURE 18-7 Creating a swatch from text

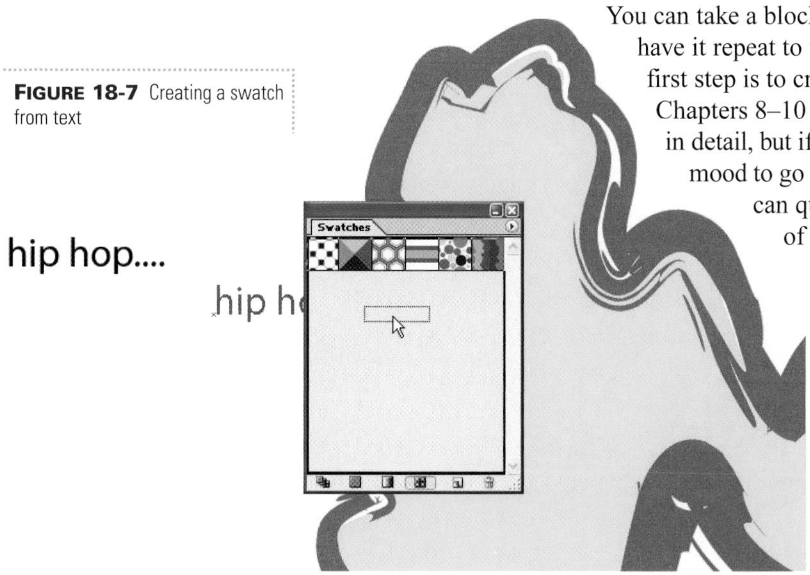

You can take a block of text and simply have it repeat to fill an object. The first step is to create a block of text. Chapters 8–10 examined text blocks in detail, but if you're not in the mood to go look that up, you can quickly create a block of text by selecting the Type tool, clicking on the artboard, and typing text.

After you've created a block of text, you can drag that text into the Swatches palette, as shown in Figure 18-7.

Felix Perez

18

Make sure that the Show Pattern Swatches tab is selected. Use the icon at the bottom of the palette to select it.

Once your pattern fill has been added to the Swatches palette, you can select any object and click the swatch you made (in the Swatches palette) to apply that fill to the selected object. Figure 18-8 shows a text swatch being assigned to fill the hip-hop figure. After you place your new fill, hold down the tilde key while you click and drag on the fill inside the shape to adjust how the fill appears within it.

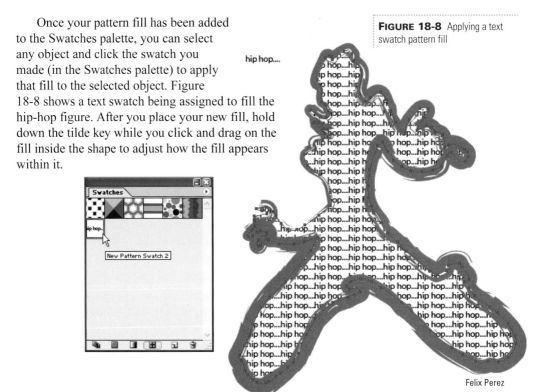

FIGURE 18-8 Applying a text swatch pattern fill

Felix Perez

Create a Basic Pattern Fill

Any graphic object can be used as a fill. It's a simple, three-step process. First, create a graphic object. Second, drag it into the Swatches palette, as shown in Figure 18-9.

FIGURE 18-9 Creating a swatch from the star

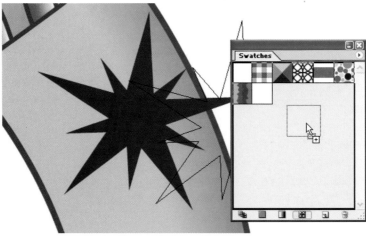

Finally, select an object to be filled, and click on the swatch, as shown in Figure 18-10.

FIGURE 18-10 Applying the star pattern fill from the Swatches palette

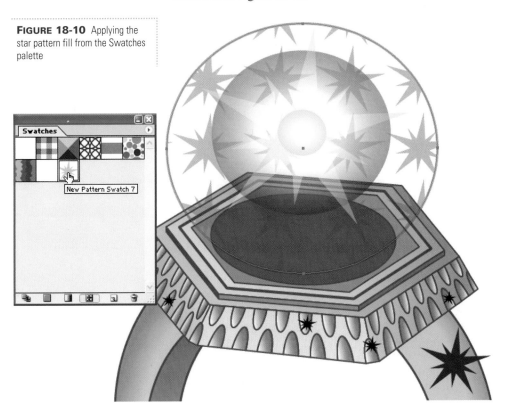

Create Repeating Fills with Bounding Boxes

For more complex fills that involve many paths or shapes, you will often want to use a bounding box to define the positioning and spacing of the tiles that make up your fill. In this context, "bounding box" means something different than the outline of a path that displays when you choose View | Show Bounding Box. Here the term refers to a shape (usually a square) that defines the outer limit of the tile you create for a pattern fill.

This concept is best explained with an example. Try these steps to create a pattern using a bounding box:

1. Draw several shapes within a small area.

2. Draw a square over the shapes you've just drawn. Assign no fill to the square, and no stroke.

18

3. With the square selected, choose Object | Arrange | Send To Back to move the square behind the shapes. Your illustration should look something like the one in Figure 18-11.

4. Use the Selection tool to select both the square and all the objects inside it. Drag the selected group of objects into the Swatches palette.

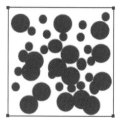

FIGURE 18-11 Collecting objects in a bounding box

Note   *Make sure the Show Pattern Swatches icon at the bottom of the Swatches palette is selected.*

5. Draw a shape and apply your new fill to it. Click in the middle of the object to select the fill with the Selection tool, hold down the tilde key, and adjust the display of the pattern fill. Because you used a square as a "bounding box" for your tile, your fill can be more complex and irregular than if you simply dragged a shape into the pattern Swatches palette. The result is shown in Figure 18-12.

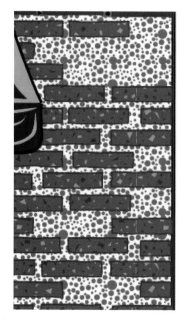

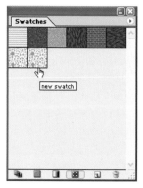

FIGURE 18-12 Applying a swatch created with a bounding box

Create Tiling Fills

Sometimes you want to create fills that don't look like they are tiled images. For example, if you look closely at the roof in Figure 18-13, you'll see that the fill is created by tiling a swatch. The pattern that the swatch was created from is also shown in the figure.

Tiling fill swatches must mesh together to create a pattern that appears seamless. You can test and edit your swatch by

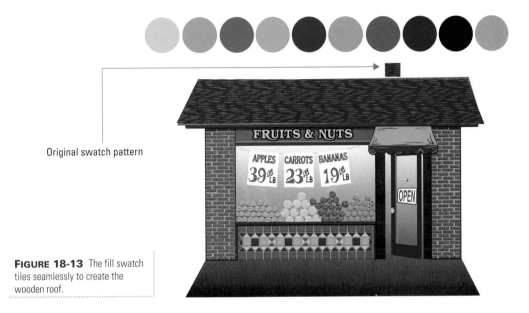

Original swatch pattern

FIGURE 18-13 The fill swatch
tiles seamlessly to create the
wooden roof.

creating duplicates and aligning them to see how they fit together,
as shown in Figure 18-14.

Tip   *You'll probably want to view grids (View | Show Grid) and turn on Snap to Grid
(View | Snap to Grid) when you are designing swatches that will tile seamlessly—
these will help you align objects within the swatch to the top, bottom, left, and right
edges of the bounding box.*

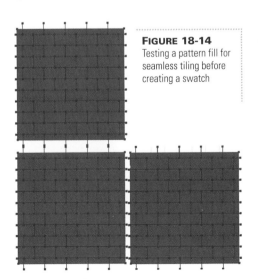

FIGURE 18-14
Testing a pattern fill for
seamless tiling before
creating a swatch

After you've tweaked your pattern so that it
tiles smoothly, you can then save it as a swatch.

Use Brush Patterns

Brush patterns are similar to pattern fills, with
two major differences: brush patterns are
applied to strokes instead of fills, and they
are adaptive in that they change depending
on the direction of the stroke path.

18

Illustrator comes with a nice set of brush libraries from which you can choose stroke patterns. Or you can mix up your own stroke pattern by adapting any vector image. You can use the existing set of brushes or make your own.

Apply a Brush Pattern

You can get some idea of how brush patterns work by selecting one from the Brushes palette and using it as a stroke pattern. To view the Brushes palette, choose Window | Brushes. Use any of the symbols in the palette as a stroke pattern.

You can get a better idea of how a brush pattern will look by choosing Thumbnail View from the Brushes palette menu, as shown in Figure 18-15.

You can apply a brush pattern to the shape tools (such as the Rectangle, Ellipse, or Star tool), the Paintbrush tool, or the drawing tools in the Line Segment tool tearoff. You can't apply a brush pattern to text or to the Symbol Sprayer tool. (Choose a pattern from the symbol library for the Symbol Sprayer.)

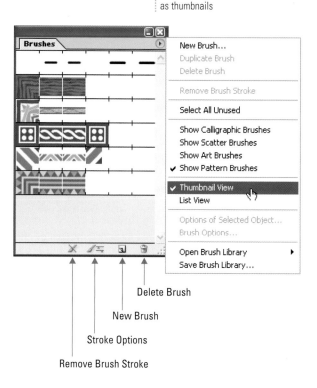

FIGURE 18-15 Viewing brushes as thumbnails

The Paintbrush tool works only with a selected brush pattern.

Follow these steps to apply a brush pattern to a stroke:

1. Click the brush pattern in the Brushes palette.

2. Select a drawing tool, such as the Pencil or Pen tool.

3. Draw a path or shape. The selected brush pattern will be applied to the outline, as shown in Figure 18-16.

After you have applied a brush pattern to an outline, you can change that stroke pattern by selecting the path and clicking on a different brush pattern in the Brushes palette. You can remove a brush pattern from a selected path by choosing

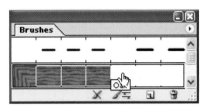

Remove Brush Stroke from the Brushes palette menu. The selected brush will continue to be applied to new paths until you choose Remove Brush Stroke from the palette menu.

Brian Miyamoto

FIGURE 18-16 Applying a brush stroke to a shape

Use Brush Pattern Libraries

Illustrator comes with many sets of brush libraries. You can access these brushes by choosing Window | Brush Libraries. The Brush Libraries submenu displays dozens of libraries of brush strokes.

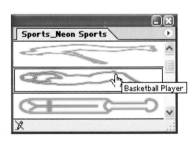

You can apply additional brush strokes from the libraries just as you apply brush strokes from the default Brushes palette. Many of the additional brush strokes work better if you use the Stroke palette to widen the stroke to which they are applied. Figure 18-17 shows a pattern from the Sports_Neon Sports library being applied to a curve. Widening the stroke to 8 points fleshes out the basketball player's shape.

Brush strokes that you assign to your document from additional libraries are added to the Brushes palette associated with your file and are available the next time you open the file.

FIGURE 18-17 Assigning a thicker stroke to a new basketball player brush stroke

18

Create Your Own Brush Patterns

There are four different types of brush patterns. Each type of pattern creates a different type of effect when applied to a path.

- **Calligraphic Brushes**   These create strokes that look like those drawn by a calligraphy pen.
- **Scatter Brushes**   These brushes "scatter" pattern objects along a path.
- **Art Brushes**   Art brushes stretch a single image—from one end of a path to the other.
- **Pattern Brushes**   Pattern brushes can include up to five different tiles that are applied to the sides, corners, and endpoints of a stroke.

Each type of brush pattern has options for different kinds of adjustments. Art brushes, for instance, can be flipped so they run from the last anchor point in a path to the first anchor point.

Because brush patterns are fairly complex, and because Illustrator comes with a large selection of pre-set ones, the easiest way to create a custom brush pattern is to modify an existing brush and save it as a new brush.

Create Calligraphic Brush Strokes

In Illustrator, *calligraphy* refers to stylized type that is designed to look like it's drawn with a pen or brush. Calligraphic brush strokes mimic real brush strokes, but they can be used with any kind of stroke. You can alter the size, angle, roundness, and randomness (variety) in the brush stroke width.

Probably the biggest factor in defining the style of a calligraphic brush stroke is the stroke shape. Shapes can vary from very round to very flat, or anything in between. Figure 18-18 shows the same type (converted to an outline), with the same width of calligraphic brush applied. The top line has a round brush shape, while the bottom has a flat brush.

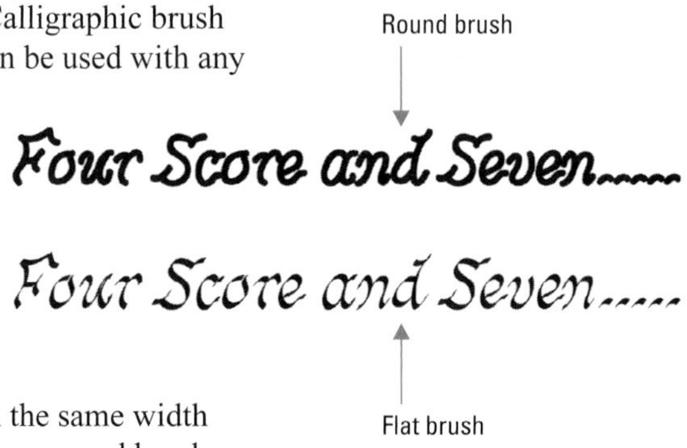

Besides the shape of the brush, you can define the *angle* of the brush (which is operative only if the brush is not round). And you can define the diameter (size) of the brush. You can

Round brush

Four Score and Seven......

Four Score and Seven......

Flat brush

FIGURE 18-18 Calligraphic strokes are affected by the shape of the brush.

elect to make brush diameter random, so that it varies as you draw. If you are using a stylus or graphics tablet, the Pressure options settings define how sensitive the brush will be to pressure on your drawing tool.

Follow these steps to create a new flat calligraphic brush stroke that is 5 points wide:

1. Choose New Brush from the Brushes palette menu.

2. In the New Brush dialog box, click on the New Calligraphic Brush button and click OK.

3. In the Calligraphic Brush Options dialog box, enter **5 Point Flat** in the Name box.

4. Type **45°** in the Angle box, and leave this setting as Fixed.

5. Type **10%** in the Roundness box to make the brush flat, and choose Random from the Roundness list.

6. Type **10%** in the Roundness Variation box.

7. Change the diameter of the brush to 5 points by entering **5 pt** in the Diameter box, as shown in Figure 18-19.

8. Click OK to save the new calligraphic brush pattern.

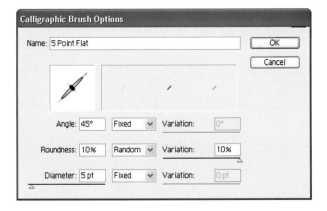

FIGURE 18-19 Defining a thin, flat, angled calligraphic brush

Once you have defined a calligraphic brush, you can assign it to any stroke or fill. If you want to apply a calligraphic stroke to type, you need to convert the type to an outline first by selecting it and choosing Type | Create Outlines.

Tip

In addition to calligraphic brushes you create on your own, some brushes in the graphic brush libraries produce results similar to calligraphic strokes. You'll find these brushes by choosing Window | Graphic Style Libraries and exploring brush sets such as the Type Effects and 3-D Effects libraries.

Create a Scatter Brush

Imagine that you could load any image—a leaf, a frog, an ink spot, or even—literally—a paintbrush...into a brush. That's how scatter brushes work. Scatter brushes allow you to quickly "paint" an image along a path on the artboard.

To experiment with one of the existing scatter brush patterns, use the Brushes palette menu to view only scatter brushes (choose Show Scatter Brushes from the Brushes palette menu and deselect the options to show other types of brushes). Select a scatter brush (try the Ink Drop for fun) and draw a path using the Pencil or Pen tool.

To create a new scatter brush, first create an object that will be "brushed" onto the artboard. Drag that object into the Brushes palette, and keep it selected. As you do, the New Brush dialog box appears. Select New Scatter Brush from the set of option buttons, as shown in Figure 18-20. Your artwork becomes a scatter brush.

After you tell Illustrator that you're creating a scatter brush, the Scatter Brush Options dialog box appears.

In the dialog box, enter a name for your new brush in the Name area. Use the sliders and lists in the dialog box to modify the pattern. *Size* controls the size of the pattern in relation to the original drawing. *Spacing* controls the space between pattern pieces. *Scatter* defines how far the pattern pieces will scatter along (depart from) the selected path. And the *Rotation* setting defines how much objects will rotate when the pattern is applied to a curved path. The Rotation setting can be applied relative to either the path or the page.

If you choose Random from the list associated with each setting, a second slider that controls variation in the setting will become active. For example, if you choose Random for the pattern size, the second slider defines the percentage of size variation of the pattern object.

If you are changing a stroke that has already been applied to existing paths, you'll be prompted to either apply the new stroke to those paths or leave them alone.

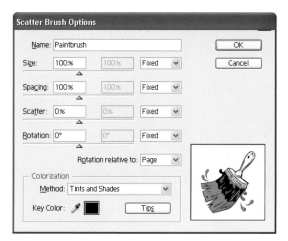

FIGURE 18-21 Defining the new scatter brush options

FIGURE 18-22 Defining an art brush from artwork on the artboard

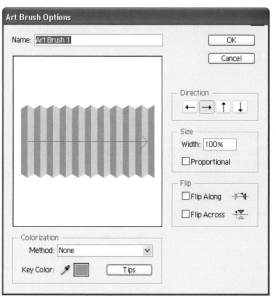

Hugh D'Andrade

The Colorization Method drop-down list in the Scatter Brush Options dialog box defines what colors (if any) are added to the original stroke color. The various options are illustrated clearly if you click the Tips button in the dialog box. You'll see a handy colorization chart that details the effect of each colorization method.

Figure 18-21 shows the Tints and Shades colorization method being used to define a scatter brush.

Create an Art Brush

An art brush stretches a pattern tile to fill the entire path to which it is applied. Therefore, most of the work of defining an art brush takes place when you create the drawing right on the Illustrator artboard.

Start with a selected drawing and choose New Brush from the Brushes palette menu. Click the New Art Brush radio button in the New Brush dialog box that appears, and click OK to open the Art Brush Options dialog box. The selected drawing will appear in the preview window of the dialog box, as shown in Figure 18-22.

Name your custom art brush by entering a name in the Name area of the Art Brush Options dialog box. Use the Direction arrow buttons to define how the pattern object will be applied as you draw a path. Use the Stroke From Bottom To Top direction arrow in the Direction area of the dialog box to have the pattern appear right side up as you draw a line from the bottom of the artboard to the top. Use the Size box to define how big the symbol will display in the stroke path, and use the Proportional check box to keep the height-to-width ratio unchanged if you resize the object. The Flip check boxes allow you to reverse the symbol either horizontally or vertically.

After you OK your Art Brush Options settings, you can apply the new custom art brush to any path—as shown in Figure 18-23.

18

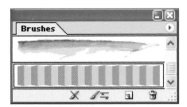

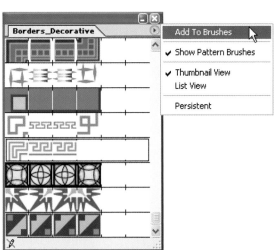

FIGURE 18-23 Bending an art brush stroke along a path

Hugh D'Andrade

After you generate an art brush, you can edit it by double-clicking on the brush in the Brushes palette. The Art Brush Options dialog box reappears, with the same options that were available when you created the brush. However, the dialog box now has a Preview check box so you can see the effect of your changes on objects in your document.

Define a Pattern Brush

Pattern brushes are the most complicated to modify or create because they involve as many as five different object panels. You can use separate symbols for the start, the finish, the side (center), the inside corner, and the outside corner panels. It's often not necessary to use all these panels.

You can see how pattern brushes work by examining some of the samples in the Borders_Decorative brush library. View these brushes by choosing Window | Brush Libraries | Borders_Decorative. You can add any of these decorative borders to the Brushes palette by choosing Add to Brushes from the Borders_Decorative brush palette menu, as shown in Figure 18-24.

Once you've added one of the available pattern brushes to your Brushes palette, you can double-click on the brush in the Brushes palette to examine, and edit, that brush. Take a look at the brush tiles for the Rectangles 2 pattern brush in Figure 18-25. You'll note that there is one tile for straight paths, one tile for outside corners, and a third tile for inside corners.

Creating a pattern brush requires a bit of thinking ahead. You can—potentially—define five tiles for your pattern: original (normal), outer corner, inner corner, start, and finish. Most pattern

FIGURE 18-24 Adding one of the pre-set pattern brushes to the Brushes palette

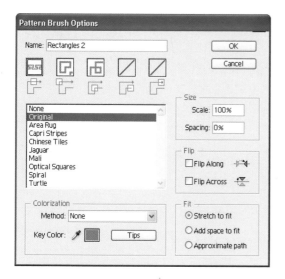

FIGURE 18-25 This pattern brush has three tiles—you can use up to five.

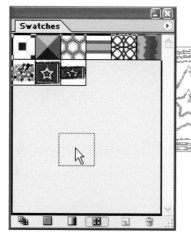

FIGURE 18-26 The first step in creating a pattern brush is to drag each tile into the Swatches palette.

brushes work well with just two tiles—one for corners and one for edges.

Follow these steps to create a pattern brush with two different tiles:

1. You need to design the tiles before you start to define your pattern brush. After you design a corner and edge (normal) tile, drag each of the tiles into the Swatches palette, as shown in Figure 18-26.

2. Double-click each of the new swatches and enter a name for each one in the Swatch Name box in the Swatch Options dialog box. This will make it easier to construct your pattern brush.

Now that you've added at least two swatches to the Swatches palette, you can use them to create a pattern brush. Once you've created your swatches, it isn't essential to keep the Swatches palette open to continue the process of defining a pattern brush.

3. Make sure that no objects are selected on the artboard, and choose New Brush from the Brushes palette menu.

4. In the New Brush dialog box, choose the New Pattern Brush radio button and click OK.

5. In the Pattern Brush Options dialog box, enter a name for your pattern in the Name text box.

6. Click the Side Tile button in the Pattern Brush Options dialog box, and then click the artwork that you added to the list of swatches that appears in the Pattern Brush Options dialog box.

7. Click the Outer Corner Tile button in the dialog box, and click the artwork you designed for corners, as shown in Figure 18-27.

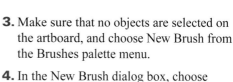

Felix Perez

18

8. Leave the rest of the default settings as they are, and click OK to define the pattern brush. Select the pattern brush from the Brushes palette, and then select a drawing tool.

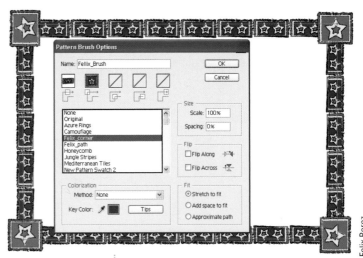

Try creating both curved paths and sharp angles. Experiment by assigning the new pattern brush to curves you create with the Pen, Pencil, or Paintbrush, or the different shape tools.

FIGURE 18-27 Defining a straight line tile and a corner tile from artwork you added to your Swatches palette

 There's also a way to create a new pattern brush without first creating new swatches. You can drag the side tile image onto the Brushes palette and then hold down OPTION *(ALT) and drag the remaining tiles.*

Share Custom Fills and Brushes

What if you want to access custom brush and fill swatches in a different file? It can be done. Illustrator lets you open the Swatch library of one file within a different file.

One useful technique is to have a special Illustrator file just to store fill and stroke swatches. From that file, you can import that set of swatches into any open document and access your full library of custom fills.

Follow these steps to open a swatch or brush library from one file into a different open file:

1. With a document open, choose Window | Brush Libraries or Window | Swatch Libraries, depending on whether you want to import brush stroke swatches or fill swatches from another file.

2. Select the Other Library submenu option.

3. Double-click the Illustrator (AI) file from which you want to import a swatch library. The new (additional) Swatches or Brushes palette appears in your open document.

4. You can access brush shapes or swatches directly from the imported Swatches or Brushes palette.

Chapter 19

Work with Bitmap Art in Illustrator

How to...

- Understand bitmap (raster) digital graphics
- Work with bitmaps in Illustrator
- Open bitmaps in Illustrator
- Bring Photoshop files into Illustrator
- Work with bitmap file formats in Illustrator
- Convert vector graphics to bitmaps
- Prepare bitmaps for Illustrator
- Edit bitmaps in Illustrator
- Apply effects and filters to bitmaps

Illustrator's unique role in the world of digital art is an unsurpassed ability to create and edit *vector* graphics. As discussed at the beginning of this book, vector artwork can be scaled, it generally creates smaller size files, and it allows unmatched editing of curves, shapes, and text.

Even with all those advantages, some artwork does not lend itself to a vector format. Photographs, for example, are composed of many tiny dots, and it is usually not effective or efficient to try to convert them to vector images. Instead, such raster-based (bitmap) images are usually edited in Illustrator's cousin—Photoshop.

Tip   *Raster? Bitmap? They refer to the same thing.* Bitmap *or* raster *graphics are digital images in which the content of the image is defined by dots mapped (located) along a raster (grid). The term* bitmap *(as in a* map of bits*) puts emphasis on the fact that* bits *(dots or pixels) are mapped, while the term* raster *emphasizes that a* grid *is used to locate the dots or pixels. The two terms are used interchangeably in this book.*

For serious raster editing, you'll want to use Adobe Photoshop or a similar bitmap editing program, such as Jasc Paint Shop Pro or Corel PHOTO-PAINT. The reason that there are bitmap editing tools in Illustrator is that many illustrations are *hybrids*—

FIGURE 19-1 The image is from Photoshop, the text from Illustrator.

combinations of both vector and bitmap artwork. For instance, the CD cover in Figure 19-1 combines a photo (stylized in Photoshop) with type layout better managed in Illustrator.

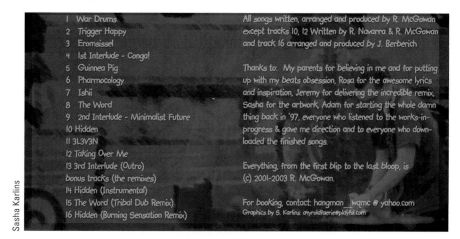

Sasha Karlins

Work with Bitmaps

Vector graphic files save information by storing descriptions of paths and fills; raster image files save information by recording the character (color, brightness, transparency, and other attributes) and location of every single pixel in an illustration. Although raster files save images less efficiently (compared to vector files), the raster file logic makes it easier to fine-tune attributes such as color on a level not available with vectors. Therefore, photographs in particular are best edited in bitmap programs.

Sometimes bitmaps are the only show in town. This is still *mainly* the case on the Web, where vector-based illustrations must rely on plug-ins such as the Flash Player to be able to be viewed in browsers.

Open Bitmaps in Illustrator

There are three ways to open a bitmap image in Illustrator. Many bitmap file formats are supported by the File | Open menu. Keep in mind, though, that when you *save* a file that was opened as a bitmap, you'll either save it as an Illustrator vector file or export it to a bitmap.

More typically, you'll place or paste a bitmap into an open Illustrator file. To place a bitmap within an Illustrator document, choose File | Place and navigate to the file in the Place dialog

19

box. The Place dialog box has a Link check box. A linked file is not embedded in the actual Illustrator document; the document simply "remembers" where that file is and displays it in the Illustrator document. If you *don't* check the Link check box when you place a file, it will be embedded in the Illustrator file.

Tip *Link vs. embed—if someone is providing you with Illustrator files, you might want to have placed bitmaps linked so you have the freedom to switch them or edit them more easily in a bitmap editor. If you are sending a file to a client, you should usually embed images so they don't get lost, or so that your client doesn't accidentally break links by moving, renaming, or deleting linked images.*

Bring Photoshop Files into Illustrator

Photoshop's PSD file format is among those bitmap formats that you can open directly in Illustrator. Many attributes of Photoshop files are supported and maintained even after the file is opened in Illustrator.

Layers are explained in Chapter 20 in this book. They are a helpful tool for organizing and editing objects in Illustrator, but they're an even more essential feature in Photoshop since bitmap images are *not* composed of easily selectable objects as vector images are. When you open or place a Photoshop object in Illustrator, layers are maintained.

Type included in a Photoshop file is editable (and formatable) when you bring the Photoshop artwork into Illustrator.

Use Bitmap File Formats in Illustrator

If the size and color of the image are defined, the bitmap is ready to be imported. Illustrator can handle more than a dozen bitmap file formats, including the following:

- **BMP (.bmp)** Bitmap, used with many Windows applications
- **GIF (.gif)** Graphics Interchange Format, used for web images
- **JPEG (.jpg)** Joint Photographic Experts Group, used for web photos
- **PCX (.pcx)** PC Paintbrush, used with some Windows applications
- **PDF (.pdf)** Portable Document Format, supports both vector and bitmap objects
- **PCD (.pcd)** Kodak Photo CD, supported by Kodak film developers

- **PSD (.psd)**   Photoshop files, which come into Illustrator with layers and other features intact
- **PICT (.pict)**   A Macintosh format, used with many Macintosh programs
- **PNG (.png)**   Portable Network Graphics, similar to the GIF format for web-compatible graphics
- **PIXAR (.pxr)**   Used for 3-D imaging
- **TGA (.tga)**   Targa, supports enhanced gamma (intensity) settings and is used with the Truevision video board
- **TIFF (.tiff or .tif)**   Tagged Image File Format, used by many scanners as a default image format

This list of bitmap formats supported by Illustrator is extensive, but not complete. So you should make sure that any bitmaps you are bringing into Illustrator have been saved to or exported to one of these formats.

Convert Vectors to Bitmaps

As noted, there are advantages to bitmap format, most notably the ability to edit the coloring of specific pixels or dots. You can convert a selected vector to a bitmap by choosing Object | Rasterize from the menu.

Tip *Just as bitmap and raster mean the same thing, pixel and dot mean* pretty much *the same thing. The smallest element of a printed bitmap is usually referred to as a* dot *(as in "dots per inch" in defining printer resolution), while the elements that make up a digital display (such as the one on your monitor) are referred to as* pixels.

You can apply raster effects to vector objects that have been converted to raster objects. But don't confuse the Object | Rasterize command with the rasterizing option available in the Effect menu. Objects that you have *displayed* as bitmaps by selecting Effect | Rasterize cannot be used with bitmap filters. They aren't really raster objects; they just display that way.

Prepare Bitmaps for Illustrator

The most important thing you should know about working with bitmaps in Illustrator is that you cannot resize them or recolor them. OK, you *can resize* bitmaps in Illustrator, but you won't want to. The reason is that if you enlarge a bitmap in Illustrator it will get grainy and lose quality. If you reduce the size of a

19

bitmap in Illustrator, it will get smaller without losing quality, but the file size will not be reduced.

 Programs such as Photoshop do have resampling tools that enable you to reduce file size as you shrink a bitmap or enhance image quality when you make a bitmap bigger.

For example, Figure 19-2 shows an enlarged image containing both vector and bitmap objects. The bitmap— the onion—is obviously distorted and displays with jagged edges, while the vector-based type has no distortion at all—even highly enlarged.

You can alter the coloration of an entire bitmap image in Illustrator by choosing Filter | Colors | Adjust Colors and then tweaking the color of the entire selected bitmap. However, these color changes are applied to all colors in the bitmap image. Tinting coloration with a filter is a useful effect, but it doesn't serve as a coloring editor.

Since resizing and recoloring bitmaps is problematic in Illustrator, you should arrange to have photos or other bitmap artwork sized and colored before you bring it into Illustrator.

FIGURE 19-2 Bitmap artwork degrades into visible pixels when enlarged, while the vector object (the type) does not.

Edit Bitmaps in Illustrator

When you bring bitmap images into Illustrator, you can use many of the editing tools and effects available for vector objects. This section of the chapter summarizes and gives examples of what you can and can't do with bitmaps in Illustrator.

For example, the following list includes editing techniques that you *can* do with bitmaps in Illustrator:

- Apply transparency and place transparent objects over other objects (including type), as shown in Figure 19-3
- Apply many filters and effects
- Place bitmaps in layers
- Group bitmaps, together or in combination with vector objects
- Use the clipboard to cut, copy, and paste (and duplicate) bitmaps

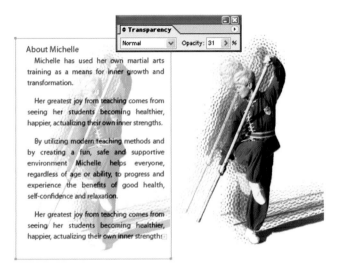

About Michelle

Michelle has used her own martial arts training as a means for inner growth and transformation.

Her greatest joy from teaching comes from seeing her students becoming healthier, happier, actualizing their own inner strengths.

By utilizing modern teaching methods and by creating a fun, safe and supportive environment Michelle helps everyone, regardless of age or ability, to progress and experience the benefits of good health, self-confidence and relaxation.

Her greatest joy from teaching comes from seeing her students becoming healthier, happier, actualizing their own inner strengths

FIGURE 19-3 Transparency can often be added to bitmaps to good effect—such as the transparent bitmap sketch overlaid on text here.

FIGURE 19-4 Many effects and filters work for both bitmaps and vectors, but some apply differently.

Vector

Bitmap

- Use the Scale, Free Transform, Rotate, Reflect, and other tools to edit the object

- Add bitmaps to your Swatches palette

- Apply crop marks for printing

What you *cannot* do with bitmaps in Illustrator:

- Make bitmaps bigger without distorting them

- Edit color (not much, anyway)

- Wrap type around bitmaps (because all bitmaps are defined in rectangular boxes)

Note *You can assign color to a monochrome (one-color) bitmap using the same fill swatch in the Toolbox that you use to assign fill colors to vector objects. But this works only for monochrome bitmap images.*

- Edit paths and fills (which don't exist in bitmap images)
- Use bitmaps as patterns for brushes

Apply Effects and Filters

Illustrator will apply to bitmaps many of the same effects and editing techniques that you use to edit vector images. These effects and filters are described in Chapter 14 and apply in a more-or-less similar way to bitmaps and vectors. The effect is *more-or-less* similar because bitmaps have different properties than vector objects. So, for example, a drop shadow filter or effect applied to a bitmap will be applied to the *rectangular box* that circumscribes the bitmap, while no such invisible rectangle exists around a vector. Figure 19-4 shows a drop shadow effect applied to a vector and a bitmap.

Note *In the case of the drop shadow illustrated in Figure 19-4, the shadow will be applied to the bitmap object and not the rectangular bounding box if bitmap transparency has been applied to the object.*

19

In addition, many effects and filters are *only* available for bitmaps. The raster fill effects on the bottom part of the Filter menu can be applied only to raster images.

Illustrator does not perform many of the basic photo-editing techniques available in the Image | Adjustments submenu in Photoshop. These options are necessary to recolor and tune up photos for publication.

On the other hand, Illustrator's set of effects and filters includes many of the effects you can apply to bitmaps in Photoshop. You don't get access to many of the extra options for editing bitmaps that are available in Photoshop plug-ins, but you do get a nice set of tools for converting your bitmap into artwork ranging from charcoal sketches to mosaic patterns.

Apply Bitmap Effects

Raster (bitmap) effects and filters work only on embedded objects, not on linked objects. Change a selected, linked bitmap to an embedded one in the Links palette by choosing Embed Image from the Links palette menu. Most raster effects and filters apply only in RGB (or Grayscale) color mode.

You apply filters and effects to a bitmap by selecting the bitmap and choosing an effect or filter from either menu. As with effects and filters applied to a vector object, you can see (and remove) effects and filters applied to a bitmap object in the Appearance palette.

Different effects provide different option sliders, but you can always preview the changes in the small preview area right in the dialog box. Use the plus (+) and minus (–) signs to zoom in and out. Zooming out shows more of your image, while zooming in displays the details of the effect. Each of the bitmap filters or effects can be previewed in a dialog box.

Artistic Effects and Filters

Fifteen artistic effects simulate a wide variety of art media, ranging from colored pencils to sponges and watercolors. These effects and filters are very memory intensive, requiring large amounts of processing resources from your computer. They produce large files when applied.

Figure 19-5 demonstrates all 15 artistic filters and effects. In most cases, the effects have been applied with high degrees of intensity to emphasize the effect.

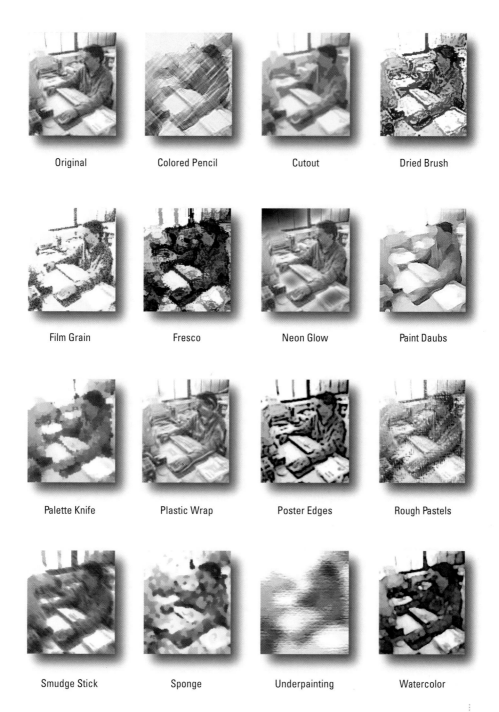

FIGURE 19-5 The artistic effects and filters simulate different art media.

19

Blur Effects and Filters

The blur effects, Gaussian Blur and Radial Blur, are available from both the Filter menu and the Effect menu, as is the Unsharpen Mask effect. To apply a blur effect to a selected bitmap, choose either Filter | Blur or Effect | Blur. Then choose either Gaussian or Radial.

The Gaussian blur does what it sounds like it would do: it creates a "heavenly" gauzy blurriness on your photo or other bitmap. Use the Radius slider to increase the blurriness, and check out the effect in the preview area of the dialog box associated with this effect, as shown in Figure 19-6.

The Radial Blur creates funhouse-mirror-type distortion. If you select the Zoom radio button in the dialog box associated with this effect, your bitmap will look like it was created with wet paint and then spun, throwing paint to the outside of the image. If you choose the Spin radio button, the image looks like it's being spun around so fast that it creates a blur. The Draft, Good, and Best radio buttons in the Radial Blur dialog box generate different resolution qualities, ranging from rough (Draft) to crisp (Best).

Brush Strokes

The eight brush stroke filters and effects apply a variety of stroke effects across bitmap images. The Effect menu versions of these transformations have a partial effect on some vector objects—like gradient fills and gradient meshes. While the Effect versions of brush strokes can be applied to some vector objects, these filters and effects are more powerful when applied to bitmaps.

The Accented Edges effect highlights edges. The Angled Strokes effect produces diagonal strokes. The Crosshatch effect creates rough edges. The Dark Strokes effect darkens shadows. Ink Outlines changes your image so it looks as if you drew over it with an ink pen. The Spatter effect makes it look like you sprayed paint from an airbrush onto your artwork. Sprayed Strokes repaints an image using its main colors with angled strokes. Sumi-e applies a Japanese-style ink-on-rice-paper look, blurring edges.

While the different brush stroke effects and filters have different dialog box options, they all allow you to preview effects before you apply them, so you can experiment with settings before you change your artwork. Figure 19-7 demonstrates the eight brush stroke effects.

FIGURE 19-6 Applying a Gaussian blur to a bitmap

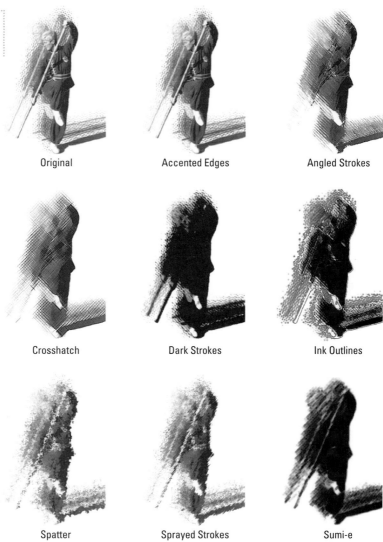

FIGURE 19-7 The brush stroke effects and filters

Original	Accented Edges	Angled Strokes
Crosshatch	Dark Strokes	Ink Outlines
Spatter	Sprayed Strokes	Sumi-e

Distort Effects and Filters

Distort effects and filters work very similarly on vector and bitmap images. Diffuse Glow adds a brightness that fades towards the edges. The Glass filter/effect makes an object appear as if viewed through a texture such as glass blocks, canvas, frosted glass, or a tinted lens. You choose a texture in the Glass dialog box before applying the filter/effect.

19

The Ocean Ripple filter/effect makes an object appear as it would if distorted by being underwater. The dialog box defines the size and magnitude of the underwater ripple. Figure 19-8 shows the three distort effects and filters.

FIGURE 19-8 The distort effects and filters

| Original | Diffuse Glow | Glass | Ocean Ripple |

Pixelate Effects and Filters

The four pixelate filters and effects distort the coloring of clumps of pixels. Only the Effect version of these filters can be applied to vector objects, while either filters or effects can be applied to bitmaps.

FIGURE 19-9 The pixelate effects and filters

Assigning the Color Halftone filter/effect generates circles that replace the original fill. The circle size is defined by the value you enter in the Max Radius box of the Color Halftone dialog box. The Screen-Angles boxes allow you to define the impact of the effect depending on the angle of dots relative to horizontal for four channels. Channel 1 is for grayscale images, and Channels 2 through 4 apply to red, green, and blue pixels respectively.

The Crystallize effect/filter groups similar colors into shapes. The Mezzotint filter/effect applies dot patterns you select from the dialog box to an object. You can preview each dot pattern before choosing one. The Pointillize effect/filter creates a kind of crazy-quilt mosaic look. You can adjust cell size and preview the effect in the dialog box before applying it. Figure 19-9 shows the four pixelate effects and filters.

Color Halftone   Crystallize

Original

Mezzotint   Pointillize

Sharpen Effects and Filters

You can define bitmap attributes within an illustration using the oddly named Unsharp Mask effect. With a bitmap selected,

FIGURE 19-10 The Unsharp Mask dialog box

choose Effect (or Filter) | Sharpen | Unsharp Mask. A dialog box with a preview area displays, as shown in Figure 19-10. This effect either unsharpens (was the word "blur" already taken?) or sharpens an image.

Sharpening is done by increasing contrast between different colors in the bitmap. The Amount slider in the Unsharp Mask dialog box defines how much sharpening to apply. (Higher values equal more sharpness.) The Radius slider defines the pixel size used to apply sharpening. Smaller values create more subtle color variation, whereas larger values create large splotches of color. The Threshold slider defines how much color differentiation will trigger sharpening.

The Unsharp Mask effect gives you a small taste of the kind of bitmap tweaking you can do with a full-featured bitmap editor such as Photoshop.

Sketch Effects and Filters

The 14 sketch effects and filters can be applied to vectors or bitmaps. They alter your image so that it appears to be created by a variety of non-digital media—ranging from charcoal and chrome to photocopier. The transformations are dramatic and can be used to transform a photograph into a sketch or to make any raster object look like it was created with the selected tools.

Most of the sketch effects/filters have self-descriptive names. Most are monochromatic. They can be previewed in their respective dialog boxes before being applied. The 14 sketch effects and filters are illustrated in Figure 19-11.

Texture Effects and Filters

The six texture effects and filters imbue selected raster objects with altered surfaces. As with other effects and filters, you tweak the effect in the dialog box for each effect/filter.

Craquelure adds *cracks* to an image. Grain adds a grainy texture to an image by simulating one of ten different types of graininess—such as Soft, Stipple, or Speckle. You choose a type of grain in the dialog box. Mosaic Tiles transforms an object into a mosaic of tiles of adjustable size. Patchwork divides an

19

Original	Bas Relief	Chalk & Charcoal	Charcoal	Chrome
Conté Crayon	Graphic Pen	Halftone Pattern	Note Paper	Photocopy
Plaster	Reticulation	Stamp	Torn Edges	Water Paper

FIGURE 19-11 The sketch effects and filters

object into squares. Stained Glass recreates an image as a stained-glass window. Texturizer offers four texture options in the dialog box: Brick, Burlap, Canvas, or Sandstone. Or you can load textures from files. Texture effects and filters are illustrated in Figure 19-12.

Video Effects and Filters

The two video effects/filters are used to move images to, or from, video. The De-Interlace filter/effect removes the interlacing that comes with images from video. The NTSC Colors effect/filter tones down highly saturated colors so that the image will not blur or bleed when viewed in video.

Bitmap Filter and Effect Tips

If you are unable to apply a filter or effect to an object, it may be that you are trying to apply the effect/filter to a vector object,

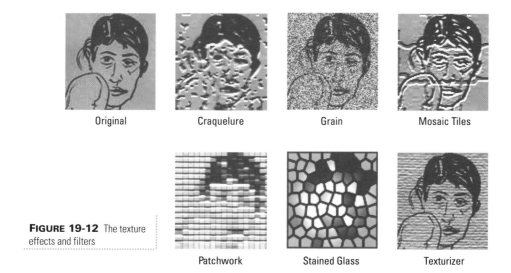

Original   Craquelure   Grain   Mosaic Tiles

FIGURE 19-12 The texture
effects and filters

Patchwork   Stained Glass   Texturizer

and that filter or effect works only on a bitmap object. You
can convert a selected vector object to a bitmap by choosing
Object | Rasterize.

You can *undo this conversion—but after you close your file, the rasterization is
frozen, and your object will no longer have the scaling and other advantages of
vector graphics.*

If you are sure you've selected a bitmap object, and you
still can't apply a raster effect or filter, check to make sure
the bitmap object is *embedded,* not linked. Raster filters and
effects work only on embedded placed objects. You can define
a selected bitmap as an embedded object by viewing the
Links palette and then selecting Embed Image from the Links
palette menu.

Finally, if you *still* can't access these filters and effects, it
may be that you have defined your document color mode as
CMYK. Remember that most raster effects and filters apply only
in RGB or Grayscale color mode. Choose File | Document Color
Mode | RGB Color to enable the filters and effects discussed in
this chapter.

19

Part VI

Use Layers and Styles

Chapter 20

Arrange Illustrations with Layers

How to...

- Get your money's worth from layers
- Use the Layers palette
- Change layer options
- Create new layers
- Use layers to organize your work
- Delete layers
- Consolidate layers
- Organize objects into separate layers
- Find objects on a layer
- Apply transparency to an entire layer
- Use scanned artwork as a template layer

Illustrator's layers allow you to both organize complex illustrations and group many effects and attributes to create compound effects.

The organizing function stems from the fact that you can separate different elements of a drawing into different layers and edit them without being distracted by the rest of your illustration. This is helpful in selecting, hiding, locking, or printing sections of your illustration.

Perhaps even more significantly, layers allow complex meshing of objects and effects to create really interesting artwork. Think of layers as transparent sheets of acetate that you can draw on. You can place any Illustrator object on a layer, including shapes and type. Because the layers are transparent, the content of different layers is visible even when you stack them on top of each other.

Objects on a top layer may cover up (or partially cover up) objects on lower layers. But you can achieve some really complex effects by controlling the opacity of each layer and of the separate objects on any given layer.

 **Get Your Money's Worth from Layers**

You use layers to organize objects in multipart illustrations and to control the properties of different objects that are grouped into layers. You can organize objects onto layers and sublayers by dragging them around inside the Layers palette. Illustrator also has tools to automatically organize objects onto separate layers.

Layer properties can include the following: hidden or visible, printing or non-printing, and locked or not locked. Hiding layers simply makes it easier to identify and work with selected objects in a crowded illustration. You can use non-printing layers as templates— as you would use a scanned photo or drawing, for instance—and build artwork around them. You can also lock layers to avoid messing up artwork on that layer while you edit artwork on another layer.

Finally, you can assign attributes to layers that affect how all objects on the layer are displayed. In this chapter, you'll learn to apply transparency to every object on a selected layer. In Chapter 21, you'll build on the knowledge of layers you get here to assign *styles*— whole groups of effects and features—to a layer.

Look at Layers

If you've bumped your head up against the difficulty of selecting and editing sections of a complex drawing, you're ready to use layers to help solve your problem. In addition, layers can be used to apply effects and other editing tools across an entire layer of objects. For example, you might want to apply the same transparency to all objects within a layer.

You can create many layers in a single illustration. Once they are defined, you can move the layers (i.e., change their order), lock them to prevent changes, group them together, and even apply styles to them. Getting into the habit of creating objects on separate layers will end up saving you time as you create more complex illustrations.

Explore the Layers Palette

To view the Layers palette, choose Window | Layers or press F7. Both of these actions are toggles, meaning that if the palette is not visible, pressing F7 or choosing Window | Layers will show the palette, and pressing F7 or choosing Window | Layers again will hide the palette.

20

Hovering the mouse over any part of the Layers palette will bring up a small tooltip that describes that part of the palette.

Figure 20-1 shows a Layers palette for the grocery store illustration.

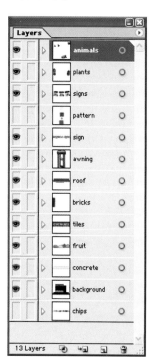

FIGURE 20-1 This illustration is broken into 13 layers.

There are two columns of icons to the left of each layer. The first column toggles visibility, allowing you to display or hide the selected layer. The second column toggles locking, which either allows you to edit a layer (unlocked) or prevents you from editing a layer (locked). Figure 20-2 illustrates the use of the Layers palette to lock the animals layer, preventing any accidental editing of the squirrel and his animal friends.

Change Layer Options

Sometimes you may want to work on a particular object and you need to have a clear, uncluttered view of it. Having your objects occupy different layers can be a real lifesaver at that time because you can control the visibility of separate layers.

FIGURE 20-2 Animals are protected—the layer is locked to prevent editing.

To toggle the visibility of any layer, simply click the Visibility icon (the small eye icon to the left of the layer's name in the Layers palette). Because this is a toggle, you can reverse the process by clicking the same area to make the layer visible again. (The eye will disappear, of course, indicating that the layer is hidden.) Figure 20-3 shows the grocery store with all but the animals layer hidden.

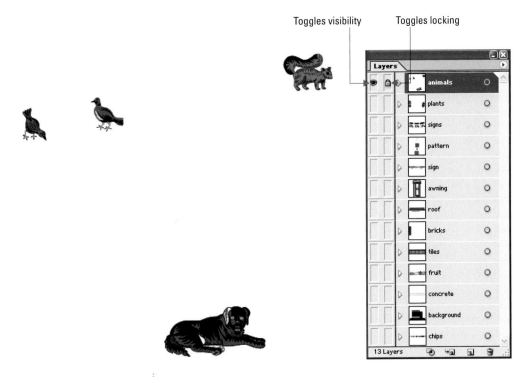

FIGURE 20-3 Each individual layer can be either visible or hidden, locked or editable.

Locking a layer prevents you from being able to select its contents. Thus, you can select objects on overlapping layers without affecting the objects on the locked layer. With a layer locked, you can click and drag the Selection tool to select partly obscured objects while preventing other objects from being selected.

To toggle the lock on a layer, click the space to the right of the Visibility icon next to the layer that you want to lock. Again, because this is a toggle, you can unlock the layer by clicking the small lock symbol that appears in the same space.

You can help the process along by using meaningful names for your layers. Naming a layer is quite easy. To name an existing layer, double-click the layer's entry in the Layers palette to open the Layer Options dialog box. In the space provided, enter a new name for the layer, as shown in Figure 20-4.

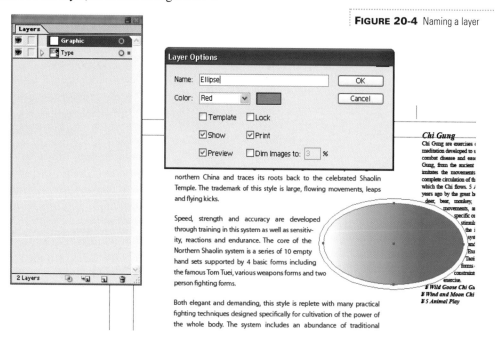

FIGURE 20-4 Naming a layer

Every layer has an icon associated with it. The icon is a small thumbnail representation of that layer's contents. Depending on the size and resolution of your screen, this thumbnail may be rather difficult to see. Fortunately, you can change the size of the thumbnail view.

Follow these steps to change the size of the thumbnail:

1. Open the Layers palette menu.

2. Choose Palette Options to open the Layers Palette Options dialog box.

3. In the Row Size area of the dialog box, choose Small, Medium, Large, or Other.

If you choose Other, enter a size (in pixels) at which you want the thumbnail to be displayed.

Layers are identified by both names and colors. You can accept the default setting for a layer color or set the color of any given layer yourself.

Follow these steps to set the color of a layer:

1. From the Layers palette menu, choose Options for "*Layer Name*". (The menu will show the actual layer name in this option instead of *Layer Name*.)

2. In the Layer Options dialog box, choose a color from the list or click the small color swatch to open the Color Picker dialog box.

3. After you select a color for your layer, click OK to close the Layer Options dialog box.

Create Layers

As you create more objects in an illustration, you should create them on their own separate layers, unless they are to be grouped together with objects on an existing layer. To create a new layer, click the Create New Layer button, located at the bottom of the

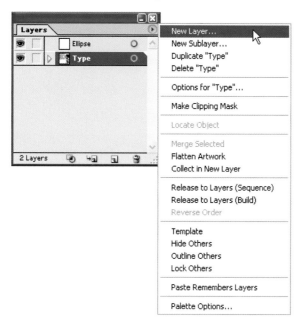

FIGURE 20-5 Creating a new layer

Layers palette, or choose New Layer from the Layers palette menu, as shown in Figure 20-5.

Sublayers, like layers, enable you to further organize your work. You can use sublayers to group like objects together under one layer and still have the same organizational control you do with layers. To create a new sublayer, click the Create New Sublayer button located at the bottom of the Layers palette.

You can create as many layers and sublayers as you need. Once you have created a layer, you can expand it to display all of its sublayers and objects by clicking the triangle to the left of the layer or sublayer (so that it points down). You can collapse the layer display by clicking the triangle again (so that it points to the right).

20

Use Layers to Organize Your Work

Sometimes you'll need to reorganize the layout of your illustrations. You may want to have certain objects appear below other objects rather than above them. With your work organized into layers and sublayers, this is an easy proposition. You can easily move layers around within the Layers palette. To change a layer's order, just click and drag it within the Layers palette.

You can drag a layer downward, effectively moving it below other layers, or drag it upward to move it above other layers. To change the order of a sublayer, click and drag the sublayer within the Layers palette. You can drag a sublayer downward, effectively moving it below other sublayers, or drag it upward to move it above other sublayers.

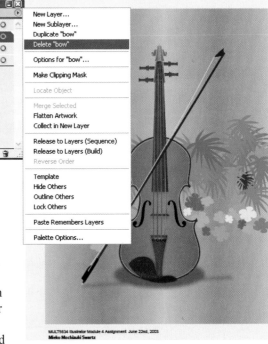

FIGURE 20-6 Deleting a layer to edit the illustration

Delete Layers

Not every object in your illustration makes it into the final illustration. For example, you might have a layer that contains a scanned bitmap image you used to build your illustration on top of. Or you might have layers that just display underlying outlines—again used to build artwork. Ditching these unnecessary layers will reduce the illustration's file size. And your client probably doesn't need to see all the elements you used to create the illustration.

You can remove layers *along with the objects they contain*. There are several ways to do this. You can remove a layer by selecting it in the Layers palette and then clicking the Delete Selection button in the lower-right corner of the Layers palette. Another way to delete a layer is to click and drag the layer onto the Delete Selection button. Mac users will find this intuitive because it follows the Mac trash bin metaphor. Yet another way to delete a layer is to select it, open the Layers palette menu, and choose Delete Selection, as shown in Figure 20-6.

Mieko Mochizuki Swartz

Duplicate Layers

Sometimes you will want to duplicate a layer. This approach is useful, for example, when you want to experiment with some of the artwork contained on a layer but want to be sure that the original artwork remains untouched. Another effective use for duplicate layers is to create animation frames. Animation often requires exact duplication of objects.

You can copy a layer by dragging and dropping an existing layer in the Layers palette onto the Create New Layer button at the bottom of the Layers palette. Or you can choose Duplicate "*Layer Name*" from the Layers palette menu, as shown in Figure 20-7.

FIGURE 20-7 Duplicating a layer

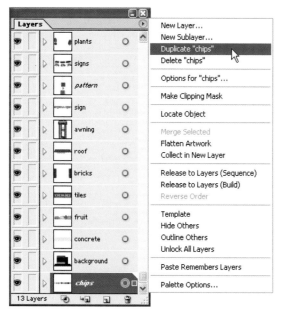

The layer will be called "Layer Name *copy", in which* Layer Name *is the actual name of the duplicated layer. To rename the copied layer, double-click it in the Layers palette and enter a new name in the Name box in the Layer Options dialog box.*

Consolidate Layers

Before you know it, you can end up with so many layers that you reduce their effectiveness. If your document has a hundred layers, applying effects or organizing your project might become unnecessarily complicated. For housekeeping purposes, you can collect layers with similar objects in them onto sublayers under one layer rather than keeping all of the objects on separate layers.

You can collect existing layers onto one layer by selecting the layers you want to collect. Start by clicking the first layer you want. You can then add to the selection by holding down SHIFT (to select contiguous layers) or COMMAND (CTRL) (to select noncontiguous layers). With the layers you want to collect selected, choose Collect in New Layer from the Layers palette menu, as shown in Figure 20-8.

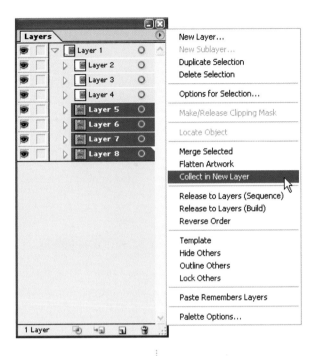

FIGURE 20-8 Consolidating several layers into a single layer with sublayers

Move Objects onto Separate Layers

Often you will begin work with a single layer or even several, but eventually your project will outgrow the layer structure you originally set up. You can move objects from one layer (or sublayer) to another by dragging them in the Layers palette. If you use large row sizes, you can see useful icons that help identify each object on a layer.

Manually organizing a major project into layers can be a big, time-consuming hassle! Fortunately, Illustrator has a couple of options for automating the process. You can automatically generate layers or sublayers for your illustration by using either the sequencing or the building feature in the Layers palette menu. You will learn to do that next.

Sequence Objects to New Layers

If you've created a number of objects on a layer and you'd like to have each of the objects on a separate layer, you can accomplish that task with relative ease. Rather than cutting and pasting each of the objects, you can release the objects to separate layers.

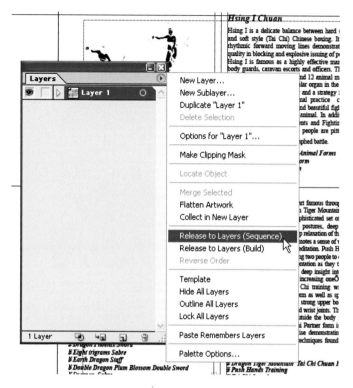

Sequencing creates a series of sublayers, each containing one of the objects from the original layer. To release objects to separate layers in sequence, choose Release to Layers (Sequence) from the Layers palette menu, as shown in Figure 20-9.

Build Layers

Another way to generate layers is to build a series of layers that contain the objects cumulatively. This technique is handy for creating series of layers for animation purposes. Each successive layer will contain one fewer object than the previous layer.

For example, you might have a layer with a rectangle, a triangle, and an ellipse. Choosing Release to Layers (Build) will create three layers; the first will have all three objects, the second will contain the rectangle and the triangle, and the last layer will contain only the rectangle.

To release objects to separate layers with the build option, choose Release to Layers (Build) from the Layers palette menu. Using this option to release objects to separate layers creates a series of sublayers containing an accumulation of the objects from the original layer, as described previously.

Merge or Flatten Layers

Earlier, in the "Consolidate Layers" section of this chapter, you learned to combine layers by reducing several layers to sublayers. For even more drastic simplification of your project, you can simply combine all the elements of two or more layers into a single layer—without any sublayers.

Reducing the number of layers saves memory. And, in some cases, it can eliminate layers that simply end up making a project unnecessarily complicated. You combine layers by *merging* them.

20

To merge a series of layers, select the layers you want to merge by holding down COMMAND (CTRL) and clicking to select the layers you want to merge. With the layers you want to merge selected, open the Layers palette menu and choose Merge Selected, as shown in Figure 20-10.

FIGURE 20-10 Making a project simpler by merging layers

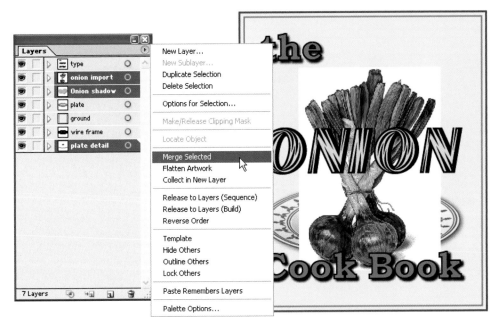

 If the layers are contiguous, you can select a group of layers by clicking the first layer you want merged and then pressing SHIFT *and clicking the last layer you want merged.*

To save space in a file, especially after you're done doing all of your tricky editing, you may want to flatten *all* of the layers in your illustration. Flattening the layers places all of your artwork onto a single layer. To flatten the layers in your illustration, choose Flatten Artwork from the Layers palette menu.

Change Layer Display

You can also use the Layers palette to change the way artwork is displayed. You can choose from Preview view or Outline view. When computers were much slower, it was often better to have objects displayed in Outline view to avoid the slow redrawing times of objects displayed in Preview view. These days, that seems less important, but it's still often handy to see selected layers in Outline view when you want to be able to easily identify paths and aren't so interested in fills.

To change the view of all objects on all layers, first select the *top* layer, and then choose either Outline All Layers or Preview All Layers from the Layers palette menu. To change the view for one layer, double-click the layer's name in the Layers palette. In the Layer Options dialog box, select or deselect the Preview check box.

Or you can select one layer and choose Outline Others from the Layers palette menu. Figure 20-11 shows the grocery store illustration with everything but the animals in Outline view.

FIGURE 20-11 All layers but the animals layer are in Outline view.

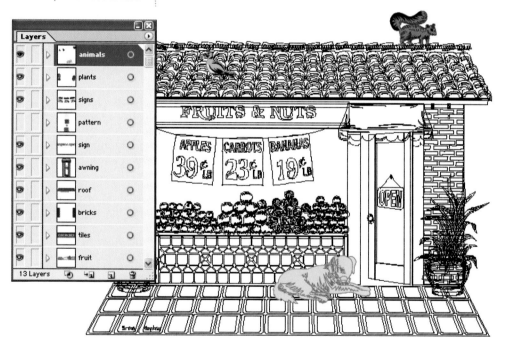

 *Another way to toggle between Outline and Preview views is to press* COMMAND *(*CTRL*) and click the eye icon in the Layers palette. The eye icon will appear hollow for layers with Outline view set.*

Find Objects on a Layer

In complex illustrations, it can be difficult to locate objects in the Layers palette. The Locate Object menu option solves the problem. When you select an object anywhere on or off the artboard with the Selection tool, you can easily locate the corresponding object in the Layers palette.

Find a selected object in the Layers palette by choosing Locate Object from the Layers palette menu. The selected artwork's expanded layer or sublayer will appear in the Layers palette, as shown in Figure 20-12.

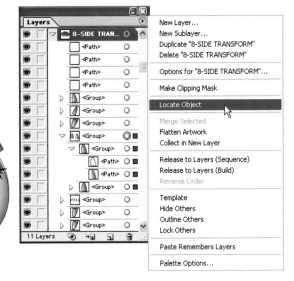

Set Transparency with Layers

One of the most powerful ways to give depth and dimension to an illustration is to have objects appear through other objects—in effect, having the uppermost objects be transparent to some degree.

You can control the transparency of layers in Illustrator by using the Transparency palette. To view the Transparency palette, choose Window | Transparency or press SHIFT-F10. This action is a toggle: it will turn on the palette if it's not visible and turn it off if it is visible.

To change the transparency of a layer, select the layer by clicking its name in the Layers palette, and then change the Opacity setting in the Transparency palette, as shown in Figure 20-13.

FIGURE 20-13 Making all of the objects on the background layer 50 percent transparent

For a full discussion of transparency and opacity, see Chapter 17.

Use Scanned Artwork as a Template Layer

A popular method of creating artwork in Illustrator is to scan in existing hand-drawn artwork to use as a template for re-creating the artwork with Illustrator's drawing tools. Many cartoonists, for example, will draw their creations in pencil or pen, scan the resulting artwork in Photoshop, and then use the scanned work as a template in Illustrator to draw the lines, shapes, and text. This artwork can then be saved and imported back into Photoshop, where final touchups and effects can be added.

Illustrator has the capacity to display layers as templates to make this process much easier. Follow these steps to automatically generate a template layer:

1. Create a layer you wish to use as a template. For example, scan a graphic and place it on a layer.

2. Double-click the layer.

FIGURE 20-14 Using scanned artwork as a non-printing layer

3. Select the Template check box in the Layer Options dialog box.

A non-printing layer is shown in Figure 20-14.

You can make any layer, not just a template layer, non-printing. To prevent a layer from being printed, deselect the Print button in the Layer palette.

Select Layer Objects

It's easy to select all objects on any given layer. You can, of course, use the Selection tool to select any object or number of objects. There are other ways to select all objects on a layer, though, by using the Layers palette itself. You may find that these options save you time.

To select all of the objects contained on a layer, click the right edge of a layer in the Layers palette or press OPTION (ALT) and click the layer name in the Layers palette, as shown in Figure 20-15.

FIGURE 20-15 Selecting all the objects on a layer

  Selecting all objects on a layer makes it easy to edit or delete them.

Chapter 21

Apply Graphic Styles, Symbols, and Actions

How to...

- Use graphic styles, symbols, and actions
- Apply graphic styles
- Create new graphic styles
- Unlink and change graphic styles
- Apply graphic styles to an entire layer
- Use actions
- Create actions
- Save and share actions
- Save time with swatches
- Use symbols
- Add, replace, and edit symbols
- Create and delete symbols

Graphic styles, actions, swatches, and symbols are all different ways to save time and avoid boring, repetitive activity while creating artwork in Illustrator.

Graphic styles are sets of attributes—such as stroke, fill, transparency, and so on—that can be applied all at once to any object.

Actions are recorded steps that can be used for anything from applying a complex set of filters to an object to saving a selected object as a browser-compatible GIF image. Illustrator comes with a nice list of carefully defined, useful actions, and it's worthwhile to check them out and use them as needed. Using an action is like applying a set of commands to the chosen artwork. In other applications, this process is referred to as "using a macro." When you apply an action, it's as if you applied a series of steps to a piece of artwork.

Swatches can save you time by storing commonly used colors. If your client provides you with a set of defined colors for his or her project, stash them in the Swatches palette to save time in designing the project.

Symbols are graphic objects that can be placed in artwork. What's special about them is that they can be easily updated or replaced throughout an illustration.

21

Use Graphic Styles

A graphic style is a named set of appearance attributes that you can apply to objects in your artwork. Using Illustrator's built-in styles is a great way to save time when you create artwork. The graphic styles don't actually change the underlying paths in your artwork; instead, they affect the *appearance* of objects. In other words, a style is *linked* to an object.

If the linked style is changed in some way, that change affects the appearance of every object to which the style is applied. In Figure 21-1, a watercolor style has been applied.

FIGURE 21-1 A watercolor style has been applied to the parrot on the right.

Tip

If you're familiar with the use of type styles in desktop publishing, or even paragraph styles in word processors (or character or paragraph styles in Illustrator), you're familiar with the concept of attached, revisable styles. The concept is the same here—except that the assigned attributes are graphical.

Open and Load Up the Graphic Styles Palette

Several palettes of different kinds of pre-set graphic styles are built into Illustrator CS. You can see them by opening the Graphic Styles palette (choose Window | Graphic Styles).

The Graphic Styles palette needs to be "loaded" with either homemade graphic styles or with graphic styles added from the various graphic style libraries. To add a graphic style, choose Open Graphic Style Library from the Graphic Styles palette menu. Click on one of the various libraries, as shown in Figure 21-2.

As you click on graphic styles in any of the graphic style libraries, those styles are added to the Graphic Styles palette for your current document. You apply a style to a selected object by clicking on the style—either in the Graphic Styles palette or in one of the various graphic style library palettes.

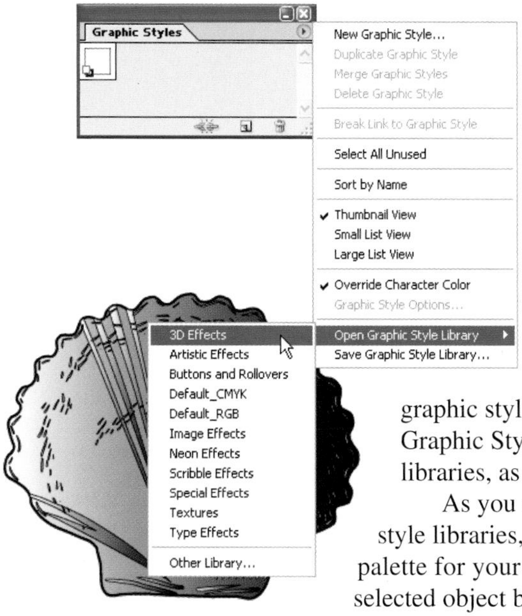

FIGURE 21-2 Checking out the graphic style libraries

You can read the fanciful names of the available graphic styles by hovering the mouse pointer over a style in the Graphic Styles palette. After a short pause, the name of the style will appear.

Apply Graphic Styles

You can apply a graphic style to any object, but that's using only a fraction of the power of these macro-effects. You can also apply a graphic style to a group of objects, a sublayer, or a layer. Keep in mind that when you apply a style to a group, sublayer, or layer, that style will be applied to all of the objects therein.

A style can store dozens of attributes (including effects, stroke and fill settings, and transparency settings), so applying a style serves as a shortcut for individually applying a whole set of graphic styles to objects one by one. Of course, all this processing adds to file size and also puts some stress on your computer's processing resources.

Caution *As you explore the various graphic style libraries, you will want to avoid applying graphic styles to an object by mistake, since many styles take a long time and a lot of memory to apply. Double-check to be sure you don't have any objects selected before you start investigating the graphic style libraries. A quick way to deselect everything in your document is to choose Select | Deselect from the menu.*

Apply a Style to an Object or Group

To apply a style to an object or group of objects, first make sure the object or group is selected. You can select an object by clicking it with the Selection tool.

After selecting the objects to which you will apply a style, simply click on a style in the Graphic Styles palette (or a graphic style library). Figure 21-3 shows a style from the Textures graphic library being applied.

Create a New Graphic Style

Graphic styles are useful time-savers. But the graphic styles feature is also a creativity tool. You can define your own graphic styles, save them, and then apply them to add continuity and

FIGURE 21-3 Applying the RGB Brick style to all the bricks

21

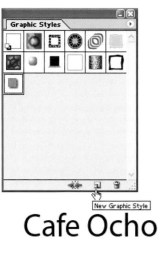

theme to an illustration. Graphic styles can contain any number of colors, fills, strokes, patterns, and so on.

This means you can create some fairly complex graphic styles. You can also create simple graphic styles such as fills and drop shadows, too. Even then, you'll find that creating a style will end up saving you plenty of time in the long run.

Follow these steps to create a style using the easiest method:

1. Create an object, either a line or a shape.

2. Apply to the object whatever effects, filters, fill or stroke color, and so on you want in your style.

3. With the object selected, click the New Graphic Style button in the Graphic Styles palette, as shown in Figure 21-4. Doing so will automatically create your new style.

4. Double-click the icon for your new style, and enter a name for your style in the Graphic Style Options dialog box, as shown in Figure 21-5.

FIGURE 21-4 Defining a style that includes a defined drop shadow, inner glow, and diffuse glow

FIGURE 21-5 Naming a style

5. Click OK in the Graphic Style Options dialog box to save the style.

Once you have defined your custom style, you can add it to any object just as you would assign a style from Illustrator's graphic style libraries: Select an object and click on the graphic style to apply it.

Tip

As you apply styles to objects, the Appearance palette will identify all the attributes assigned via the style.

Unlink a Graphic Style

As mentioned, graphic styles are linked and applied to objects in your artwork. But they are not *permanently* applied to them. You can break the link between an object, or set of objects, and its graphic styles.

Breaking a style link *does not remove the appearance of the style*. Instead, it makes the changes you applied via the style permanent changes to the object.

 You can always select Edit | Undo to undo this change, but only if you haven't closed and reopened your file—and, of course, if you've done a lot of work since you assigned the style, you'd have to undo it all to undo the graphic style.

Follow these steps to unlink a style from an object or set of objects:

1. Select the object or objects.

2. Click the Break Link to Graphic Style button in the Graphic Styles palette, as shown in Figure 21-6.

FIGURE 21-6 Breaking a style link

Clear Formatting and Delete a Graphic Style

Trying to *get rid* of the effect of a style? If you want to *clear* all the formatting applied by the graphic style, you can select the object and click on the Reduce to Basic Appearance button in the Appearance palette.

If you no longer need a particular style, you can delete it. Deleting a style breaks the link to objects that have had the style applied, but it does not remove or change the appearance of those objects. To delete a style, drag it onto the Delete Graphic Style (trash bin) button at the bottom of the Graphic Styles palette.

Change a Graphic Style

As is true with styles that are applied in a word processor, a desktop publisher, or web-supported style sheets, Illustrator's graphic styles are changeable. After you create a style, you can later edit its appearance, and the changes will be applied automatically to every object to which the style is linked.

You can edit graphic styles using a combination of the Graphic Styles and Appearance palettes. Use these steps to edit an existing style:

FIGURE 21-7 Examining attributes associated with a style

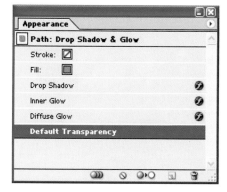

1. Deselect any selected objects (choose Select | Deselect) so that you look at and edit only the attributes of a style.

2. Select the style by clicking its icon in the Graphic Styles palette.

3. View the Appearance palette (choose Window | Appearance). Here you'll see all the attributes assigned to your style, as shown in Figure 21-7.

4. In the Appearance palette, double-click any of the attributes of the selected style to open the appropriate palette. For example, if you click Default Transparency, the Transparency palette opens, and you can change the opacity/ transparency setting for the style.

5. With the changes made, select Redefine Graphic Style "*Style Name*" from the Appearance palette menu, as shown in Figure 21-8.

FIGURE 21-8 Redefining a style to add new attributes

 Other changeable style attributes include stroke and fill.

Remember, changing a style *affects the appearance of any objects to which the style has been applied.*

Use Graphic Styles with Layers

In addition to applying graphic styles to objects, you can target layers and sublayers for graphic styles. You can apply predetermined graphic styles, such as drop shadows, buttons, and textures, to the objects located on any given layer or sublayer. Applying these types of effects would normally require a great deal of work if you were to try to apply them without the use of Illustrator's graphic styles.

You get graphic styles and layers to work together by using the target icon in the Layers palette and the available graphic styles in the Graphic Styles palette. The target icon, which has four different appearances, is just to the right of a layer's name in the Layers palette. This rather tiny icon displays with subtle (hard to see!) differences that vary depending on the graphic styles that are associated with the layer.

Normally, when not all of the objects on a layer are selected, the icon will appear as an empty circle, even if some of the objects are selected. If all of the objects on a layer are selected, the target icon will have another circle drawn around it: that is, the icon will consist of two circles, one inside the other. Figure 21-9 shows a layer whose objects are all selected.

If the inner circle is empty, it means that the layer is targeted but has no style or appearance attributes associated with it. If the target icon has a single circle with a filled, three-dimensional appearance, the selected layer has style or appearance attributes associated with it but is not currently targeted, as shown in Figure 21-10.

If the target icon has a filled, three-dimensional appearance and an additional concentric circle outside the inner circle, the layer has a style or appearance attribute associated with it and is currently targeted.

Selected layer

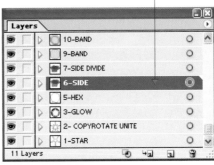

FIGURE 21-9 The second circle indicates that all objects on the layer are selected.

FIGURE 21-10 A selected layer with a style applied to the entire layer.

A filled-in circle showing that a style is applied

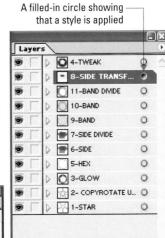

To target a layer, click the target icon on the layer. To target a sublayer, click the target icon on the sublayer. With a layer or sublayer targeted, you can apply a style by clicking the style you wish to apply in the Graphic Styles palette.

Note   *Graphic styles are saved along with your artwork when you save your Illustrator file.*

Use Actions

Actions are like macros—they collect and automate many functions and allow you to apply a whole set of collected keystrokes or mouse-clicks. You can use actions for a wide range of purposes, from automating printer settings to applying a set of effects to an object.

Illustrator comes with an underrated and useful set of pre-defined actions. Using one of these built-in actions is as simple as selecting it from the Actions palette. To view the Actions palette, choose Window | Actions.

The Actions palette includes sets of steps that apply formatting changes, such as rotation or path simplification, to a selected object. Other actions allow you to perform file operations, such as exporting a selected object to a browser-friendly JPEG image. The Actions palette is shown in Figure 21-11.

FIGURE 21-11 Exploring the Actions palette. The Transparency action is assigning 60-percent opacity.

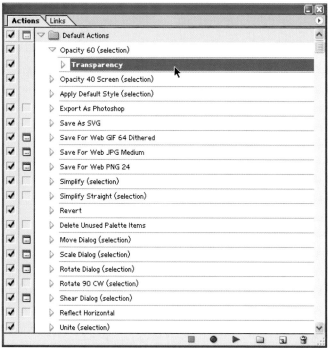

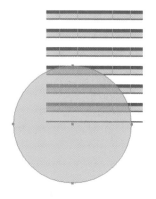

If you expand an action (click the triangle next to it so
that the triangle is pointing down), you can see all the tasks
that action will perform. For example, the action selected in
Figure 21-12 will save the selected object as a GIF image, with

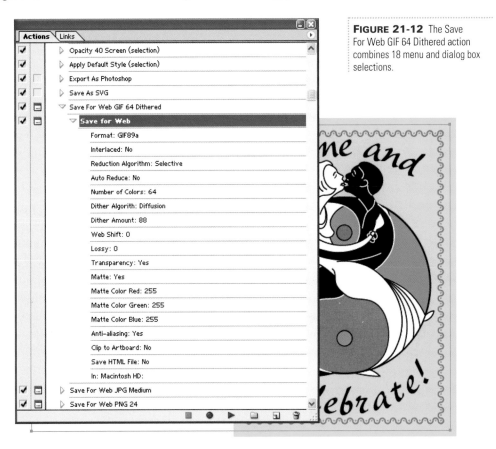

FIGURE 21-12 The Save
For Web GIF 64 Dithered action
combines 18 menu and dialog box
selections.

transparency (the background color will be hidden) and no
interlacing (it won't phase in, but instead will appear all at once
in a browser). And the action even includes instructions about
which folder to save the file to on the hard disk. That not only
saves a bunch of work, it also helps you make sound decisions
about the best file attributes to use when exporting a selected
image for the Web.

Note *Some of the default actions require that an object be selected. This is usually reflected by*
the fact that the word "selection" is displayed parenthetically after the action's name.

To apply an action, simply click the action's name in the Actions palette and then click the Play button in the Actions palette, at the bottom of the palette.

Create an Action

Creating an action can be an elaborate process. How elaborate depends on what you're trying to accomplish. Something like creating rounded rectangle buttons for a web page can be done without too much effort. Of course, the more elaborate the effort in the beginning, the more work your action will save you in the long run.

The following steps use a simple example to illustrate how actions work. The action you define will create a simple rounded rectangle button that you can use on a web page. Follow these steps to create this action from scratch:

FIGURE 21-13 Beginning to define a new action

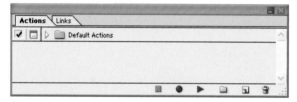

1. Click the Create New Action button at the bottom of the Actions palette, as shown in Figure 21-13. It resembles a page with its lower-left corner bent upward.

2. The New Action dialog box appears. Enter a name for your action and choose a set where it will reside. It's safe to leave it at the default, Default Actions, if you wish. (You'll explore what sets are and how to create them in the "Save an Action" section later in this chapter.) Click Record. As soon as you do so, the new action begins capturing your keystrokes.

3. Select the Rounded Rectangle tool and draw a rounded rectangle somewhere on the artboard.

4. Select the Gradient tool and set the gradient to a white-to-black linear gradient in the Gradient palette. (Gradients are explained in Chapter 16.)

5. Drag the Gradient tool from the left side of the rectangle to the right side to fill the object with the gradient.

6. Choose Edit | Copy.

7. Choose Edit | Paste In Front to duplicate the object.

8. Choose Object | Transform | Scale, and enter **90 percent** in the Scale window under Uniform.

9. Choose Object | Transform | Rotate, and enter **180 degrees** in the Angle box.

10. Click the Stop Playing/Recording button at the bottom of the Actions palette.

If you followed the steps above, you created an action. To test the action, first select the objects you created and press DELETE to clear the artboard. Then select your action in the Actions palette and click the Play button. If everything worked right, the action should create a rounded rectangle button for you.

Tip *If you click in the Toggle Dialog On/Off column in the Actions palette (next to the action name), you can turn on (or disable) dialog boxes for options in your action. Turning on dialog boxes allows the person playing the action to make selections in dialog boxes throughout the process, while disabling dialog box applies default dialog box settings or settings you define as you record the macro.*

Manage Actions

The beauty of actions is that all you need to do is click the mouse a couple of times to have all the work done for you. Even better, though, is that you can create your own actions and *share them*.

You share actions by first saving them. Then they can be reused—in other files on your computer, or even by other users. If you no longer need an action, you can clear a little memory by deleting it.

Save an Action

To save an action, you must create it in a new set. You can create a new set when you first create an action, or you can create a set by clicking the Create New Set button (it looks like a folder) at the bottom of the Actions palette. If you create a set after you have defined an action, you can drag the action into the new set folder in the Actions dialog box to include it among those to save.

 *To clarify: you can only save a set of actions, you can't save actions that are not part of a set. The easiest way to do this is to define a new set and then, with the new set selected in the Actions palette, start defining a new action.*

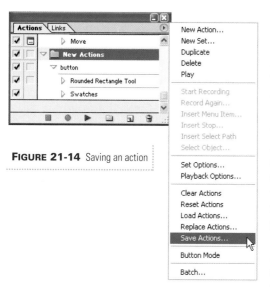

FIGURE 21-14 Saving an action

Once you have created a set, choose Save Actions from the Actions palette menu, as shown in Figure 21-14. The Save Set To: dialog box will open. From within that dialog box, you can choose a location for your action set and give it a filename.

Share Actions

Any set of actions that you've saved can be shared with other files or with other Illustrator artists. To share a set of actions, simply locate the file that you saved the set to and copy that file onto a disk, e-mail it to someone, or place it on the Web for others to share.

An action set file is saved with the extension .aia, and these files are cross-platform compatible. That is, actions created on a PC should work on a Mac, and vice versa. Once you have an action on disk, you can add it to the Actions palette by choosing Load Actions from the Actions palette menu and then navigating to the file.

Delete an Action

If you have an action that you have no further use for, you can delete it by selecting it in the Actions palette and clicking the small trash bin button in the Actions palette. Alternatively, you can drag and drop the action from the palette onto the trash bin button, or you can select the action and choose Delete from the Actions palette menu.

Use Swatches to Save Work

Chapters 16 and 18 briefly noted the use of *swatches* to store color sets and customized patterns. Here it's helpful to focus on how you can save time by building up a collection of swatches—including color, gradient, and pattern swatches—to use and reuse as you create your artwork.

The Swatches palette is fairly simple to work with. If it is not visible, simply choose Window | Swatches (which works as a toggle). The buttons at the bottom of the palette offer these options (from left to right): Show All Swatches, Show Color

Swatches, Show Gradient Swatches, Show Pattern Swatches, New Swatch, and Delete Swatch.

After you've created a swatch, Illustrator assigns it a default name. You can rename the swatch by double-clicking its thumbnail. The Swatch Options dialog box opens, as shown in Figure 21-15, enabling you to rename the swatch.

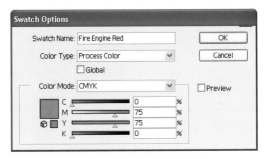

FIGURE 21-15 Renaming a swatch

To delete a swatch that you've created, select the swatch's thumbnail in the Swatches palette and either drag and drop it onto the trash bin button or simply click the trash bin button with the thumbnail selected. Note that deleting a swatch has no effect on objects that have had the swatch applied to them.

Use Symbols

Like swatches and graphic styles, *symbols* are great time-savers. They can be especially helpful when you need to add clipart-like images to your artwork. Symbols, like graphic styles, can be updated throughout an illustration.

So, for example, if your organization's logo changes midway through an art project, you can instantly update that object throughout an illustration if the logo was saved as a symbol. In this sense, symbols in Illustrator are similar to symbols in Macromedia's Flash and other programs that use stored, editable symbol objects.

The Symbols palette displays all of the currently available symbols. At the bottom of the palette are several buttons that help you control and use the available symbols. They are identified in the Figure 21-16.

Like the Graphic Styles palette, the Symbols palette has to be "loaded" with symbols from libraries. Choose Open Symbol Library from the Symbols palette menu, and then choose one of the symbol libraries from the submenu. With the Symbols palette open, just click on symbols in any symbol library palette to add them to the Symbols palette and make them easily accessible.

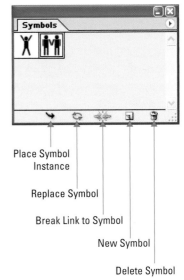

FIGURE 21-16 The symbols palette

Place Symbol Instance

Replace Symbol

Break Link to Symbol

New Symbol

Delete Symbol

Add, Replace, and Edit Symbols

You can easily add existing symbols to any open file. To add a symbol to your artwork, select the symbol you want from the Symbols palette and click the Place Symbol Instance button at the bottom of the Symbols palette.

You can also apply a kind of search-and-replace procedure using symbols, substituting one symbol for another throughout an illustration. Follow these steps to replace an existing symbol in your artwork:

FIGURE 21-17 Replacing one selected symbol with another

1. Select symbol instances (on your artboard) using the Selection tool.

2. Select the new symbol you want to use in the Symbols palette.

3. Click the Replace Symbol button at the bottom of the Symbols palette, as shown in Figure 21-17.

Breaking a link to a symbol removes the link between the symbol and the object. The object then becomes the series of editable objects that were used to create the symbol. Use the steps below to break the link to a symbol:

1. Select the symbol object using the Selection tool.

2. Click the Break Link to Symbol button at the bottom of the Symbols palette.

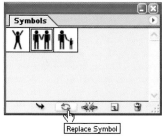

Create or Delete Symbols

You can create your own symbols, which can be handy when you want to create multiple instances of objects and preserve objects for later use.

Follow the steps below to create a new symbol:

1. Create an object or group of objects.

2. Select the object or objects with the Selection tool.

3. Click the New Symbol button at the bottom of the Symbols palette.

You can remove any symbols you no longer need. To delete an existing symbol, simply select the symbol in the Symbols palette and click the Delete Symbol button at the bottom of the Symbols palette.

Part VII

From Illustrator to Print and Web

Chapter 22

Print Illustrations

How to…

- Understand print options
- Print an Illustrator document on a desktop printer
- Export an Illustrator document to a printer-friendly format
- Prepare a file for commercial color printing
- Define process colors for your document
- Prepare process color separations
- Prepare for spot color printing
- Create crop marks

There are basically three possibilities for printing your artwork. The first is to print it yourself on your desktop printer or on one of the increasingly affordable commercial-quality color printers available for the office. The second is to send it to a commercial printer. The third and probably most widely used option is to submit your artwork to someone else for inclusion in a book, brochure, newspaper, magazine, or other publication.

For those of you who will be taking their artwork to a commercial printer or submitting it to someone else for inclusion in a publication, the advice in this chapter boils down to one sentence: Check with your printer or publisher and find out what specifications they have for file types!

If your artwork will be incorporated into a larger publication, someone is probably going to embed it in a file managed with a desktop publishing program such as Quark, InDesign, PageMaker, or even a Microsoft Office application such as Word, PowerPoint, or Publisher. In that instance, you will probably need to export your artwork into a file format accessible to the team managing the publication.

Preview Print Colors on Your Monitor

You can have Illustrator "tune" your monitor to display colors that look more like the colors you'll get when you print your

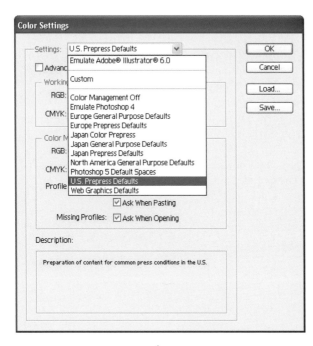

FIGURE 22-1 The U.S. Prepress Defaults setting reflects color settings used by many commercial print shops in the United States. Many other regional options are also available.

document. The first step in doing that is to select a color setting. Do that by choosing Illustrator (Edit) | Color Settings. The Color Settings dialog box appears. From the Settings drop-down menu in the dialog box, choose the appropriate prepress default settings for your part of the world. Figure 22-1 shows settings for the United States.

If you are previewing work that will be produced by a commercial print shop, you can consult your print shop for advice on which setting to select. Or they may provide you with more detailed setting information and you can customize the Color Settings dialog box based on that information.

Once you have defined a color setting in the Color Settings dialog box, click OK. Now (and only now) you can tune your monitor colors to more closely match print output. Follow these steps to synchronize your monitor colors with your printer's colors:

1. With your document open, choose View | Proof Setup | Custom.

2. In the Proof Setup dialog box, choose your printer or one close to it from the Profile list.

3. Click OK in the Proof Setup dialog box.

4. Choose View | Proof Colors to enable your monitor to simulate printed color.

Usually printed colors will be darker than the backlit RGB colors generated by your monitor.

Print on Your Own Printer

If you need to produce just a small number of copies of your illustration, it might be appropriate to use your desktop printer. Modern desktop printers do a reasonably good job of presenting the colors you have assigned in Illustrator.

Beyond that, technological developments have made it possible and financially wise for many companies and organizations to invest in commercial-quality printers for runs of up to several thousand copies of a publication. You'll manage your print job using Illustrator CS's improved Print dialog box. The new Print dialog box allows you to preview how your document will be cropped when printed. By default, the printable section of your illustration is generally the section of the artboard within the page layout.

Select File | Print to open the Print dialog box. The General category replaces your operating system's basic print dialog box and allows you to control basic print features such as choice of printer and scaling. (The options are no scaling, scaling to fit your printed page, and custom scaling.) In addition, you can use the Print Layers drop-down list to choose between printing visible and printed layers (the default), visible layers, or all layers.

FIGURE 22-2 Choosing options for cropping a document

You can define cropping options in the Setup category of the Print dialog box. Aside from cropping to the artboard, you can crop to the artwork's bounding box (the rectangle around the actual artwork in your document) or to crop marks (created by drawing over your document with a rectangle and choosing Object | Crop Area | Make). Figure 22-2 shows the options for cropping in the Print dialog box.

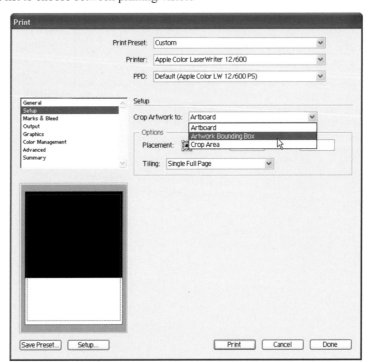

The Marks & Bleed category in the Print dialog box allows you to print any or all of the trim marks, registration marks, and other information a commercial printer *might* want. Normally you won't use these features when printing from your own printer.

The Output category allows you to print separate sheets for separated colors (cyan, magenta, yellow, and black). Color separations are not normally used for projects that are printed from your own printer.

The relevant option for using your own printer in the Graphics category of the Print dialog box is the Flatness slider. The Automatic check box is usually appropriate for printing on your own computer, but you can deselect it and manually define flatness using the slider, electing any setting from Quality (the best quality for curves) to Speed (the lousiest quality—curves will be distorted but printing is fastest).

The Color Management category in the Print dialog box reflects the color settings you have defined for your document.

The Advanced category allows you to choose printer resolution—either High, Medium, Low, or custom settings (click the Custom button). These options vary depending on the capacity of your printer. You can also use the Overprints drop-down menu to define how to manage overprints. The concept of overprinting is explained in the "Overprint" section later in this chapter.

The Summary category of the Print dialog box lists your settings and even allows you to save them as a text file by clicking the Save Summary button. The Summary category also lists potential issues that can affect your printing.

Export to Other File Formats

Illustrator has four native vector file formats to which you can save files: Illustrator (AI) format, Encapsulated PostScript (EPS) format, Portable Document File (PDF) format, and Scalable Vector Graphics (SVG or SVG compressed) format. Save to any of these formats by choosing File | Save As and choosing a format from the Save As dialog box. (The specific options available vary depending on your operating system.)

There are advantages and disadvantages to using each of these formats.

■ Illustrator's AI files open fully editable in Illustrator. If you use the File | Export dialog box to save to an older version of Illustrator, you'll create a version of the file that can be opened in the older version. In general, all of the features that you have assigned are preserved in the down-versioned file, but some features, such as transparency, will not be editable. Therefore, if you save to an older version of Illustrator, you should save a separate version of the file in Illustrator CS.

- Encapsulated PostScript (EPS) files also open fully editable in Illustrator. This format is more widely supported than Illustrator's AI file format. Your print shop or desktop publisher is likely to prefer EPS files to AI files.

- Portable Document File (PDF) files preserve only some of the features and effects assigned in Illustrator, and they are not fully editable. PDF files are very widely supported and can be opened and read by anyone with Adobe Acrobat Reader.

- Scalable Vector Graphics (SVG) files (or Compressed Scalable Vector Graphics SVGZ files) are used with XML and web publishing and are not editable in Illustrator.

When you save to either EPS or PDF formats, you can generate a *thumbnail* (a small preview version of the illustration). Saving to either of these formats also allows you to embed fonts with the file so that it can be opened even if the recipient's system does not have all the fonts in the document.

All four of the native file formats preserve the scalability and reduced file size typical of vector graphics.

 *If you save a file without embedding fonts, and if the recipient does not have those fonts on his or her system, the recipient will be prompted to substitute a different font when opening the file.*

More Export Options

Along with supporting popular generic raster file formats, Illustrator also allows you to export to various proprietary formats, including Adobe's own Photoshop format. However, you can open Illustrator files right in Photoshop, so in most cases that's a simpler and more effective option.

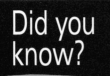 **Export to Raster Formats**

It's generally preferable to maintain a vector format for Illustrator artwork. However, sometimes publication specs require a file to be submitted in a raster format such as TIFF (Transport Independent File Format) or PICT. Saving Illustrator artwork to raster formats is covered in Chapter 23.

22

Illustrator CS has added the Save for Microsoft Office option to the File menu. Microsoft's Office suite (including Word, PowerPoint, and Excel) uses the PNG format as its native compressed image format. While most Office installations can import or use dozens of graphic file formats, PNG is the standard and most widely supported, even for users who have elected to do minimal installation for Office. When you choose File | Save for Microsoft Office from the menu, Illustrator saves your open document in PNG format.

Other supported file formats include the CAD format used in technical design programs such as AutoCAD, the TGA (Targa) format used in video production, and the Windows Metafile (WMF) format that incorporates vector images into Windows documents.

Prepare Files for Commercial Color Printing

Your computer monitor creates colors by mixing together tiny red, green, and blue pixels. In contrast, printed color is created by mixing and overlaying different ink colors. There are two basic approaches to color printing. The *spot color* method usually involves two or possibly three colors. The other option, process color, will be discussed later in this chapter.

While spot color usually involves just one color (in addition to black), you can use different gradations of spot colors to produce complex color effects. For example, if you use red as a spot color, you can overprint a 50-percent-transparency red over a black design to achieve a redish tint, or you can use 50-percent-transparency red to create pink.

Tricks and Tips for Printing

As you prepare your artwork for commercial printing, you'll find that an understanding of a few helpful terms and concepts will allow you to communicate clearly with your printer and ensure that your artwork appears as you want it to look.

Caution *The explanations that follow are—as noted—to help you communicate with your printer if he or she asks you to apply any of these processes to your document. Normally, your printer or publisher will manage these features, and in any case, you won't want to tamper with or experiment with any of these features unless you've been given specific instructions from your print shop on how to apply them.*

Bleeding is not as violent as it sounds; it's a process for allowing ink to extend to the edge of a piece of paper or other material. *Trapping* is a way of handling four-color printing that minimizes the tacky look you sometimes see in color newspaper photos when the different colors aren't properly aligned. And *overprinting* is a way to manage how colors are laid down on top of one another.

Bleed

Many times you will want your final artwork to extend to the very edge of the material on which it is printed. Because no printing press prints all the way to the very edge of the paper, fabric, plastic, or whatever, material is trimmed after printing so that it conforms to the edge of the artwork.

To a viewer, it will appear as if your artwork was printed to the very edge of the paper or other material, but in reality, this effect will have been achieved by the trimming of the material. You can define a bleed area in the Print dialog box, or you can ask your printer or preprint service bureau to bleed your artwork to the edge of the page. In either case, you will want to design an area of your artwork that extends beyond the area that will appear in the final output.

In other words, you need to create a bit of artwork that will be cut off and thrown away during the final production process. A simple way to do this is to create a large filled rectangle behind your artwork that can be trimmed.

Trap Colors

Because printers apply colors by using up to four color plates, the plates must match perfectly so that the final output doesn't have a blurry, mismatched look. The process of matching plates is called *registration.* However, in the real world, plates don't always match perfectly.

Trapping is a technique for creating some overlap between colors to avoid registration errors. Before you assign trapping, make sure you are using the CMYK color model. One quick way to do this is to choose File | Document Color Mode | CMYK Color.

Follow these steps to assign trapping for two or more overlapping objects:

1. Select the overlapping objects to which you will apply trapping.

22

FIGURE 22-3 Applying a trap to overlapping objects

2. View the Pathfinder palette by selecting Window | Pathfinder.

3. Select Trap from the Pathfinder palette menu, as shown in Figure 22-3. The Pathfinder Trap dialog box opens.

4. In the Thickness area of the Pathfinder Trap dialog box, enter a stroke width. The value must be between 0.01 and 5000 points.

5. The Height/Width box allows you to change the relative size of the horizontal trap compared to the vertical trap. For now, leave this at the default setting of 100 percent.

6. The Tint Reduction box defines how much of the overlap area will have the color of the lighter color in the overlap. For now, leave this at the default setting of 40 percent, which creates a smooth merging between lighter and darker colors.

7. Select the Traps With Process Color check box to convert spot colors to process colors.

8. Generally, trapping is done by expanding the lighter color of the overlapping colors. In some rare cases where the overlapping colors are close in darkness, you might want to reverse the process and expand the darker color. You can select the Reverse Traps check box to reverse trapping.

9. After you have defined your trap options for the selected objects, click OK.

Overprint

Overprinting is another way to guard against misregistration in process color printing. When two different-colored objects overlap in process printing, the bottom object is normally cut away during printing. This ensures that the color of the top object and the color of the bottom object do not mix or blend. This method of printing produces clean, uncorrupted colors just as you assign them in Illustrator.

The downside is that if registration is slightly off, odd spacing or awkward overlapping will occur between the objects. By assigning overprinting, you can add the color of a top object to that of a bottom object when objects overlap. The printed result is less vulnerable to misregistration.

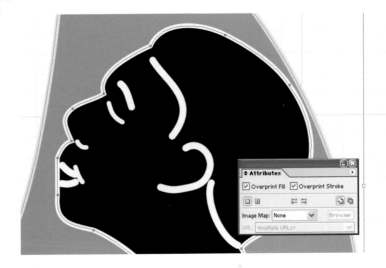

FIGURE 22-4 To prevent misregistration errors and blurriness, the top object will be overprinted on the background.

Follow these steps to assign overprinting to overlapping objects:

1. Select both (or all) objects to be overprinted.

2. Choose Window | Attributes to display the Attributes palette.

3. Click the Overprint Fill check box to assign overprinting to the fill of the top object(s).

4. Click the Overprint Stroke check box to assign overprinting to the stroke of the top object(s). Figure 22-4 shows both check boxes selected.

To see the effects of the overprinting options on your monitor, choose View | Overprint Preview.

The Overprint Black check box in the Output tab section of the Print dialog box automatically overprints black objects in your illustration. Because black covers over other colors, this is a helpful way to prevent mismatched layers in your final output.

Prepare Process Color Separations

Once you define CMYK as your document color model, all colors will be defined as relative mixes of cyan, magenta, yellow, and black. Cyan is a color close to turquoise. Magenta is close to a bright plum color.

Set Up Color for Process Printing

When an illustration is prepared for process color printing, it must be separated into four color plates. These plates are made from film prepared by a preprint service bureau. And your service bureau will use Illustrator to generate separate film for cyan, magenta, yellow, and black.

The most important thing to remember when you are preparing an illustration for process color is to work exclusively with colors from the CMYK color palette. There are different ways to do this, but two of the easiest are these:

- Choose File | Document Color Mode | CMYK Color.
- Choose CMYK from the Color palette menu.

Tip   *Some print shops now use six plates instead of four to provide an increased color spectrum. The same basic process described here is used to prepare six-color printing, but additional color plates are created.*

You can get a general sense of the final color output from your monitor by choosing View | Proof Colors. And you can see an approximation of your final print colors by using your desktop color printer. However, onscreen color proofing and printing to your desktop color printer are not accurate enough to verify how your print job will look after it comes off a commercial color printing press. For an accurate color proof, you must have your commercial printer prepare test proofs.

The test pages you print on your desktop printer will help your commercial printer verify and apply process color.

Follow these steps to print color separations on your own printer:

1. Choose File | Print and select a PostScript printer from the list of available printers. The appearance of the dialog box that opens will vary depending on your operating system and the printer you select, but the basic options will be similar.

2. Choose the Output category from the list box on the left side of the dialog box.

3. Choose an available separation option from the Mode drop-down menu.

4. The Document Ink Options area at the bottom of the dialog box will show a list of the four process colors, as shown in Figure 22-5.

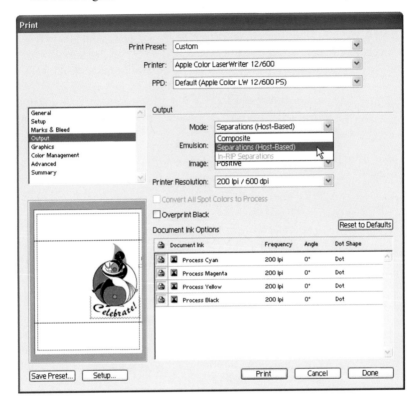

If you applied colors using a different color setup than CMYK, those colors will be listed as well. You can convert them to process colors by clicking the Convert All Spot Colors To Process check box to convert them to one of the four process colors.

5. You can deselect the Printer icon along the left side of the Document Ink Options area for any of the four process colors to *not* print that particular color. To create four separate test sheets (to simulate printer plates), you can deselect all but one color and print four separate versions of your document.

6. After you define printing options, click Print to print a separate page for each color. You can provide these pages to your service bureau and printer to help them check and create the real separation plates that will be used for your print job.

Prepare for Spot Color Printing

Spot colors are defined by a wide range of commercial color sets. The most widely used is the Pantone color system, but there are many others as well. If you are preparing a job for two-color printing, spot printing is more economical than four or six color printing because instead of mixing cyan, magenta, yellow, and black in four press runs to produce your color, the selected ink color is simply applied in one press run.

Because there are so many sets of available process colors, they are difficult to simulate on a monitor. You really need to rely on the process color pattern sheet provided by your printer to know which color to expect in your final output. Spot colors are applied by running the paper, fabric, or material through a printing press more than once, so the basic procedure for preparing illustrations for spot color is very similar to that for preparing illustrations for process color.

The two main differences are that with spot coloring you usually use only one color (plus black), and that that color does not have to be a product of mixing cyan, magenta, yellow, and black but can be any color of paint or ink provided by your printer.

Create Crop Marks

Sometimes a production manager or a printer will require you to crop your illustration. Crop marks must be defined by a non-rotated rectangle.

Follow these steps to create crop marks:

1. Draw a rectangle around the area that you wish to define with crop marks.

2. With the designated rectangle selected, assign no fill and no stroke to the rectangle.

3. Select Object | Crop Area | Make.

Figure 22-6 shows crop marks in the document window.

"SPACE" - a series of digital prints
by Bruce K. Hopkins

FIGURE 22-6 These crop marks do print but are trimmed off by your print shop as part of the publication process.

You can convert the crop marks back to a regular rectangle by selecting Object | Crop Area | Release. Because you use only one set of crop marks in a document, you can replace the assigned crop marks by creating and selecting a new rectangle and assigning crop-mark properties to that shape. The old crop marks will revert to a regular shape. When you print color separations for spot or process printing, the crop marks you set on the artboard define the printed area for separations.

Service Bureau Dos and Don'ts

Printers and print service bureaus are experts at converting your Illustrator files into the desired final output. As early as possible in the development process, you will want to establish a relationship with a printer and a service bureau, explain to them exactly what kind of final output you want, and carefully note and comply with the advice they give you for preparing your artwork in Illustrator.

The following checklist will help you prepare your illustration for commercial printing:

1. Which version of Illustrator or EPS file will the printer and service bureau accept?

2. How do they want fonts handled? Do they want you to embed fonts? Do they have a set of fonts that you are allowed to use? Or do they want you to convert fonts to outlines? (If so, select all of the type in your document and choose Type | Create Outlines before submitting the file to the printer.)

3. If you are doing two-color printing, which set of spot colors do they use, and what advice do they have about how they come out?

4. How should you handle sizing and scaling?

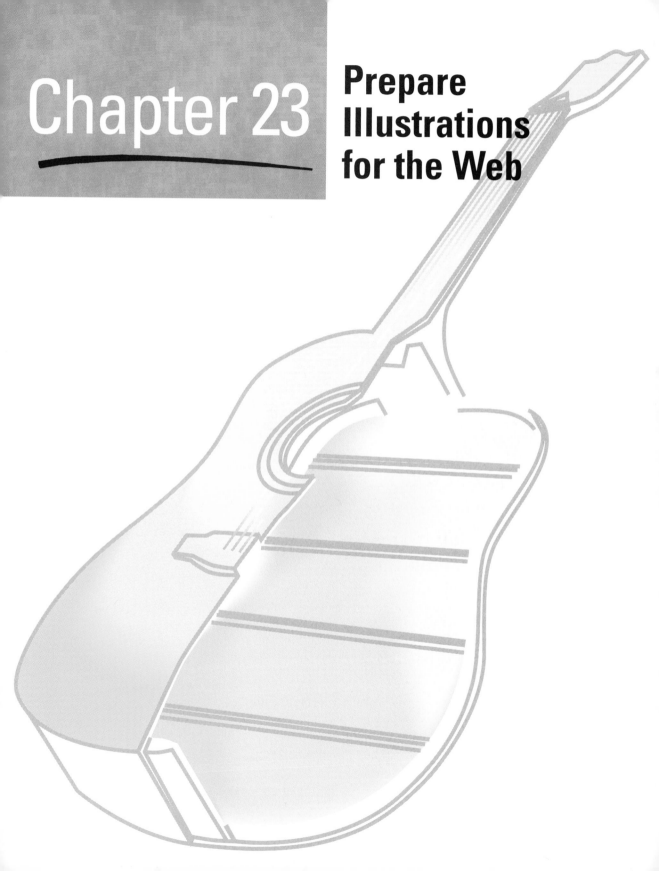

Chapter 23

Prepare Illustrations for the Web

How to...

- Prepare illustrations for the Web
- Understand the challenges of placing vector art on the Web
- Use new vector graphics options for web graphics
- Assign web links in Illustrator
- Create image maps
- Use web-safe colors in Illustrator
- Define a web-sized artboard
- Export to GIF or PNG format
- Export to JPEG format
- Save Illustrator files to SWF format
- Export to SVG format
- Generate HTML web pages from Illustrator
- Save to PDF format

Vector Art in a Still (Mainly) Raster World

Once you have created your web artwork, you face an interesting challenge in presenting your Illustrator artwork on the Web. The Web is (mainly) a raster environment, while Illustrator excels at vector-based images. The basic problem is that the Web displays artwork with a limited set of colors on grainy, low-resolution monitors and, for the most part, without scalable graphics.

Illustrator helps you meet this challenge with the Save for Web dialog box. Here you can experiment with different file formats, tweak how coloring is managed, and even assign different attributes to different "slices" (selected areas) of an illustration.

Web browsers usually support two image file formats: GIF (the *G* is pronounced either as in "get" or as in "gee") and JPEG ("jay-peg"). A third widely interpreted web graphic file format, the PNG ("ping") format, is similar to GIF.

Configure Illustrator for Web Graphics

If you are preparing your illustration for the Web, you'll want to define the Illustrator environment so that web-friendly features are assigned and accessible. You can confine yourself to web-safe colors (a set of colors that are supported by the widest variety of web browsers and devices), and you can view illustrations as they will appear when exported to raster format. Finally, you can define your artboard so that it simulates a web page instead of a printed page.

Use Web-Safe Colors

To minimize the variation in color display for web graphics, you can use web-safe colors. An easy way to view and assign web-safe colors is to view a special swatch palette that is buried in Illustrator. To access that palette, choose Window | Swatch Libraries | Web, and use the swatch palette that appears to assign browser-safe colors.

You can find another web-safe set of swatches in the swatch libraries. It's called Visibone2, and it displays the same set of browser-safe colors, but organized slightly differently. It's based on a popular online color resource (www.visibone.com/colorlab).

To display in a digital environment, illustrations created with CMYK colors must be converted to RGB mode. To convert CMYK colors to RGB, choose Filter | Colors | Convert to RGB. Just remember to save a separate version of your file with CMYK colors if necessary.

Define a Web-Sized Artboard

With all the contradictory developments in browsing environments (from larger monitors to PDAs and web-viewing phones), the consensus generally remains that you should design graphics assuming that your image will be embedded in an 800-pixel-wide web page. Whatever page width you determine to be your target, you can define the artboard to match that size.

Follow these steps to change the artboard size to a typical web page width:

1. Choose File | Document Setup.

2. In the Document Setup dialog box, choose one of the preset web page widths, as shown in Figure 23-1. Or choose Custom in the Size drop-down list, choose Pixels in the Units drop-down list, and enter values in the Width and Height boxes.

3. Click OK to close the Document Setup dialog box and assign a web-sized artboard to your document.

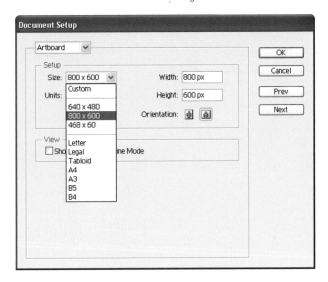

FIGURE 23-1 Defining an 800 pixel by 600 pixel artboard for web design

Save Images as Web-Compatible Raster Files

As you already learned, the two main file formats for the Web are GIF and JPEG. The PNG file format is a variation on GIF that has minor improvements, but it is somewhat less widely interpreted by web browsers.

JPEG format is usually used for photographs. The JPEG format supports more colors than the GIF format. And JPEG provides compression options that allow you to reduce file size (although image quality decreases with file size). GIF images support transparency (and animation). To save a file as a GIF (or PNG) or JPEG image, choose File | Save for Web. The image appears in the Save for Web dialog box. The most powerful way to experiment with file options is to choose the 4-Up tab in the Save for Web dialog box. By default, the upper-left window of the four display windows shows your original illustration. Figure 23-2 shows the Save for Web dialog box with the 4-Up display.

You can click any of the other display windows to apply and preview different file attributes. The Save for Web dialog box

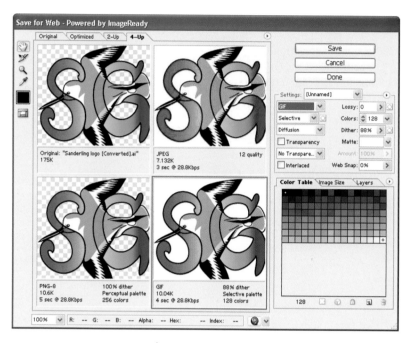

preview menu (a pop-out menu that works like palette menus) lets you define which download speed you expect most visitors to use when they see your graphics on the Web. Selecting a speed from this menu lets Illustrator calculate download time for your images depending on which file format and other attributes you select.

You can resize an image as you export it by selecting the Image Size tab in the Save for Web dialog box. Here you can define size by entering values in the Width and Height boxes. With the Image Size tab selected in the Save for Web dialog box, keep the Constrain Proportions check box selected to keep the image's height-to-width ratio unchanged as you resize. Or you can use the Percentage box to resize an image as you export it.

FIGURE 23-2 Comparing an original image with three web export options

To trim the exported illustration to only that portion within the artboard, choose the Clip to Artboard check box.

The Image Size tab of the Save for Web dialog box also includes the Anti-Alias check box. Anti-aliasing helps smooth out the jagged edges that often result when you convert a vector image to raster art.

Use the Hand tool in the toolbox in the upper-left corner of the Save for Web dialog box to move images around within preview windows. Once you have experimented with different export settings and previewed how they will look, you can save to your defined export settings. To do so, click the Save button in the Save for Web dialog box.

The Save Optimized As dialog box appears, and the settings you defined already are incorporated into how the file will be exported. Navigate to the folder to which you'll save the file, assign a filename, and click Save in the Save Optimized As dialog box to export the image to a new file format.

Export to GIF Format

Once you have opened the Save for Web dialog box (choose File | Save for Web), you can configure it for GIF export by choosing GIF from the Optimized File Format drop-down list, at the top of the Settings area in the dialog box. The Settings drop-down list in the Save for Web dialog box lists many different GIF file options. You can experiment with any of these settings and test the effect in the selected preview window.

FIGURE 23-3 Exporting a logo to GIF format and constraining the color set to browser-safe colors

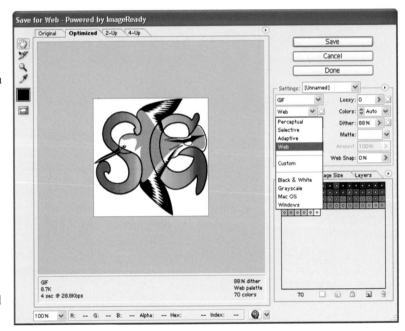

To export your image with the browser-safe color palette, choose Web from the Color Reduction Algorithm drop-down list in the Settings area of the Save for Web dialog box, as shown in Figure 23-3. A new color palette will appear in the Color Table area with the web-safe colors needed to display your image. If you don't use all 216 of the browser-safe colors, Illustrator will create a restricted palette that will reduce the size of your GIF file.

To assign transparency to your image, choose one of the four display windows and click the Transparency check box in the Save for Web dialog box. The Matte drop-down list provides options for tinting the transparent color.

Tip *Here the term transparency means something completely different than when we talk about transparency/opacity as an effect in Illustrator. Transparent web graphics do not employ the same kind of finely tuned opacity/transparency settings allowed for Illustrator effects. Instead, "transparency" applies to only one color and is applied completely— making the one color disappear.*

23

Increasing the value of the Lossy slider decreases file quality and increases download time. You can see the changes reflected in the preview window.

Interlaced images fade in as they download into a web site. Instead of appearing in strips, from top to bottom, the entire image is visible in low resolution at first and then fills in more detail as the entire file downloads. You can add interlacing to GIF (but not JPEG) images by clicking the Interlaced check box in the Save for Web dialog box.

Dithering generates colors not available from the limited 216-color web-safe set by mixing pixels of different colors—such as red and blue to make purple. The Dither slider allows you to experiment with different percentages of dithering for your illustration. The Dither Algorithm drop-down list allows you to experiment with different dithering techniques. Dithering sometimes produces inaccurate coloring, and your illustration uses lots of colors. The JPEG format has a wider range of colors and is usually a better option for photos and other web graphics with many shades of colors than GIF dithering.

FIGURE 23-4 Lower compression creates a higher-quality web graphic with a slower download time

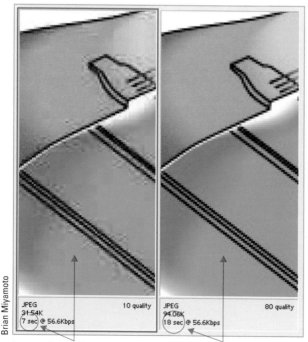

Brian Miyamoto

Low-quality JPEG image will download in 7 seconds

Best-quality JPEG image will maintain gradient mesh much better but will download in 18 seconds

Export to JPEG Format

To export your image to JPEG format, choose one of the preview windows in the Save for Web dialog box (choose File | Save for Web) and then choose JPEG from the Optimized File Format drop-down list.

The Compression Quality drop-down list and the Quality sliders do the same thing: they allow you to use more or less compression. More compression produces faster download times. (Check the listed download time in your preview window as you adjust compression.) But more compression also reduces quality. Figure 23-4 compares high and low compression options for exporting an illustration to JPEG.

You can use the Matte drop-down list in the Save for Web dialog box to change a JPEG image's background color. The Blur slider literally causes a JPEG image to become blurry, and it has limited usefulness in diffusing jagged edges in images.

The ICC Profile check box creates and embeds a monitor profile with your exported image. This profile is not widely supported enough to be useful in exporting for web display.

Add Web Attributes to Illustrations

You can define a link target for an image in Illustrator so that when the object is placed in a web site it serves as a link. You can also create *image maps*: graphics that contain several links in a single image. For instance, you can create a map with different clickable areas that lead to different link targets. Links and image maps are defined the same way in Illustrator—the only difference being that an image link covers the entire image, while an image map is applied to a portion of an image (and usually image maps consist of *several* clickable regions in an image).

FIGURE 23-5 Defining a clickable area associated with a rectangle around an object

You assign links to objects by using the Attributes palette. First select the object to which you want to assign a link, and then use the Attributes palette to define the link itself. Links in Illustrator can be assigned either to a rectangular area or to a polygon.

A rectangular link generates a rectangular clickable area around the selected image that includes space that is not part of the image itself. Figure 23-5 shows the clickable area for a logo generated by a rectangular link.

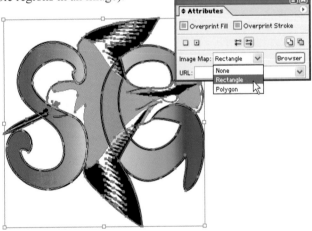

Follow these steps to assign a link target to an object in Illustrator:

FIGURE 23-6 Defining a link target for a clickable object

1. Select an object or objects.

2. Choose Window | Attributes to display the Attributes palette.

3. From the Image Map drop-down list in the Attributes palette, choose either Rectangle or Polygon.

4. In the URL text box in the Attributes palette, enter a URL, as shown in Figure 23-6.

If you are defining an image map, you will draw several clickable areas on the image, one at a time.

5. When you save your file, the URL you selected will be embedded in the graphic.

 You can click the Browser button in the Attributes dialog box to test your link by opening the target URL in your system's default browser.

Export to Web-Friendly Vector Formats

The process of exporting Illustrator images to the SWF and SVG vector formats is very similar to exporting to the JPEG and GIF raster formats. It's all done in the Save for Web dialog box (choose File | Save for Web). You can experiment with different settings and preview the results before you export.

The Image Size tab in the Save for Web dialog box works with SWF and SVG files, as does the download speed calculator. You'll find fewer options when you export to SWF and SVG than you have to confront when you export to JPEG or GIF. That's good. There are fewer options because there is less to convert. Your scalable, smooth, small-file-size vector images retain most of their Illustrator qualities when you export to SWF and SVG.

Save to SWF Format

SWF files can be viewed with any web browser that has the Flash (aka Shockwave) Player. They can also be opened in Flash and used by Flash developers. Other vector graphic programs also support the SWF format.

You can export to the SWF file format in the Save for Web dialog box (choose File | Save for Web). When you choose SWF from the Optimized File Format drop-down list, you can select the Read Only check box to keep people from opening the file in Flash and editing it.

The Curve Quality slider defines image quality for exported SWF files. Higher values on the Curve Quality slider create smoother curves and take longer to download. You can preview quality and download time as you experiment with curve quality.

The Type of Export list allows you to export the entire image as a single SWF image or create a separate SWF frame for each layer in your image. In effect, you can create simple Flash animations by exporting layers to frames. When you do, each layer becomes a separate frame in a Flash movie. This strategy is most useful when you (or someone else) are going to edit the exported images in Flash. Figure 23-7 shows a multilayer image being exported to Flash, with layers being converted to frames.

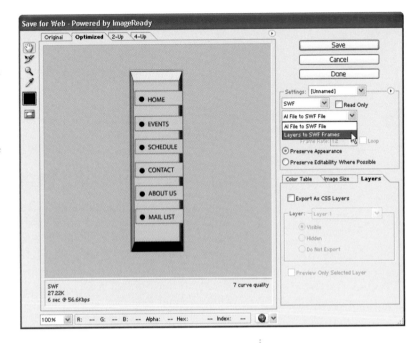

FIGURE 23-7   Each button in this navigation bar is a separate layer, and each will become a separate frame in Flash.

Export to SVG Format

Partly because Adobe is associated with and is promoting the SVG format, the Save for Web dialog box provides more options for exporting to SVG than to the Macromedia-based SWF format. As with other web options, the easiest way to initiate the process of exporting to SVG format is to choose File | Save for Web and work through the Save for Web dialog box. Choose SVG from the Optimized File Formats drop-down menu.

The Font Subsetting options allow you to attach fonts if necessary. The Only Glyphs Used option includes only the characters necessary for the file and is sufficient for most web uses.

You should almost always choose Embed Images from the Image Location list so that your images don't get lost or disassociated from your file. As long as you are exporting to SVG, you might as well stick with the default Presentation Attributes setting in the CSS Properties list. The Decimals setting defines image quality—higher settings create better images and slower download times.

Create HTML Web Pages in Illustrator

Illustrator provides minimal options for saving a document as an HTML web page. A general word of advice if you plan to design web pages in Illustrator: Don't. If you are serious about creating web pages, you'll need to take up HTML or use Illustrator in conjunction with a web design program such as Dreamweaver, FrontPage (for Windows only), or GoLive. The fatal flaw in Illustrator's (and Photoshop's) web page generation tools is that Illustrator (and Photoshop) do not provide the ability to save text as HTML text. So when you export your document as an HTML page, all of the text is converted to images.

Because Illustrator is not much of a functional web page design program, we'll take only a quick look at how it can be used to generate web pages. The key feature and concept to understand is *slicing*. Slicing has a lot of different meanings in web graphic design, but here it refers to the Illustrator feature that allows you to designate individually exportable objects within a single document.

Slice Illustrations

Slicing can be used to break a large image into smaller chunks, which some web designers consider more suitable for web pages. And slicing allows you to assign different attributes to different elements of an image. For example, you can slice up a large illustration and export one slice as a high-quality JPEG to preserve a gradient while exporting another slice as a low-quality JPEG to speed up download time.

If you do not do any slicing, you can still convert an Illustrator element into an HTML page. But the page will have just one graphic file that includes all of the objects on the page.

Follow these steps to create slices from an illustration:

1. Select an object or objects on the artboard.

2. Choose Object | Slice | Make. The document will appear "sliced" into rectangular, as shown in Figure 23-8.

 If you want to generate a single slice out of all your selected objects, choose Object | Slice | Create from Selection.

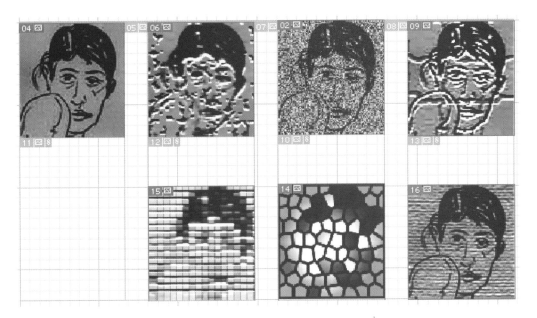

Another technique for defining slices is to create a grid on your page using guides and then generate slices based on those guides. Follow these steps to generate slices from guides:

FIGURE 23-8 Each mug shot has been defined as a separate slice.

1. Choose View | Show Rulers to display rulers.

FIGURE 23-9 Generating many slices from one object using guides

2. Click and drag from either the horizontal or vertical ruler to place guides on the artboard.

3. After you place guides on the artboard, choose Object | Slice | Create from Guides to generate slices from the grid you defined with horizontal and/or vertical guides, as shown in Figure 23-9.

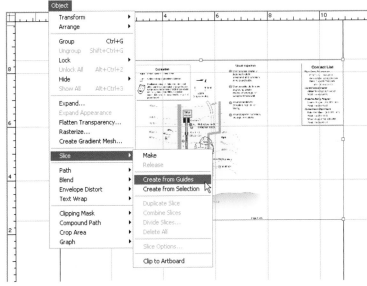

Export Illustrator Documents to HTML

Illustrator's Save for Web feature allows you to export distinct web graphics from each slice image, and Illustrator will generate HTML (web page layout) code that will place all of your exported images in a layout grid using HTML tables.

Follow these steps to save an Illustrator document as an HTML page:

1. Choose File | Save for Web.

2. If you have sliced objects on your page, choose the Slice Select tool from the Save for Web dialog box toolbox (in the upper-left corner of the dialog box) and select one of the sliced objects.

FIGURE 23-10 Saving a slice of an illustration as a medium-quality, progressive JPEG file

3. Define specific image export attributes for the selected slice (if you created slices), as shown in Figure 23-10.

Slice Select tool   Selected slice

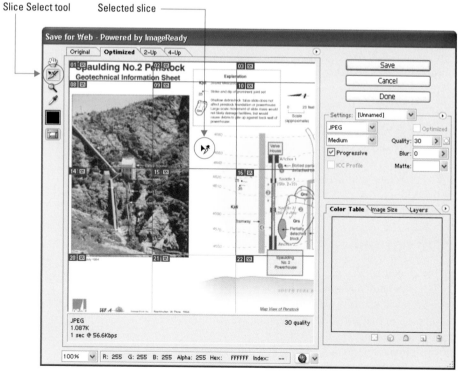

4. Define additional specific export attributes for other slices.

5. After you've defined your web export settings for each slice in the Save for Web dialog box, click Save.

6. In the Save Optimized as dialog box, choose HTML and Images in the Save as Type drop-down list.

7. Navigate to a file folder and enter a filename in the Save Optimized as dialog box.

8. If your document will be used as a (template) background image on a web page, choose Background Image from the Settings drop-down list in the Save Optimized as dialog box.

 If you know HTML, you can use the Other option in the Settings drop-down list to open the Output Settings dialog box and define how Illustrator will generate HTML.

9. Click Save to save your file. If you are replacing an earlier version of your HTML page (or if there is a different HTML page with the filename you selected), the Replace Files dialog box appears. You can deselect the check box(es) next to the file(s) that you don't want to replace. Then click Replace.

The web page you generate using the export options in Illustrator will have images embedded within it. Those images are saved in an Images folder that is generated during the export process. You can open your HTML file in any editor for further refinement.

Save to PDF Format

The Portable Document Format (PDF) file format is supported on the Web and in hardcopy printing. To view (and print) PDF files on the Web, visitors to a web site must have the Adobe Acrobat Reader, but that software is available free from Adobe, and it's easy to download.

To save an Illustrator document as a PDF file, choose File | Save as and choose Illustrator PDF as the file type. Enter a filename, navigate to the folder to which you'll save the PDF file, and click Save. The Adobe PDF Options dialog box opens and displays six categories, as shown in Figure 23-11.

FIGURE 23-11 Defining PDF export options

The General category has a Compatibility drop-down menu to set version compatibility. The check boxes allow you to select or deselect Preserve Illustrator Editing Capabilities, Embed Page Thumbnails (small icon-size versions of the illustration used in Acrobat Reader), Optimize for Fast Web View, and View PDF after Saving.

The Compression category has a Preset drop-down menu that allows you to assign optimal compression (reducing file size) for Press (print projects), Acrobat 6 (a format that preserves layers), or Default. The options in this category allow you to micro-tune your compression settings.

The Marks & Bleeds category lets you define printer marks—consult with your commercial printer to see if this is appropriate for your file.

The Advanced category defines how colors, fonts, overprinting, transparency, and layers are saved in the PDF file. The default settings embed fonts, which is almost always helpful and useful when documents are shared, so unless you have good reason to do otherwise, leave these default settings alone.

The Security category allows you to assign password protection for viewing and/or editing the file. The Summary category provides a report on your settings.

Behind the Scenes

A GALLERY WITH TECHNIQUES FROM THE PROS

As a way of returning to and getting a new perspective on the techniques covered in this book, I invited several of my favorite Illustrator digital artists to contribute projects to this gallery. They've all been cool enough to share their Illustrator files so that their secret techniques could be demystified, dissected, and deconstructed.

As you explore the projects in this gallery, you'll get an inside, behind-the-scenes look at how real professional graphic designers put projects together in Illustrator. Surprisingly, perhaps, you'll see that the techniques they use tend to be pretty basic—lines created with the Pen tool, fills, blends, transparency— the same procedures and tools focused on in this book. Of course, years of experience have imbued the hands of these artists with an almost magical efficacy.

The projects in this gallery represent the broad gamut of Adobe Illustrator's uses—technical illustrations, fine art, business cards, architectural renderings, CD covers, logos, posters, postcards, maps, and anatomical illustrations.

Switch Poster

Mike Kohnke

Mike Kohnke is a cutting-edge typographer who uses Illustrator both to design his type fonts and to create promotional materials for them. The poster he contributed to this gallery illustrates the use of Illustrator to design type fonts as well as a wonderful poster design.

Step

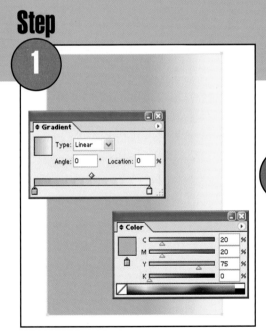

For this poster, the artist built semi-transparent layers of type and texture against a background that was a simple linear gradient fill, shown here. The gradient fill for the background object runs from yellow mixed with cyan and magenta to light yellow on the right.

Overlaid on the background is a 20-percent opaque repeating pattern. The pattern subtly adds depth and texture without detracting from the content of the poster.

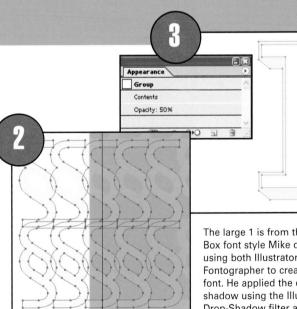

The large 1 is from the Switch Box font style Mike developed, using both Illustrator and Fontographer to create the font. He applied the drop shadow using the Illustrator Drop-Shadow filter and applied 50-percent opacity to the character in the poster.

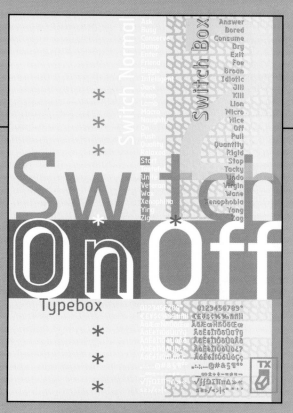

Mike's Switch poster was created to promote his Switch typeface. The typeface has two styles, Normal and Box (hence the "on/off" theme in the poster). You can see more of Mike's typefaces at

http://www.weassociated.com/html/Td.html
http://www.typebox.com/fontbox.cgi/index.html

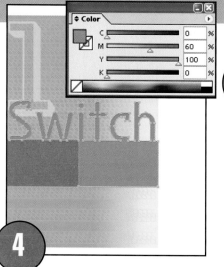

4 The type for "Switch" matches the color of the rectangular block on the right, further adding to the concept of transition. The block on the left is full magenta, while the orange rectangle on the right mixes magenta and yellow.

5 The text of the poster combines type rotated 90 degrees with type in narrow columns. All type was converted to outlines to facilitate printing; it is fully opaque white and magenta fill.

Logo
Hugh D'Andrade

Hugh D'Andrade's unique, avant-garde illustrations have been displayed at the Oakland Museum in Oakland, California; at Burning Man; and at galleries around the country. Hugh teaches illustration in the Graphic Design program at UC Berkeley Extension.

Step

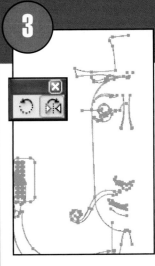

Hugh imported the painting into Illustrator as a non-printing template layer. The template layer has a linked JPEG file. It is non-printing and dimmed 50 percent—the default settings for imported bitmap template layers.

Hugh traced the image with the Pen tool. So that he could see his work, he drew with a bright red line. Since the image is designed to be more-or-less symmetrical, he first drew the left half of the art.

To reflect and duplicate the half-a-figure, hold down the OPTION/ALT key while dragging on selected paths with the Reflect tool. The Copy button in the Reflect dialog box will duplicate a reflection of the image.

Hugh's specialty in the world of digital graphic design is print design with a rough, hand-tooled appearance. He created this logo by vectorizing a painting.

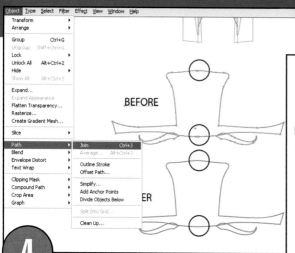

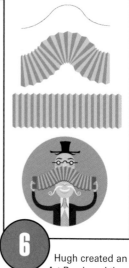

4 Hugh created the hat by using the Object | Path | Join command to combine the paths in the hat. The Join command joins end anchors of an open path to create a closed path. Or, if you select two open paths, the command connects the end anchors of the two paths. In this case, the command is being used to combine the two halves of the hat.

The shirt and tie are just artfully combined shapes, lines, and fills, as shown in the enlarged section of this figure. The two pieces of the tie are overlaid on a yellow rectangle, and the stripes are narrow Pen lines on top of everything.

6 Hugh created an Art Brush and then assigned it to a curved path to simulate an expanding accordion. After that, he placed the whole image in front of a teal circle, completing the logo.

Folding Business Card

Bruce K. Hopkins

Bruce K. Hopkins has been a full-time professional illustrator for 20 years. He creates every type of artwork, from technical illustrations for major manufacturers to fine art. He has been the designer of fabric prints for Joe Boxer shorts since their inception. Bruce is the main illustrator for this book.

Step 1

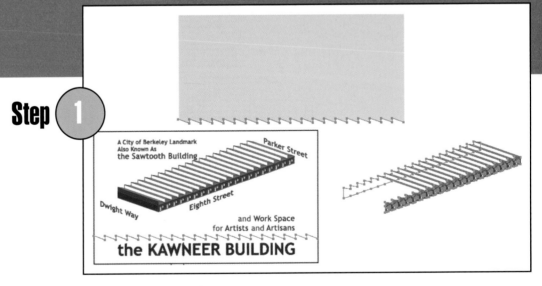

This folding card has a top that flips up to reveal more detail on a larger "second page" that extends below the bottom of the top "page." The graphical theme of the card revolves around the "sawtooth" concept taken from the shape of the building and the building's nickname.

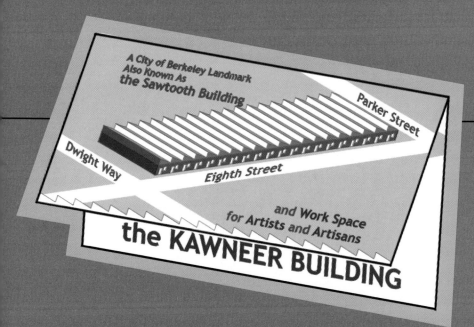

Bruce created this folding business card for the Kawneer Building (aka the Sawtooth Building), a Berkeley, California complex that hosts a hundred artists, performers, and craftspeople.

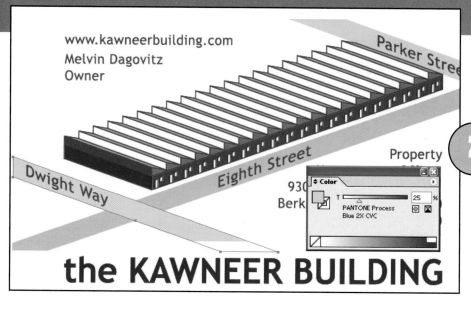

To keep printing costs manageable, the card uses two Pantone (spot) colors, but with different degrees of saturation. The streets are 25-percent saturation, the roof 75-percent, and the type 100-percent.

Technical Illustration

Adam Sadigursky

Adam Sadigursky creates technical illustrations for Hewlett Packard and other high-budget, demanding clients. Adam contributed a major project involving both technical illustration and artistic design.

Step

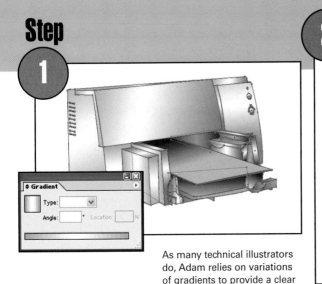

1

As many technical illustrators do, Adam relies on variations of gradients to provide a clear visual effect for each object. Over two dozen different linear gray-and-white gradient fills highlight different parts of the printer, with different rotation angles on the fills. One of the gradients is displayed here.

2

To create the person sitting at the table, Adam took several digital pictures of a person sitting at a table. He used a photograph to trace a vector path. The path was filled with white, as shown here.

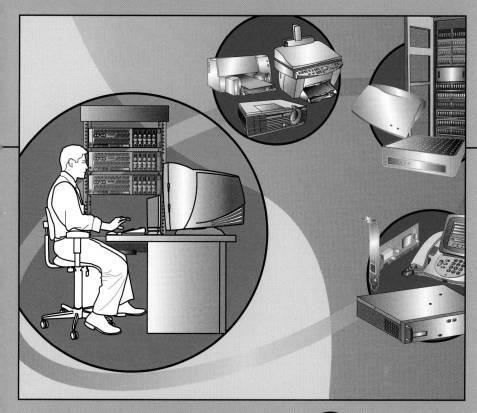

A huge number of technical illustrations are created in Adobe Illustrator each year for manuals, diagrams, and instructional brochures. Adam's poster combines several technical illustrations.

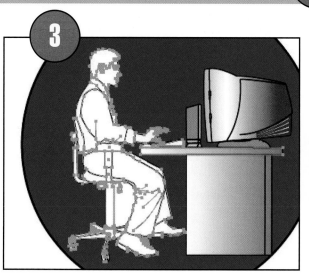

After creating a white background shape, Adam traced the man at work over an embedded digital image that was converted to a filled vector shape.

The ellipse combines a gradient fill with 50-percent opacity and runs over the illustration. The fill is actually all reddish-brown— the blue and yellow belong to underlying objects that show through the semi-transparent gradient fill.

Museum Rendering

Gary Newman

Gary Newman is a world-class architectural rendering artist whose Sebastopol, California design firm, NewMango.com, designs web sites, logos, brochures and flyers, catalogues and books, consumer and trade ads, and maps.

Step

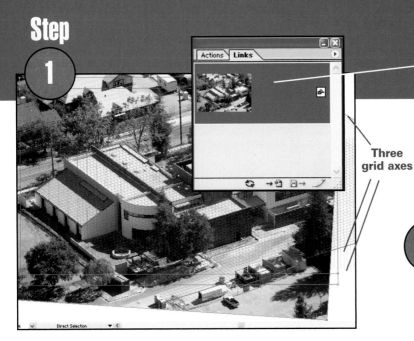

1

Actions | Links

Embedded Image

Three grid axes

2

Transparency
Normal | Opacity: 70 %
Clip
Invert Mask
Isolate Blending | Knockout Group
Opacity & Mask Define Knockout Shape

Direct Selection

After selecting the view he wanted, Gary embedded the image in an Illustrator file, locked its layer, and on a new layer drew three sets of axes.

By blending between these axes, he created a convincing perspective grid on which to base his illustration.

Building on the grid and the locked bitmap layer, Gary made roofs and walls translucent to show the interior features of the building from an exterior view. The semi-transparent (70-percent transparent) wall shown here reveals the lobby behind it. For other revealed elements, lightened colors create the illusion that the viewer is looking through a semi-transparent roof or wall.

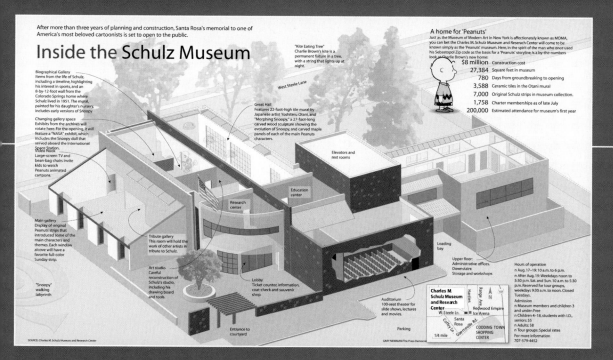

Gary sent a photographer up in a plane to take the photos that were used as a basis for this architectural rendering. The final artwork was published in a feature article in *Newsweek* magazine covering the opening of the Charles Schulz Museum in Santa Rosa, California.

3 The key to being able to pull off this complex project was the use of many layers. Locking, viewing, and hiding layers allowed the artist to focus on different areas of the museum as he worked. Here, all the layers are locked and outlined except for the Admin layer.

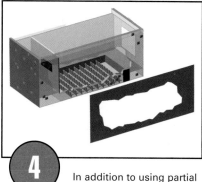

4 In addition to using partial transparency and lightened colors to let the viewer look "through walls," Gary created a cutaway shape to reveal part of the auditorium. The shape is duplicated here to expose the technique.

Globe

Javier Romero

Javier Romero Design Group is among the most successful Illustrator-based design firms in the world. People see Javier's work everywhere in the world every day—his VW logo, Amnesty International logo, *Time* magazine covers, CD covers, Coca-Cola ads, *Newsweek* covers, and much more.

Step

1

The design was built on very basic shapes and colors—orange and blue rectangles and a star filled with a yellow-to-orange gradient.

2

The globe itself is a four-color gradient fill. The blue used for the earth is mixed with the yellow theme in the illustration.

Javier's images can be disarmingly simple or very complex. The globe he contributed to this gallery combines simple shapes with complex layering.

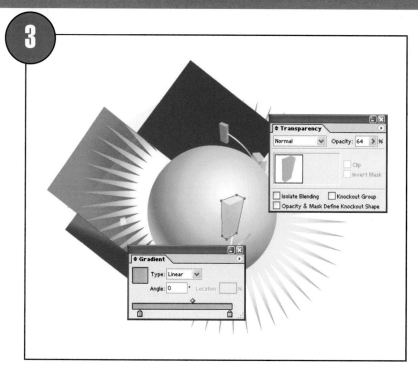

The building icons combine a two-color gradient fill with 64-percent opacity and mixed transparency to reveal part of the underlying planet earth.

Postcard

Bruce K. Hopkins

Bruce is one of the very few artists who use Illustrator to create fine art. A recent project is his "Space" series of spectacular full-sized framed posters. Bruce created this postcard to promote the series. (The biography for Bruce K. Hopkins was included with his "Folding Business Card" entry earlier in this gallery.)

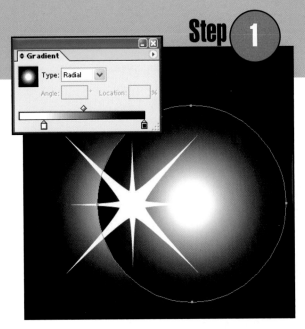

Step 1

Bruce created the star in the poster by creating two four-point stars and rotating one 45 degrees. The glowing bulb in the background relies on a black-to-white gradient fill to create depth and glow.

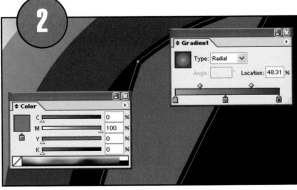

2

To ensure the integrity of the colors in printed posters, Bruce used a small color palette, relying on pure colors from the CMYK color model. Much of the illustration is pure cyan or magenta.

Bruce's Space poster series is brilliant in its simplicity, relying on precisely executed paths and finely tuned gradients. Designing for print output, and requiring exact color matches, Bruce creatively turned the constraints of CMYK process printing into an aesthetic theme.

3

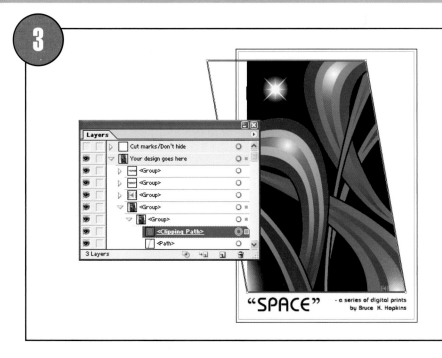

The shapes in the illustration are ordered on top of each other. Since the postcard is a section of a larger illustration, Bruce used a clipping mask to constrain the size of the cropped piece. The clipping object is on one layer, while the border is on a higher layer and thus not affected by the clipping mask. Here you can see the clipping mask skewed to the side to expose the effect.

Map

Mark Stein

Mark Stein specializes in custom map design for advertising and for publications including travel guides, textbooks, and magazines. His design firm has created maps for book publishers such as Fodor's and St. Martin's Press. His recent map work can be seen in *The Cousin's Wars* by Kevin Phillips.

Step 1

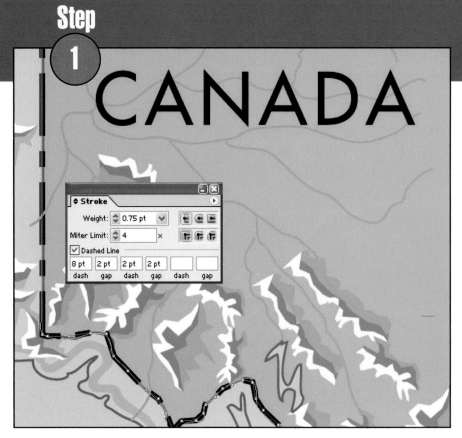

The border between the United States and Canada was drawn with a custom stroke—alternating eight-point and two-point dashes separated by two-point gaps—defined in the Stroke palette, as shown here.

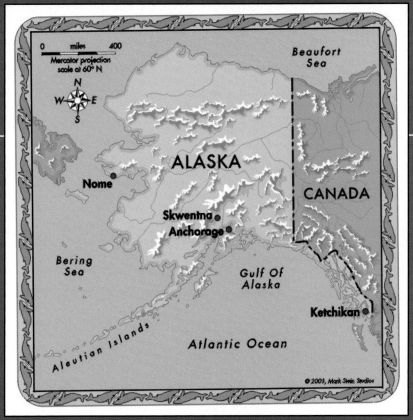

Mark's map of Alaska utilizes type, borders, scaled objects, and shadows to create a geological map that looks three-dimensional.

2 Mountain ranges were drawn with the Pen tool and shaded with white to the north and a darker shade to the south. The blue path is a river.

3 Rather than use a Pattern Fill, the border around the map was created by duplicating a fish to create one side of the border. Once one side is completed, copying, scaling, and rotating complete the frame.

Anatomy Illustration

Jared Schneidman

Jared Schneidman's firm creates information graphics for advertising, corporate, and editorial use. He specializes in charts, maps, diagrams, architectural renderings, products, scientific, and technical illustrations. Here he allows us to look "behind the scenes" at one of his anatomical illustrations.

Step 1

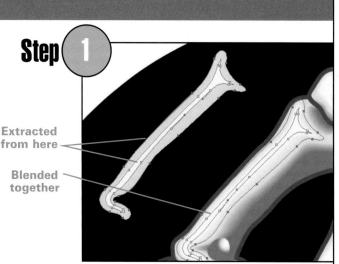

Extracted from here

Blended together

It took plenty of tedious work with the Pen tool to create the objects used to detail each organ or other body part. The softening effect in the skeletal parts was achieved by using smooth blends of white and tan shapes. Here, one part of a finger bone has been duplicated and the blend removed to show how the softening look was created.

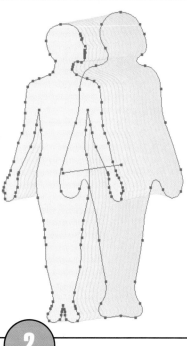

2

A smooth color blend was also used to soften the line between the inner and outer body shapes. The two silhouettes have been separated to reveal the blend at work.

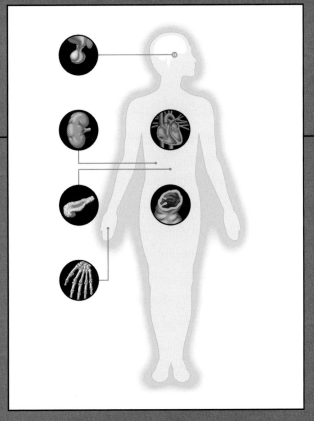

The two word version of how Jared created realistic anatomical elements is "hard work." Each finger, each blood vessel, each organ part combines multiple paths with intricately managed blends between them.

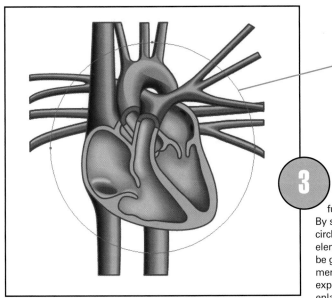

Object clipping mask

3 The heart organ has been cropped by a circle that functions as a clipping mask. By selecting both the overlay circle and the underlying organ elements, a clipping mask can be generated from the Object menu. The clipping mask is exposed here. The figure also enlarges a gradient fill used to soften edges in organs (as well as bones).

Logo

Gary Priester

Gary W. Priester is the guru of North American logo design. Clients such as American Cinema Editors, EZ Metrics, and others pay Gary thousands of dollars to design their logos.

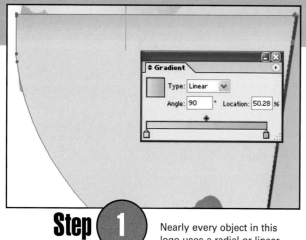

Step 1

Nearly every object in this logo uses a radial or linear gradient fill. This illustration shows how the interactive Gradient tool was used to customize a gradient fill that appears to make the top of the wall curve back. The line on the screen indicates the length and direction used by the Gradient tool to define the fill.

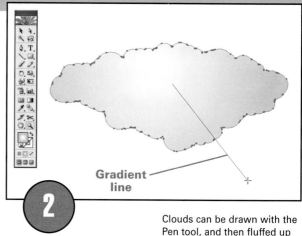

Gradient line

2

Clouds can be drawn with the Pen tool, and then fluffed up with a radial gradient.

Gary often uses color schemes for his logos that reflect the spectacular landscape of the Southwest region of the United States, as he did with this one.

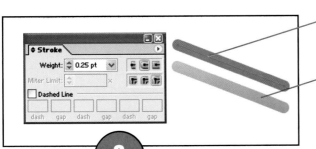

Original stroke with round cap

Stroke converted to outline and filled with gradient

3 Even the plant shoots are filled with gradients. Gradients can be applied to paths, but not to strokes. It would take an insane amount of work to create the plants by drawing shapes for each shoot. But the plants can be drawn with the Pen tool, and the paths converted to shapes by choosing Object | Path | Outline Stroke. Here you can see a stroke (created with a round cap), and its cousin, a stroke that has been converted into an outline and filled with a gradient.

CD Cover

Eileen Starr Moderbacher

Eileen Starr Moderbacher's studio creates corporate illustrations, academic and medical art, fine art, and CD covers. Among the books Eileen has illustrated is *Cells, Embryos, and Evolution.*

Step 1

The screening overlay on the painting is a bitmapped gradient created in Photoshop. It takes on transparency through 70% opacity being assigned to the *layer.*

Illustrator provides a template for designing CD covers. The File | New From Template menu options includes many CD and DVD templates. Eileen's CD cover uses the same painting as a base for both the cover and the label.

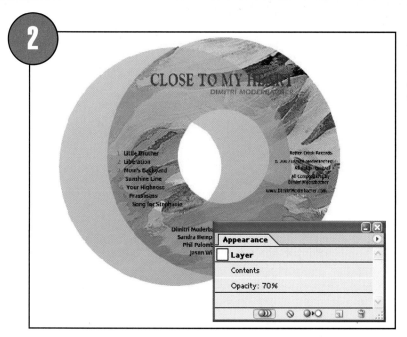

2

The same painting and gradient bitmap were used for the CD sticker: the filtering layer is a bitmap, with transparency assigned.

Artists

Hugh D'Andrade
San Francisco based illustrator and designer
www.hughillustration.com

Hannelore Fischer
heartist7@earthlink.net
www.hannelorefischer.com

Jason Holmberg
jholmbe1110@earthlink.net

Bruce K. Hopkins
ILLUSTRATION, DESIGN, FINE ART
930 Dwight Way, Suite 3
Berkeley, CA 94710
bruhopk@aol.com
www.bkhopkins.com

Mary Jensen
www.marylew.com

Sasha Karlins
a4yroldfaerie@playful.com

Mike Kohnke
mike@weassociated.com

Brian Miyamoto

Eileen Starr Moderbacher
eileen@studio-star.com

Gary Newman Design
www.newmango.com

Felix Perez

Gary W. Priester
The Black Point Group
Placitas, New Mexico
gary@gwpriester.com
www.gwpriester.com

Javier Romero
Javier Romero Design Group
www.jrdg.com

Adam Sadigursky
http://home.earthlink.net/~adam308/

Jared Schneidman Design
www.jsdinfographics.com

Mark Stein
Mark Stein Studios
73-01 Juniper Valley Road
Middle Village, NY 11379
(718) 326-4839
steinstudios@att.net
www.steinstudios.com

Susan Steinhauer

Mieko Mochizuki Swartz
kirin@obakezukan.net
www.obakezukan.net

Nathan Alan Whelchel

Index

INTERNATIONAL CONTACT INFORMATION

AUSTRALIA
McGraw-Hill Book Company
Australia Pty. Ltd.
TEL +61-2-9900-1800
FAX +61-2-9878-8881
http://www.mcgraw-hill.com.au
books-it_sydney@mcgraw-hill.com

CANADA
McGraw-Hill Ryerson Ltd.
TEL +905-430-5000
FAX +905-430-5020
http://www.mcgraw-hill.ca

**GREECE, MIDDLE EAST, & AFRICA
(Excluding South Africa)**
McGraw-Hill Hellas
TEL +30-210-6560-990
TEL +30-210-6560-993
TEL +30-210-6560-994
FAX +30-210-6545-525

MEXICO (Also serving Latin America)
McGraw-Hill Interamericana Editores
S.A. de C.V.
TEL +525-1500-5108
FAX +525-117-1589
http://www.mcgraw-hill.com.mx
carlos_ruiz@mcgraw-hill.com

SINGAPORE (Serving Asia)
McGraw-Hill Book Company
TEL +65-6863-1580
FAX +65-6862-3354
http://www.mcgraw-hill.com.sg
mghasia@mcgraw-hill.com

SOUTH AFRICA
McGraw-Hill South Africa
TEL +27-11-622-7512
FAX +27-11-622-9045
robyn_swanepoel@mcgraw-hill.com

SPAIN
McGraw-Hill/
Interamericana de España, S.A.U.
TEL +34-91-180-3000
FAX +34-91-372-8513
http://www.mcgraw-hill.es
professional@mcgraw-hill.es

**UNITED KINGDOM, NORTHERN,
EASTERN, & CENTRAL EUROPE**
McGraw-Hill Education Europe
TEL +44-1-628-502500
FAX +44-1-628-770224
http://www.mcgraw-hill.co.uk
emea_queries@mcgraw-hill.com

ALL OTHER INQUIRIES Contact:
McGraw-Hill/Osborne
TEL +1-510-420-7700
FAX +1-510-420-7703
http://www.osborne.com
omg_international@mcgraw-hill.com

Know How

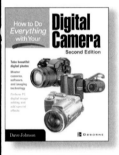

How to Do Everything with Your Digital Camera
Second Edition
ISBN: 0-07-222555-6

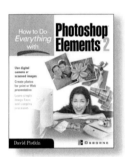

How to Do Everything with Photoshop Elements 2
ISBN: 0-07-222638-2

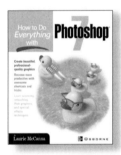

How to Do Everything with Photoshop 7
ISBN: 0-07-219554-1

How to Do Everything with Your Sony CLIÉ
ISBN: 0-07-222659-5

How to Do Everything with Macromedia Contribute
0-07-222892-X

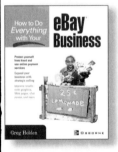

How to Do Everything with Your eBay Business
0-07-222948-9

How to Do Everything with Your Tablet PC
ISBN: 0-07-222771-0

How to Do Everything with Your iPod
ISBN: 0-07-222700-1

How to Do Everything with Your iMac, Third Edition
ISBN: 0-07-213172-1

How to Do Everything with Your iPAQ Pocket PC
Second Edition
ISBN: 0-07-222950-0

Sound Off!

Visit us at **www.osborne.com/bookregistration** and let us know what you thought of this book. While you're online you'll have the opportunity to register for newsletters and special offers from McGraw-Hill/Osborne.

We want to hear from you!

Sneak Peek

Visit us today at **www.betabooks.com** and see what's coming from McGraw-Hill/Osborne tomorrow!

Based on the successful software paradigm, Bet@Books™ allows computing professionals to view partial and sometimes complete text versions of selected titles online. Bet@Books™ viewing is free, invites comments and feedback, and allows you to "test drive" books in progress on the subjects that interest you the most.